GENESIS
AND
EXODUS

GENESIS
AND
EXODUS

With an Introduction by
John Goldingay

John W. Rogerson,
R.W.L. Moberly
and William Johnstone

Sheffield
Academic Press
www.SheffieldAcademicPress.com

Part I originally published by JSOT Press 1991 as J.W. Rogerson, *Genesis 1–11* (Old Testament Guides, 1)

Part II originally published by JSOT Press 1992 as R.W.L. Moberly, *Genesis 12–50* (Old Testament Guides, 2)

Part III originally published by JSOT Press 1990 as W. Johnstone, *Exodus* (Old Testament Guides, 3)

Copyright © 2001 Sheffield Academic Press

Published by
Sheffield Academic Press Ltd
Mansion House
19 Kingfield Road
Sheffield S11 9AS
England

www.SheffieldAcademicPress.com

Typeset by Sheffield Academic Press
and
Printed on acid-free paper in Great Britain
by MPG Books Ltd
Bodmin, Cornwall

British Library Cataloguing-in-Publication Data

A catalogue record for this book is available
from the British Library

ISBN 1-84127-191-8

CONTENTS

Part III

EXODUS
William Johnstone

ABBREVIATIONS

ÄAT	Ägypten und Altes Testament
AB	Anchor Bible
ANET	James B. Pritchard (ed.), *Ancient Near Eastern Texts relating to the Old Testament* (Princeton: Princeton University Press, 3rd edn, 1969)
BA	*Biblical Archaeologist*
BAR	*Biblical Archaeology Review*
BETL	Bibliotheca ephemeridum theologicarum lovaniensium
Bib	*Biblica*
BibSem	The Biblical Seminar
BJS	Brown Judaic Studies
BK	Biblischer Kommentar
BZAW	Beihefte zur *Zeitschrift für die alttestamentliche Wissenschaft*
CBQ	*Catholic Biblical Quarterly*
CBQMS	*Catholic Biblical Quarterly*, Monograph Series
ConBOT	Coniectanea biblica, Old Testament
EHPR	Etudes d'histoire et de philosophie religieuses, Faculté de théologie protestante, Strasbourg
ExpTim	*Expository Times*
FOTL	The Forms of the Old Testament Literature
FRLANT	Forschungen zur Religion and Literatur des Alten und Neuen Testaments
GKC	*Gesenius' Hebrew Grammar* (ed. E. Kautzsch, revised and trans. A.E. Cowley; Oxford: Clarendon Press, 1910).
HKAT	Handkommentar zum Alten Testament
HSM	Harvard Semitic Monographs
HTR	*Harvard Theological Review*
ICC	International Critical Commentary
IDB	George Arthur Buttrick (ed.), *The Interpreter's Dictionary of the Bible* (4 vols.; Nashville: Abingdon Press, 1962)
IDBSup	*IDB*, Supplementary Volume
JBL	*Journal of Biblical Literature*
JETS	*Journal of the Evangelical Theological Society*
JJS	*Journal of Jewish Studies*
JNES	*Journal of Near Eastern Studies*

JSOT	*Journal for the Study of the Old Testament*
JSOTSup	*Journal for the Study of the Old Testament*, Supplement Series
JTS	*Journal of Theological Studies*
NEB	New English Bible
OBO	Orbis biblicus et orientalis
OTL	Old Testament Library
OTP	James Charlesworth (ed.), *Old Testament Pseudepigrapha*
REB	Revised English Bible
RSV	Revised Standard Version
TOTC	Tyndale Old Testament Commentaries
VT	*Vetus Testamentum*
VTSup	*Vetus Testamentum*, Supplements
WBC	Word Biblical Commentary
WMANT	Wissenschaftliche Monographien zum Alten und Neuen Testament
ZAW	*Zeitschrift für die alttestamentliche Wissenschaft*
ZTK	*Zeitschrift für Theologie und Kirche*

INTRODUCTION TO GENESIS AND EXODUS

John Goldingay

Ways of Reading a Text

How do we go about studying Genesis and Exodus? How do we discover what they meant to their first readers and what they might mean for readers today?

It is possible to identify various possible interests for the task of interpretation. I will work here with a way of categorizing them that distinguishes three fundamental objectives for the task.

- We can look at the world of the text itself, at the way it works as a narrative, at the story it tells, the characters it portrays, and the way it discusses certain themes.
- We can look at the worlds behind the text, so as to try to discover its origins and to ask about the possible historical realities it refers to.
- We can look at the worlds in front of the text, at the way it interacts with the lives and thinking of its readers. We can ask in what way its significance differs for (say) Christians and Jews, or men and women, or first world and third world readers.

Reading the Text Itself

In due course the Old Testament includes many kinds of texts—prayers, poems, hymns, accounts of visions, laws and others. But it begins as a narrative; indeed, narrative dominates the Old Testament. In due course we will ask about the historical nature of the narratives in Genesis and Exodus, a question which was a major concern of their study in the modern period. But initially I invite the reader to leave that question on one side and consider the books themselves, to look at the story they tell. Whether a narrative is more factual or more fictional, there can be a number of foci for reading it. Among the chief ones we can consider are the plot or theme(s) of the story, and the characters who appear in it.

Genesis and Exodus as Narrative

Genesis and Exodus form the first two parts of the eleven or twelve parts that comprise the huge narrative extending from Genesis itself to the end of 2 Kings. There are 'eleven *or* twelve', because the English Bible has Ruth as part of this narrative, whereas that story comes later in the Hebrew Bible, among the 'Writings'.

Like the episodes in a mini-series, each of these parts has a degree of completeness and closure, but in addition each of them treats themes that also appear in other parts that precede and/or follow. It is thus not totally complete in itself. So Genesis takes the story of the world's origins and the story of Israel's ancestors from the making of a series of promises by God to the fulfilling of some aspects of these promises. A tiny family has become a sizeable people. Equally clearly, it leaves other aspects of these promises unfulfilled. This people does not yet have the land promised to it—indeed, it looks further away from possession of that land. The reader is thus encouraged to turn over the page or take up the next scroll. Similarly Exodus comes to some closure: the people have built the tent shrine that God commissioned. Yet God also commissioned the ordaining of a priesthood, and this has not yet taken place. The reader again turns over the page or takes up the next scroll to discover whether it does take place. This process continues through the eleven or twelve parts of the work as a whole. Arguably the series is still incomplete in substance when we reach 2 Kings 25, but we know that there is no more to the series because when we again pick up the next scroll, we find it is Isaiah, which begins a different mini-series. Or when we again turn over the page in the English Bible, we find ourselves in 1 Chronicles, back at the beginning of the long story, once more making the acquaintance of Adam. We are beginning to watch a remake of the first series.

While the division into those eleven parts is quite intelligible, it may have been made partly for convenience. Though the parts are not all of the same length, they are within a certain range—thirty to fifty pages in an English Bible. And some of the divisions may seem a little strange. In terms of content, for instance, one might outline the opening of the work as follows:

Genesis 1–11:	How God related to the world from the beginning
Genesis 12–50:	How God related to Israel's ancestors
Exodus 1–18:	How God delivered Israel from Egypt
Exodus 19–Numbers 10:	How God met with Israel at Sinai

But as parts on their own, Genesis 1–11 and Exodus 1–18 would be much shorter than the others, while Exodus 19–Numbers 10 would be much longer (Exodus 19–Leviticus 27 would mark a plausible 'part', but this division would still leave Exodus 1–18 looking truncated).

So we might follow the series editor's version of the long work and think of Genesis and Exodus as two parts of it. Or we might think of them as four shorter parts. Either way, the parts are in some respects self-contained, but they also look beyond themselves. It is a nice fact that the three 'Guides' which this volume includes preserve one way of looking at the matter in the treatment of Genesis (which appears as two parts) and the other way in the treatment of Exodus (which appears as one).

The Characters in the Story

In our own experience we are used to a difference between characterization as it appears in a book and as it appears in a film. In books authors can tell us about their inner workings or about those of other people, and can make evaluative comments on matters ('She was grieved', 'I was angry', 'He was an honest man'). In films this is unusual; only when directors are desperate do they have characters talking to camera. Films have to *show* rather than *tell*. They show people acting in certain ways and leave us to work out what this says about their character.

In general, the narrative in Genesis–Exodus works more like a film than like a book. Genesis 1–3, for instance, tells us nothing of God's motivation in creating the world. It tells us that God thought the elements in the created world were good, and it tells about God's reflecting on the need not to let Adam and Eve eat of the tree of life after their disobedience. But the first time we are taken right inside God's character is when we are told that God was sorry and grieved that the world subsequently went so wrong (6.6). Similarly in Exodus 32 we are told for the first time that God has got angry that Israel has gone wrong. But we are never told (for instance) that God loved the world or that God chose Israel. We are left to work that out from God's actions.

In the cast of a story, there are major characters and minor characters. The major characters are the ones we most get to know, though some minor characters play such clearly etched cameo roles that we also get to know them quite well. While the major characters come across as people with the complexity that attaches to being a person, the minor characters may seem simpler. Some minor characters are there only to 'play a role' or fulfil a function.

In this mini-series, one character is central. This person appears in the very first scene simply as 'God', then in the second as 'Yhwh

God'. 'God' is the all-purpose word for deity, which also applies to the deities of other peoples. In the second scene it is thus juxtaposed to the particular name by which Israel addressed God. The story that will unfold in these books concerns God, but a God known specifically as Yhwh, though generally the two words God and Yhwh appear separately rather than being juxtaposed. (In deference to the Jewish practice of neither pronouncing the name nor writing it in its pronounceable form, in this volume we use the vowel-less form Yhwh. Most English Bibles replace the name Yhwh by the expression 'the LORD', or by 'GOD' if the regular Hebrew word for 'the Lord' itself appears in the context. See the note at the end of this Introduction.)

Different facets of the being of this character unfold as the story itself unfolds. In Genesis 1, God is a person who is in complete control of what goes on, who acts systematically, carefully, and reflectively. In Genesis 2–3, God turns out to be someone who can also act impulsively, experimentally, and collaboratively. The God with a name is interested in a relationship with human beings and likes to visit them in the cool of the afternoon to ask how the day has been. Admittedly Yhwh God is also direct and confrontational, and gives rather puzzling instructions to people, expecting them to obey the instructions even if they are surprising. In Genesis 4, too, Yhwh acts in puzzling fashion, welcoming one person's worship but not another's, and not explaining why. At the same time, Yhwh shows an openness to being argued with and a flexibility about decision-making which fit with the collaborativeness and the relational instinct, and will play an important part in the story on other occasions. The negative side to that flexibility soon appears in Genesis 6 when Yhwh responds to human (and heavenly) intransigence by regretting making the world and deciding virtually to clean the slate and start again. As God started off by being someone who could be thrilled at the sight of the world as it comes into being, so now God is someone who feels hurt that this world has turned out as it has.

It is possible to trace the further unfolding of this character through the rest of Genesis–Exodus. In Genesis 12–50 God comes to be known by some new names. On one hand, God is 'El'. This name first appears in Gen. 14.17-23, initially as the name of the God worshipped by the priest-king of Salem, Melchizedek. Specifically, this God is El Elyon, which NRSV renders 'God Most High'. Such a rendering assumes that El is a common noun meaning God rather than a name; some passages imply the one, other passages imply the other. Abram glosses the name that Melchizedek uses by adding Israel's own name for God to produce the phrase 'Yhwh El Elyon'. So in some sense

Yhwh can be identified with the God whom the other inhabitants of the land worship, even if Abraham's comment indicates that more needs to be said about God than the people of Salem are aware.

Subsequently, the God of Israel's ancestors is identified by several other expressions involving this name El:

- *El Roi*, which some translations take to mean 'God who sees me', but which Hagar takes to mean 'God whom I see' (16.13).
- *El Shaddai* (17.1; 28.3; 35.11; 43.14; 48.3; Exod. 6.3); the meaning of this expression is uncertain, but it is traditionally taken to signify 'God Almighty'.
- *El Olam*, 'one who has been God from long ago' or 'one who will long be God' (literally 'God Age') (21.33).
- *El [of?] Bethel* (31.13; 35.7).
- *El, God of Israel* (33.20 – 'Israel' in the sense of the individual Jacob who has just been re-named Israel).

Another facet of this character appears when God speaks as 'El, the God of your father' (46.3; cf. 49.25). So far we have seen that God is one with a particular name, Yhwh, and also one who can be identified in a qualified way with the God of the peoples among whom Israel's ancestors live and can be linked with specific places such as Salem and Bethel. The self-description just quoted marks God as also one who establishes a special relationship with the successive leaders of the family whose story Genesis tells, with Abraham, Isaac and Jacob. Yhwh is thus 'the God of my father'. The specificity of the special relationship is expressed in God's being 'the God of Abraham, the awe of Isaac and the strong one of Jacob'. The link with a leader and not merely with a place means that this God relates to the people in a way that meets the needs of a family that is often on the move under the authority of its head. God is one who guides and provides.

There is another feature to the way God is portrayed in Genesis 12–50. At the beginning, in the story of Abraham, God is one who takes the initiative in speaking and acting. By the end, in the story of Joseph, God is much more behind the scenes. Joseph's life originally receives its dynamic from a prophetic dream, but the fulfilment of the dream comes about through the ordinary human activity of people such as himself and his brothers. God is capable of operating both ways. By the beginning of the next part of the story, in Exodus, the trouble is that God seems to have given up being involved at all, and Israel has to call God back to the kind of supra-natural activity that the earlier story described.

When we turn to Exodus 1–18, we also find new facets of God's character emerging. In Genesis 14, Abraham had had to get involved in fighting, and as the God of Abraham, Yhwh had got dragged into that, but generally there had been no need for such activity. The situation in which Abraham's descendants now find themselves requires a different form of activity, or rather requires a more dedicated application of the kind of capacity Yhwh showed in Genesis 14. In fulfilment of the promise to Abraham, Israel has become a sizeable ethnic group. In itself that means it needs to learn to function in the political arena, and Yhwh will have to show the kind of characteristics required in that arena. But in addition, Israel is actually under the harsh control of another nation. Although Israel is nation-sized, it does not have nation-status. Indeed, whereas Genesis had spoken of its becoming a great 'nation', Exodus's own preferred term for Israel is 'people'. It has no *national* identity. Yhwh still has work to do, and this is different work from that involved in taking it from family-size to people-size. So in Exodus 1–18 the character of Yhwh reveals more consistently confrontational, conflictual, martial features from the ones it shows in Genesis 12–50.

In Exodus 19–40 things change again. The guide who became a warrior now becomes a rule-maker. In Genesis there had apparently also been no need for instructions on how to behave, or at least there had been no place for these. One way of expressing the need for Yhwh now to show this capacity is to note again that Abraham's family has become a nation, or at least a nation-sized people. A nation needs laws. Its life needs boundary markers. It needs ways of handling conflict and other problems in the community. It needs a common framework for considering matters such as property, employment, marriage, justice, personal injury and loans. Even as a family, the people would have needed some such common framework, but a family can work on the basis of a moral authority resting within the family itself ('this is the way we have always done things'). A nation needs a more formalized framework for its life. Yhwh has to become a lawgiver in order to relate to Israel as a nation.

God is *the* major character in this story. It is God's character that emerges most fully and therefore in most complexity. Because this character is on stage on-and-off throughout the drama, we see God acting and reacting in a series of different contexts, playing those different roles (creator, punisher, guide, deliverer, lawgiver) and revealing different emotions (e.g. grief and anger).

In the Old Testament story as a whole, the major 'character' opposite Yhwh is the Israelite people. In Genesis this people does not exist—at least not until the closing pages, which refer to the twelve clans of Israel. Genesis tells of Israel's background in the story of a small family that is destined to become a great nation. The last of the three great fathers in the family history, Jacob, is one who comes to bear the very name 'Israel', and he is the father of twelve sons to whom the clans trace their origin. His name 'Israel' is suggestive. He receives it from a mysterious wrestler at the River Jabbock (32.28). The wrestler implies that the name denotes Jacob as someone who wrestles with God (and with human beings) and wins. More literally, the name means 'God wrestles'—presumably with Jacob. Either comment on the name constitutes a telling introduction to the character.

In Genesis, then, the foreshadowed Israel is a family that is destined to be a nation. The idea that Israel began as a family will be a feature to which the Old Testament appeals from time to time. Deuteronomy will argue that as members of one family, Israelites ought to treat each other as brothers and sisters. Meanwhile, at the beginning of Exodus Israel is first described as now having become a 'people' (Exod. 1.9). The word identifies Israel as a community with a common racial or ethnic identity—a family writ large. The word comes on the lips of the Egyptian Pharaoh, for whom this family is writ large enough to seem a threat to Egypt itself. He responds by seeking to squash it. From there it is taken onto Yhwh's lips when Yhwh for the first time describes Israel as 'my people' (3.7). At the moment the Pharaoh compels Israel to live as if he owned it—as if Israel were the Pharaoh's people. It has to be involved in 'service' to the Pharaoh (e.g. 2.23). Actually, Israel belongs to Yhwh, and Yhwh intends to be the object of Israel's 'service' (e.g. 3.12). Words such as 'serve', 'service', 'servants', 'slavery' and 'worship' are of key importance in these chapters. All come from the Hebrew verb *'ābad* and related nouns.

On what basis does Yhwh claim ownership of Israel? Perhaps part of the basis implicitly lies in the covenant commitment to Israel's ancestors. It was this that made God accept an obligation to do something about the situation when the people cried out under their oppression. In other respects, describing Israel as 'my people' anticipates a new situation—indeed, it brings it into being. At Sinai Yhwh and Israel will enter into a formal relationship whereby Yhwh becomes Israel's God and Israel becomes Yhwh's people. But that event will have its background in a decision Yhwh has apparently made by this time. To say 'my people' constitutes a decision to stake a claim to Israel. It might be seen as an instance of performative language. On the basis of this claim, Yhwh intends to take Israel from the one who currently 'pretends' to own them, by force if necessary.

To put it another way, Yhwh is adopting Israel and treating the people as firstborn son, and the job of such a son is to serve his father (4.22). The Pharaoh had better not dispute the claim. Israel is leaving Egypt to start serving Yhwh.

The trouble is that Israel is a resistant servant as the Pharaoh is a resistant rival. As the Pharaoh resists having his slave-people taken away, so the slave-people resist being taken away by Yhwh, when in the short term it means their life gets harder. After their double escape from the Pharaoh, they do come to revere and trust in Yhwh, and to trust in Moses (14.31), but they resist the down sides to their enforced trek through the desert. At Sinai they commit themselves to being Yhwh's people, but they are soon making up their own minds about how to worship Yhwh. Exodus does close with great acts of generosity to provide the raw materials for building Yhwh's shrine, but at its end the narrative leaves us uncertain whether they will eventually settle into a pattern of such responsiveness to Yhwh, or one of resistance to Yhwh, or whether they will continue to move between the two.

Among the individual human characters in Genesis and Exodus, the ones who emerge most clearly are Abraham, Sarah, Hagar, Jacob, Joseph and Moses. Cain, Noah, Esau and Miriam play significant cameo parts. Aaron is on stage for a long time, but he is more a man playing a role than someone who comes into focus as a person, as are Lot and the Pharaoh of the exodus. Adam and Eve, too, seem to be there as the means of discussing a theological theme. We do not get to know them as people. Among the minor players, Enoch has especially intrigued readers and inspired a substantial literature in the Second Temple period. Isaac is an oddly underdeveloped character, given his significance as one of the sequence of ancestors in Genesis 12–50.

The Plot and the Themes of the Story
So what is this story about? We might see the themes of its four parts as blessing, promise, liberation and lifestyle.

Genesis 1–11 is about whether and how far the world stands under God's blessing or under God's curse. The linguistic basis for seeing it that way is that the words 'blessing' and 'curse' recur a number of times through the chapters. The story of the world's origins includes a declaration that God blessed the creatures of the sea and the sky, blessed humanity, and blessed the Sabbath (1.22, 28; 2.3). But the story of Adam and Eve and their children tells us that there is a curse on the cleverest of the land creatures, a curse on the land that Adam was to tend and a curse on Adam and Eve's surviving son (3.14, 17; 4.11).

After that, we are admittedly encouraged by the reminder that God did bless humanity at the beginning (5.2), but this does not stop the story proceeding to describe the curse working itself out in a destructive flood. The other side of that flood, however, once more we are encouraged to read about God's blessing Noah and his family (9.1). Yet soon Noah is himself putting a curse on his grandson (9.25). How long is this to go on? It seems that the story of the world is a story in which blessing and curse wrestle for the victory, and it is not clear which will win. The opening of chapter 12 reassures us that God's purpose to bless will win out.

We could portray Genesis 12–50 as the story of how that comes about, as 'blessing' talk continues, while talk about curse falls more into the background. But Genesis 12–50 has a distinctive way of making the point, and nuancing it. Its initial reference to blessing comes in the setting of a charge to Abram to go to a new land, apparently to complete a journey begun by his father. In between talk of a land and talk of blessing is a promise that Abram will become a great nation and will gain a great name (see Gen. 12.1-3). The rest of Genesis is the story of how these promises found partial fulfilment against a variety of odds. The promises are imperilled by a sequence of factors. Abram's wife and a number of other women in Genesis cannot have children. God's own requirement almost involves Abraham in offering to God the son through whom his family is to grow. Will this one family really become a nation? Another people lives in the land that God sends them to, and anyway Abram is soon on the way out of this land again because of a famine. A later famine causes Jacob's entire family to leave the land. Will this people ever possess it? Instead of gaining a great name, ancestors such as Abraham, Jacob and Joseph often earn themselves a bad name or gain one when they do not deserve it. Instead of being a blessing, they bring trouble.

Yet the story shows how the promise does find forms of partial fulfilment. One man and his infertile wife have grown to become a large family. Abraham does gain a foothold in the land and Joseph closes the book with a dying reaffirmation of the promise that will take his family back there. Joseph has made a name for himself in Egypt. Jacob brings blessing to Laban (30.27), Joseph brings blessing to Potiphar's house (39.5) and Jacob blesses Pharaoh (47.7, 10). Genesis 12–50 tells of how God's promise is continually reaffirmed, often endangered, partially fulfilled, and always standing before Israel's ancestors to lure them on.

Exodus 1–18 are about liberation. Their story starts with the promise of increase spectacularly fulfilled, but with this family-become-people in bondage to another nation. The story of its liberation opens with the preparation of a leader who will lead them out from bondage. It goes on to describe the conflict between him and the leader of the oppressor nation. The dual highpoint of the story is the people's departure from Egypt and the subsequent drowning of their oppressors when they eventually decided to pursue the escapees. The close of the story takes the people to the destination announced earlier, a meeting with God at a mountain in the desert where the leader had once himself met with God.

The meeting with God issues in a multiform revelation on the mountain. In at least three respects Exodus 19–40 compares with the opening of Genesis. First, God lays before the people the style of life that God expects of them, but does so in much more detail than was the case in Genesis 2. The wide giving of permission and the single prohibition that placed one limitation on people's lives is succeeded by a complex sequence of commands and prohibitions that lay down boundaries for Israel's life. Second, the hearers immediately disobey. The 'original sin' of the people of God replaces the 'original sin' of the first human beings. But third, despite the disobedience at the bottom of the mountain while God is speaking to Moses on the top of the mountain, the people can still fulfil the commission to build God a home among the people, which images God's heavenly home, and God comes to dwell there.

The meeting at Sinai takes Israel into a covenant relationship with Yhwh. A covenant is a solemnly ratified, formalized commitment. It may be a one-sided commitment by one party, which requires nothing of the other party except to let it happen. Or it may be more reciprocal. If both parties make a commitment, then the covenant depends on both keeping them.

There are a number of covenants between God and humanity in Genesis–Exodus, of varying kinds. In the creation story, admittedly, there was no covenant. The implication may be that it is only when sin has entered into the equation that commitments need to be solemnly ratified and formalized. On the other hand, one of the covenants in Exodus is the 'permanent covenant' involved in keeping the Sabbath, which is a sign that looks back to creation (Exod. 31.12-17). In this sense Genesis and Exodus do assume that creation involved a covenant.

The link between covenants and sin may be implicit in the first actual account of covenant-making, God's commitment to Noah and the humanity to descend from him. This commitment is that henceforth God will maintain the structure of life on earth, and part of its background is the fact of human wickedness (Gen. 8.21). The second account of a covenant tells of God's commitment to Abraham. It, too, is virtually one-sided, in that the only response it requires is the circumcision of male babies. The third account of a covenant describes the sealing of a covenant at Sinai (Exod. 19–24) and its renewing after the people's transgressing of it there (Exod. 32–34). This covenant again emphasizes God's initiative, but it differs in basing itself on the fact that God has actually done what was pledged to Abraham. On that basis it looks for a reciprocal commitment on Israel's part. The 'laws' in Exodus define the nature of that commitment.

The suitability and the unsuitability of the word 'law' emerge here. The English word is apt to suggest a quasi-legal understanding of the relationship between Israel and God. The Hebrew word 'torah' is a more general one suggesting 'teaching'. The narrative in Genesis is as much part of the Torah as are the instructions about behaviour in Exodus. Neither Old Testament Israel nor subsequent Judaism has an inherently legal or legalistic understanding of their relationship with God.

On the other hand, in Exodus the relationship between Yhwh and Israel is being articulated in quasi-political terms. Yhwh is like a king and Israel is like this king's people. It is thus quite natural for the king to use quasi-legal terms in portraying the lifestyle expected of the people. This is one way in which a king attempts to ensure that the life of his people is what it should be.

We have noted that there was a change in the way God was involved with people as Genesis 12–50 unfolded. There is a parallel development within Exodus. In his commentary on Exodus John Durham characterizes it as follows.

- Exodus 1–18 is the story of God in Israel's midst, 'acting'. Yhwh is Israel's redeemer or deliverer.
- Exodus 19–40 is the story of God in Israel's midst, 'speaking'. Yhwh is revealing the demands of the covenant to Israel.
- Exodus 40 marks a transition to the story of God in Israel's midst, 'being'.

Part of that revelation on Sinai concerned the building of a home for Yhwh, a place where Yhwh could dwell and where Israel could therefore always find Yhwh. Chapters 25–31 give the instructions for building this mobile home. Chapters 35–40 then repeat them virtually word-for-word, except that they are now report rather than instruction (without the institution of the priesthood; we have noted that this comes in due course in Leviticus). In some ways this rounds off Genesis–Exodus. At the beginning of Genesis God created heaven and earth as a home, achieving much of the work by speaking (e.g., 'There is to be light'). At the end of Exodus God comes to live in a home, made in accordance with the words God had spoken, and designed to embody the ordered nature of that large-scale home of God that comprises heaven and earth.

Behind Genesis and Exodus

When people read Genesis and Exodus in their English Bibles in the pre-modern period, the books were headed 'The First/Second Book of Moses, Called Genesis/Exodus'. These heading told them that Moses wrote these books. He was clearly in an excellent position to give them accurate historical information on the story in Exodus, and this encouraged them to assume that they were reading a straightforward historical account of events. One could therefore add up the years in Genesis and work out approximately (or even exactly) not only the dates of the exodus and of Israel's ancestors, but the date of the world's creation.

The modern period introduced a new set of attitudes. Those headings are not part of the text of Genesis and Exodus; they do not appear in the Hebrew Bible. Traditions about the origin and meaning of the text were no longer accepted simply on the basis of their being traditions. They needed to be tested. The books needed to be studied historically.

There are two aspects to the historical study of Genesis and Exodus. One of its concerns is to work out who actually wrote the books, and when, and where. The other is to establish what were the actual historical events to which the books refer. Who actually was Abraham, when did he live and what did he do? What actually were the origins of the Israelite people?

The Origin of the Books

Moses was in a position to write Exodus on the basis of personal experience of nearly all the events, but he could not have written Genesis on this basis. If he wrote it, where did he get his information? One might look behind the text of Genesis itself for clues. Perhaps there were existent collections of stories about people such as Abraham and Joseph, and these were strung together. Or perhaps there was an earlier version of the whole story, though filled out by material from elsewhere. Or perhaps there were several versions of the same stories, and these were subsequently interwoven. This last process would then have anticipated what happened a millennium or so later, when the first Christians wrote several versions of the Gospel story. While these were included in the New Testament separately, the second-century Christian theologian Tatian turned them into one, his Diatessaron, a Harmony of the Gospels.

In the study of Genesis and Exodus, it was a version of the last possibility that convinced the world of scholarship for a hundred years, from the late nineteenth century until the late twentieth century. But the idea that it was Moses who did the interweaving had long been abandoned. It became clear that the stories in Genesis had been adapted to speak to the needs of a much later time than that of Moses. Sometimes the indications of this are quite small details. For instance, the story of Abraham refers to his having come from Ur of the Chaldeans (11.31). But the Chaldeans did not arrive in Ur until several centuries later. Technically this is therefore an anachronism, but referring to the Chaldeans helps later readers identify the city in relation to the politics of their day.

A famous instance of adaptation to speak to a later time is the creation story in Genesis 1 itself. In the nineteenth century, some scholars described this as borrowed from a Babylonian creation story. That is hardly right, because the Genesis story is so different from the Babylonian story. But we can say that the Genesis story is written to communicate with people who know the Babylonian story, and who might be tempted to believe it. Against that background, the Genesis story reckons to tell its readers the real truth about creation in a way that confronts key features in the Babylonian story.

The result of attempts to look behind the story in Genesis and Exodus (and subsequent books) and to date the material that appears there was the view that these two books interweave two or three major earlier versions of the story, conventionally known as J, E and P. J takes its title from the name Yhwh (Jhwh in German), the name this strand uses for God in Genesis. E takes its title from the ordinary Hebrew word for God, *ʾelōhîm*, which it uses for God in Genesis. P stands for the Priestly Work, named after its interest in matters that concerned priests, such as Sabbath, food laws, and circumcision. P also uses the word *ʾelōhîm* for God in Genesis, but its priestly interests make it possible to distinguish P from E. The scholarly consensus dated J in the early monarchy, the time of David and Solomon or soon after. It dated E a century or so later. It dated P in the exile or after. A fourth source, D, is largely confined to Deuteronomy, which the scholarly consensus dated between E and P, though in the treatment of Exodus that follows, William Johnstone shows how the 'Deuter-onomists' might have edited Exodus.

The trouble is that it is a highly speculative business to get behind a narrative work in order to discover the sources it used and the time they belonged to—as John Rogerson and Walter Moberly note in their treatments of Genesis 1–11 and 12–50 in this volume. The author(s) of Genesis and Exodus wanted us to read these books themselves, and would not have wanted to give obvious clues to any sources out of which the books were constructed. Their aim was that we should focus on Genesis and Exodus. But for a century the world of scholarship was keen to have an answer to the question of the material's background, and it agreed to take the JEDP scheme as a working hypothesis.

At the end of the twentieth century, however, that agreement collapsed, and there is currently no consensus on the question. This does not mean that the scholarly world is inclined to think that perhaps Moses wrote Genesis and Exodus after all. The data that convinced people in the 1880s that this cannot be so remained convincing in the 1980s. The novelty in our current situation is this fact that there is no new consensus to put in the place of the old one.

In this last part of the twentieth century the scholarly world in general, in the sciences and the humanities, was taken with the hypothesis of Thomas Kuhn concerning 'paradigm shifts' in the sciences, which also came to be applied to the humanities. People often imagine that science proceeds by a process that involves scientists collecting raw data and watching a hypothesis emerge from it. In practice, scientists operate with a collection of already existent, supposedly proven hypotheses, and they fit data into these hypotheses. Their question then is, what do they do with data that do not fit the existent hypotheses? They can live with a small quantity of such data, but when the quantity increases, so does the pressure to formulate a hypothesis that will better account for it. Kuhn emphasized that generally people do not abandon theories easily, even when they can see that there is so much intransigent data that it can no longer be ignored. They continue to use a theory that is manifestly unsatisfactory *until a better theory emerges*.

A striking feature of the history of the study of Genesis and Exodus over the past three hundred years is that it fails to illustrate Kuhn's theory. The world of scholarship abandoned the tradition that Moses wrote the books, without having another theory to put in its place. To judge from scholarly work on these two books published in the last decades of the twentieth century, it has now largely abandoned the

JEDP framework for understanding the books' origin, again without there being another consensus on an alternative theory. In conformity with Kuhn's thesis, however, it may be that the silent majority in the world of scholarship still assumes that working hypothesis, in the absence of another. In the same way, ordinary people continue to assume that Moses wrote Genesis and Exodus, and it may be that most students of theology heave a sigh of relief and revert to that assumption after they graduate.

This is a particularly hazardous procedure for people who want to understand the Bible because they believe it is the word of God. The way in which a document communicates with people depends in part on the way in which it interacts with their situation and needs. To cite a less complex example, the great difference between the message of Kings and Chronicles derives in part from the different circumstances of the community in the Babylonian period, when Kings was written, and that in Persian period, when Chronicles was written. Chronicles would communicate quite differently in the former period, Kings quite differently in the latter period. So we have to locate the audience in its time if we want to overhear the narrators telling these versions of Israel's story to their audience and to hear them as it would.

In an ideal world, the same would be true of Genesis and Exodus. The trouble is, it seems that we do not know when they were written, and that we never will. The following considerations may help to mitigate the difficulties caused by our inability to date the books.

First, the books' relative lack of concrete indicators of their origin may reflect a desire not to be tied to a context in the way that Kings and Chronicles are. The four Gospels in the New Testament were written by individual authors and may have been first read to particular communities, but each is a 'Gospel for All Christians' (to use Richard Bauckham's phrase). In the same way, from the paucity of concrete information about the intended audience of Genesis–Exodus we should perhaps infer that the books were intended for the Israelite/Judean community as a whole. They were not so slanted to the circumstances of the community in one period.

Second, the books themselves, and/or the wider context of the Old Testament, implicitly invite us to read them against the background of times such as the exodus period, the united monarchy, the exile, and the Persian period. This is so even if we cannot be sure which of these periods generated the books. What I mean by this is that (for instance) the story of the exodus refers back to Yhwh's promises to Israel's ancestors. I do not believe that Genesis was written by Moses or in Moses' day, but I can appropriately follow the invitation in

Exodus and study the period of the ancestors as background to the events of Moses' day. In general the regulations in Exodus presuppose the settled life of Israel in a period such as the monarchy, so I can follow their implicit invitation and study them against that background. The way Genesis tells the Abraham story also links with realities in the period of the monarchy: the promises to Abraham reappear in part as promises to David. It also links with the exile: the position of Abraham living by the *promise* of land rather than by its possession corresponds to the position of Judean exiles, and we have noted that Genesis draws attention to the Chaldeans, who ruled Babylon in the exilic Judeans' own day. Then Ezra–Nehemiah tells us of the way the story in Genesis–Exodus and the rules for life in Exodus were applied to the community back in Judah in the fifth century. We can reckon to read Genesis and Exodus against these historical contexts because the books invite us to do so, whatever may turn out to be the facts of their origin.

Third, to put the same point another way, studying the books historically can be heuristically illuminating even if our conclusions about dating turn out to be wrong. Scientists sometimes find that a theory is illuminating in enabling them to make further discoveries, even though the theory itself turns out to be wrong. That has been true of the study of Genesis and Exodus over the past two centuries. Much of it must be wrong in its assumptions or conclusions about the books' origin. But this has not stopped it enabling us to understand aspects of the text that we might otherwise have missed.

The Books' Historical Value
In his book *The Eclipse of Biblical Narrative*, Hans Frei attempted to trace the course of a fateful development in the study of books such as Genesis and Exodus in the seventeenth and eighteenth centuries. At the beginning of his period, as part of the set of attitudes that we now call pre-modern, people assumed that the narrative and the history were the same thing. Creation, ancestral history, exodus and events at Sinai happened as Genesis and Exodus describe them. Modernity brought an awareness of the difference between history and story. The question was, which was to be the focus of study and the place where truth could be found? For two reasons, it was inevitable that history won. One reason was modernity's general commitment to history. The other was the fact that this enabled new questions to be asked, and thus opened up the possibility of new discoveries being made. The energy behind the development of the JEDP theory (or any other theory about the origins of the books) derived from the

conviction that a theory about the books' origins was of key importance if we were to answer this second question, that of the historical
events to which Genesis and Exodus refer. By implication, these
events would turn out to be not merely ones that took place in the
second millennium BCE but events that took place through much of
the first millennium BCE. It was in the first millennium that the books
were written, and like any documents, the books give subconscious
witness to the history of the period in which they were written as well
as their conscious witness to the period they portray.

There are a number of reasons why someone might be interested in
establishing the actual history of Israel, and the people's pre-history. I
might be interested in it for the same reason that I might be interested
in (say) the history of Peru or Indonesia: I might find history inherently interesting and illuminating. Or I might be interested in it
because in some sense I view it as 'my' history. Jews obviously do
that, but Christians also do so. My self-identification with the history
gives an extra impetus to my study. Thus the history that may lie
behind Genesis and Exodus has been studied much more intensely
than the history of Israel's contemporaries in the Middle East, because
so many people have become involved in this study because of that
self-identification. (Many, many Babylonian documents lie in
museums unpublished because there are not enough people interested in them to get around to deciphering them and publishing
them.)

The down side to the self-identification is that we may have a clear
idea of the sort of historical results we want to reach. Most Jews and
Christians do not want to conclude that Abraham or Moses never
existed. It requires a rather sophisticated sort of religious faith to say
that this does not matter. Indeed, Genesis and Exodus imply that it
does matter. It is Yhwh's making promises to Abraham and fulfilling
them, and Yhwh's delivering Israel from Egypt, that provide evidence
that Yhwh is God and show what kind of God Yhwh is. If Yhwh
made no promises and effected no deliverance, this does not quite
provide evidence of the opposite or directly undermine the picture of
the kind of God Yhwh is, but it does leave Yhwh's identity and status
floating in the air. Jewish and Christian scholars thus have a vested
interest in the results they come to. That is all the more the case if they
work for educational institutions identified with their faith, so that
their jobs depend on the kind of results to which their scholarship
comes. (Of course, all this also means that an atheist or an agnostic
might be subject to converse pressures.)

One may perceive two quite contrary trends in the scholarship of the last part of the twentieth century. One is that there continue to be works arguing that Genesis and Exodus look more historically accurate than the JEDP hypothesis suggests. If they were indeed written between the time of Solomon and the exile, one would not expect them to contain much reliable information concerning the middle half of the second millennium BCE when Israel's putative ancestors lived and when the people were in bondage in Egypt. But studies such as those of Walter Moberly and Augustine Pagolu have shown how Genesis 12–50 portrays a religion very different from any religion known from later Israel. They argue that this most likely indicates that Genesis offers an accurate portrayal of the time of Israel's ancestors. Similarly, studies such as those of James Hoffmeier have argued afresh that the Exodus portrayal of the Israelites' life in Egypt and their escape from there corresponds to evidence from Egyptian sources. Neither of these approaches offers hard evidence that the stories Genesis and Exodus tell are factual. Both offer circumstantial evidence that reckons to raise difficulties for the view that the narratives were written from scratch many centuries after the period they portray.

The contrary trend in scholarship works in quite the opposite direction. The JEDP theory always assumed that Genesis and Exodus reached their final form in the Persian period. We have seen that the books contain detailed indications that they were written in the exile or afterwards, such as the reference to Ur of the Chaldeans. The description of Ezra the *scribe* (that is, writer) bringing the Torah from Persia to Jerusalem fits with the assumption that the books were written in the Persian period. The JEDP theory sought to look behind the books as we have them for the indications that they used earlier sources. But suppose that the Persian period was *the* period in which the creative work that produced Genesis and Exodus was done? Indeed, suppose there were no such earlier sources and that the books were written from scratch in the Persian period? An illustration of the way this trend works itself out is Samuel Balentine's study of *The Torah's Vision of Worship* (pp. 39-57). Balentine shows how the creation stories, the codification of laws, and the formalization of regulations for worship could have been a means of Persia exercising control of this part of its empire. If Genesis and Exodus indeed came into being more or less from scratch in the Persian period, it becomes unbelievable that they accurately portray events nearly a millennium previously. There must be some other explanation for the portrayal of a distinctive lifestyle in Genesis 12–50. Perhaps it reflects not a style of life that obtained long before the books were written, but one that obtained in a different area or among different groups from the ones whose lives lie behind other parts of the Old Testament story.

One difficulty here, however, is that there is no positive pointer to this being the background of the story, any more or any less than there are pointers to the background lying in (say) the early monarchy or the exile. This again illustrates the problem about the entire enterprise of attempting to determine when Genesis and Exodus were written. The collapse of the scholarly consensus at the end of the twentieth century and the reopening of questions that seemed settled a century before suggests not only that we will never know when the books were written but also that the attempt to discover what historical events lie behind Genesis and Exodus, while vitally important, is fraught with difficulties that may never be overcome.

The Worlds In Front of Genesis and Exodus

Behind Genesis and Exodus lie ancient historical contexts and events. In front of the text stand readers who come from their own worlds to the text and who may find that their worlds illumine the text, giving them access to aspects of the world of the text itself. In the treatment of Genesis 1–11 in this volume, John Rogerson pays particular attention to the way this works out with regard to those chapters.

Admittedly the worlds behind the text and in front of the text overlap. Even in undertaking historical study, we construe the world behind the text in the light of who we are as readers and what we think history is. On the other hand, as readers we are probably seeking access to the world behind the text in the sense of a world that truly exists. We do not wish merely to see ourselves at the bottom of the well, nor merely to visit a world within the text that only exists there and has no links with the 'real world'.

The Doctrinal World

In the past, most people's reading of Genesis and Exodus was guided by the doctrinal beliefs of the church. Since the early Christian centuries, Genesis in particular has been a focus of Christian study and has been of key significance for a Christian understanding of creation and of what it meant to be human.

Among the first attempts to see the significance of Genesis for Christian belief was Paul's discussion of Genesis in Romans. First, he infers from it the importance of the principle that God does not relate to human beings on the basis of acts that we do. God does not accept people because they perform the right kind of religious rites, nor does

God love people because they live the right kind of lives. God relates to them on the basis of grace and love—or to use something closer to Genesis's own way of expressing the matter, on the basis of making promises in which they simply put their trust. Paul argues from the plot of Genesis–Exodus that it is when grace and love have won a response that God indicates what that response needs to look like in life. So Genesis 12–50 establishes that God's reaching out to Israel comes first, and Exodus 19–40 shows what the response is to look like. This construction is not explicit in Genesis–Exodus, but it fits important aspects of the books' own dynamic.

Elsewhere in Romans Paul looks behind Abraham to Adam, and traditionally the doctrinal significance of Genesis and Exodus has lain chiefly in Genesis 1–3. In the second century CE, Christian theologians such as Tertullian formulated a 'guideline for the faith', an outline understanding of the Christian faith designed to provide a framework for a Christian approach to scripture. It was eventually embodied in the Apostles Creed. The only Old Testament event to which it refers is creation. These and subsequent theologians such as Augustine also took up the use in the New Testament of the story of the first human beings' disobedience in Genesis 3, and developed the doctrines of 'the fall' and 'original sin'. The difficulty with this process has been that subsequent Christian doctrine has read Genesis not only via Paul but also via Augustine.

The idea of a fall presupposes that Adam and Eve were in an exalted position in Eden, from which they then fell. But much of the outworking of this belief seems to be at best absent from Genesis, at worst in conflict with it. Nor does it appear in Paul, though some aspects of the idea appear there. Talk in terms of a 'fall' comes first in a Jewish work called 2 Esdras, which takes the form of a work by Esdras (=Ezra) discussing the destruction of Jerusalem in 587. It was actually written some time after the destruction in 70 CE, but it became part of the Roman Christian canon of the Old Testament. In 7.118, Esdras implies that human beings were created immortal and that their sin brought their 'fall' from immortality. Language in terms of 'fall' then began to appear in the work of Christian theologians. But Genesis 2–3 does not imply that Adam and Eve were inherently immortal. They needed to eat from the tree of life if they were to live forever. This fits the fact that the human body seems to be designed to go through a cycle of birth, maturing, senescence and death, like a plant's or an animal's. It is difficult to imagine a human body of a form that did not follow this cycle. From the beginning it would thus have needed to be transformed if human beings were to live forever.

It is in the sense that this transformation will not happen that death came about as a result of Adam and Eve's disobedience.

The idea of a fall has other implications that are difficult to fit with Genesis. It implies that the first human beings lived a life of happiness and closeness to God. As a result of the fall their relationship with God was broken. But Genesis 1–3 does not say anything about how their life actually was in the Garden, while Genesis 4 pictures human beings as involved in working together with God, in worshipping and in conversing with God.

The idea of a fall implies that the first human beings could obey God, but that after the fall human beings could not. Yet when Christians read Genesis 3 they find the same dynamics of temptation and disobedience as they themselves experience, and Genesis 4 assumes that Cain can obey God.

The idea of a fall implies that originally the world worked in a harmonious way. There were no earthquakes, and lions lay down with lambs. As a result of the fall, the world is spoiled. But Genesis 3 says only that God cursed the snake and the soil, which would henceforth therefore produce desert plants rather than garden plants—presumably because it lacked the abundant water of Eden. When Romans 8 describes the world as subject to futility, it does not say when or how this came about, and specifically it does not link it with human sin.

A reading of Genesis 3 that does not start from the Christian idea of the fall suggests that what the story describes is not a fall from a state of bliss but a failure to realize a possibility. As Paul put it, human beings 'fell short of the glory of God' (Rom. 3.23).

Now Genesis 1–11 offers extensive insight on the nature of human sin, and thus theological reflection on this subject on the basis of these chapters can be a fruitful exercise. They portray God forming a world that constituted an ideal environment where human beings could live, work and grow. Such a world would not be without challenges and problems, because it is through handling these that people do grow. There is some taming of the world to be done on God's behalf. God expected human beings to accept certain constraints in living in God's world, and their first failure lay in declining to do that. Their disobedience was trivial, and it is not called sin, but it was disastrous, because it involved taking no notice of the one constraint under which they were challenged to live.

In Genesis 1–11 it is the story of Cain that introduces us to 'sin' (4.7). Sin consisted in one human being's violence to another. The story of wrongdoing is taken further in the story of divine beings getting involved in sexual relationships with human women (6.1-4). A cumulative account of the 'fall' of humanity runs through Genesis 1–6, leading to God's decision to end it all and start again. The new start recognizes the deep-seated nature of human sinfulness (8.21) and soon witnesses fresh evidence of it, within Noah's family (9.20-27) and in the hopes, aims and resistance to God's purpose embodied in the life of the city-builders of chapter 11.

It is thus possible to study the text of Genesis for the doctrinal truths that it implies, on a subject such as sin, but in doing so readers need to lay on one side for a while the church's doctrinal tradition if they are to see what Genesis itself says.

The possible fruitfulness of doing this may be further illustrated by consideration of the doctrine of God. At the beginning of Genesis, human beings are created in God's image, and not long after the end of Exodus, Israel is urged to be holy as Yhwh is holy (Lev. 19.2). Humanity is designed as God-like, and Israel is called to realize that purpose by being a distinctive people in line with the distinctiveness of Yhwh as God. The creation and the urging might make one read through Genesis and Exodus asking, Who then is this God whom humanity is designed to image and whom Israel is to resemble? Among the answers are that God is

- creative, life-giving and order-bringing (Gen. 1–2)
- easily hurt, realistic and not inclined to give up (Gen. 3–11)
- giver of hope, land space and scope (Gen. 12–50)
- attentive to people's pain, open and self-revealing, active against oppression and giver of freedom (Exod. 1–18)
- frightening, categorical, concrete and practical (Exod. 19–24)
- present, flexible and more merciful than judgmental (Exod. 25–40).

Many of these aspects of God's character and of the human vocation are not prominent in Christian doctrine. So a doctrinal question can enable us to perceive aspects of the text and can generate answers that broaden the framework of the question.

The Political World

Readers have brought to Genesis and Exodus two very different political worlds, the world of the powerful and the world of the powerless. Nations such as Britain and America have seen themselves as a chosen people in succession to the people of Abraham and Moses. This self-understanding undergirded European emigration to America and British policy in Southern Africa. If European and British peoples were in the position of Abraham or Moses, then in both areas local people, Native American or African peoples, were in the position of Canaanites, and could be treated accordingly.

At the same time, American pioneers saw themselves as like Israelites escaping from Pharaoh Britain, and in the modern world it has often been powerless peoples who have identified themselves with Israel oppressed by the Egyptians. In the 1970s liberation theology paid considerable attention to the exodus story in this connection, taking it as a model for what God might be expected to do for the powerless in Latin America today.

One strength of this lay in its capacity to recapture central aspects of the text of Exodus itself. In the 1960s there had been four dominant modes of reading the exodus story, two more academic, two more confessional. In the world of Old Testament criticism, the focus lay on the attempt to recover the historical world behind the text. We have seen that this leads to minimal conclusions, conclusions of 'academic' interest but not capable of having an impact on the way people think about their lives or live them. In the world of Old Testament theology, the focus lay on the idea of 'God who Acts', an idea clearly proclaimed in the story. More surprisingly, however, this theology was also of largely 'academic' interest. Theologians who studied the idea 'in the text' did not have clear ideas on what it might represent in the world behind the text or in our world, the world in front of the text.

In the Jewish world, the exodus story constituted a vital element in people's self-understanding, a role reinforced every year in its retelling at Passover. In the Christian world, the story was read typologically. The story itself spoke of God's this-worldly deliverance of a people from this-worldly oppression, incorporating the death of thousands of actual lambs whose blood was literally spattered over the homes of the community. In the Christian world, the story became a figure for God's deliverance of people from inner oppression through the death of a person, whose blood was metaphorically spattered over people.

Liberation theology abandoned historical speculation, theological theorizing, ceremonial re-enactment, and typological reinterpretation, for a literal reading of the story and an expectation that it should have literal implications. It was able to do that because there were real parallels between Exodus and the context from which it read the book. It is perhaps not surprising that there were only half-acknowledged limitations to the literalness of its reading. It no more expected a supernatural intervention by God than mainstream Old Testament theology did. It saw the story more as a possible inspiration for human action to effect a people's deliverance. But it at least read the story politically.

Liberation theology's approach has subsequently been taken up and taken further by black theology in South Africa and in the United States, and by other forms of ethnic and post-colonial interpretation.

The Gendered World

In front of Genesis and Exodus is also a world in which readers' identity as men and as women is of far-reaching significance for the way they read texts. The last quarter of the twentieth century also saw the development of feminist theology and of feminist biblical interpretation. The latter had implications for the study of all four parts of Genesis–Exodus.

Feminist interpretation began with Genesis 1–3 and suggested that these passages had long been read in an androcentric and patriarchal fashion. Christian theology had affirmed that women were spiritually and mentally the weaker sex, and it justified a commitment to men's headship over women by the story of the woman's creation after the man and her yielding to the serpent's temptation before the man. Starting from the conviction that women were just as strong as men spiritually and mentally, feminist interpretation suggested that Genesis 1–3 had analogous implications. It had been read patriarchally but was not a patriarchal text. It remains a matter of dispute how far this argument can be sustained.

In Genesis 12–50 feminist interpretation focused on the stories of the matriarchs and not just the patriarchs, and in Exodus 1–18 looked at the roles of Miriam and the other women in the story and not just at those of Moses and other men. In Exodus 19–40 it considered the sexist nature of the regulations for life that appear in these chapters.

Questions about gender apply to men as well as women, and a further aspect of interpretation out of a gendered world asks about the images of maleness that find expression in the text. One can again ask this question about the stories in Genesis 1–11, in Genesis 12–50 and in Exodus. One can ask about the people whom the 'Ten Words' in Exodus 20, and the subsequent regulations, address and benefit. One can ask about the gender implications about the key rite of circumcision, the mark of the covenant that applies only to males.

Here it is the distinction between the world in front of the text and the world of the text itself that collapses, because the asking of such questions establishes that the text itself naturally reflected a gendered world. It is possible that the modern Western world is over-preoccupied by questions about gender, though the people who think so are usually men whose exercise of power is imperilled by the question. Nevertheless, approaches to Genesis and Exodus that begin from these questions succeed in pointing to aspects of the text that other approaches have not noted, and sometimes succeed in solving problems that other approaches leave unsolved.

An example is the riddle of the three stories in Genesis 12–50 about a patriarch passing off his wife as his sister. Among all the stories that could have been told about Abraham and Isaac, why should this one be told three times (even if it happened three times)? Cheryl Exum has suggested a plausible explanation arising out of the gendered world in which we live and from which Genesis emerged. These stories represent three expressions of a male need to express their ambiguous feelings about their wives' sexuality.

A Note on the Name Yhwh and the Terms 'LORD' and 'GOD'
We noted that most English Bibles replace the name 'Yhwh' by the expression 'the LORD', or by 'GOD' if the regular Hebrew word for 'the Lord' actually appears in the context (see Gen. 15.2, 8). In either case the whole word is thus printed in capitals, to draw attention to the fact that the Hebrew word there is the actual name, not the word for Lord or God. Because people stopped pronouncing the name and replaced it by the equivalents of the words for 'Lord' or 'God' in Hebrew, then in Greek, then in Latin and then in modern languages, we cannot be absolutely sure how the name was once pronounced, though comments by early Christian scholars suggest that this involved 'a' in the first syllable and 'e' in the second. Two pieces of logic may have lain behind the replacement of the name by the common noun.

- Giving God a particular name could give the impression that Yhwh was merely the God of the Jewish people and not the God of the whole world.
- One of the Ten Words from Sinai bade people not to 'take Yhwh's name in vain' or not to 'make wrongful use' of this name (NRSV; Exod. 20.7). Indeed, 'blaspheming' the name of Yhwh could incur death (Lev. 24.16). It may have seemed safer not to take the name at all.

On the other hand, a number of positive significances attach to God's having a name, and these are lost when the name is replaced by a more general word.

- Having a name marks someone as a person with a specific personal identity.

- Telling people your name invites them into a relationship with you. As well as declining that, replacing the name by the expression 'the LORD' gives a significantly more patriarchal caste to the portrait of God.
- In traditional cultures, names have meanings. They signify something about a person's background or destiny. Thus the name 'Yhwh', which recalls the verb 'to be/happen', could point to this being a God who will always be there with Israel, relating to the people in the ways that different situations need.
- Sometimes the point about the name is precisely that it distinguishes the God of Israel from other 'gods'. In a context where people worship many such gods, declaring that 'Yhwh' is 'my God' (see Exod. 15.2, 11) is a significant commitment. Declaring that the LORD is my God has different significance, while declaring that 'the LORD is God' may seem a tautology.

(See further William Johnstone's discussion of the revelation of the divine name in the treatment of Exodus in this volume.)

References

I have referred to the following works in this introduction.

Samuel Balentine, *The Torah's Vision of Worship* (Overtures to Biblical Theology; Minneapolis: Fortress Press, 1999).

Richard Bauckham *et al.*, *The Gospels for All Christians: Rethinking the Gospel Audiences* (Grand Rapids: Eerdmans; Edinburgh: T. & T. Clark, 1997).

John I. Durham, *Exodus* (WBC; Waco, TX: Word Books, 1987).

J. Cheryl Exum, 'Who's Afraid of "The Endangered Ancestress"?', in J.C. Exum and D.J.A. Clines (eds.), *The New Literary Criticism and the Hebrew Bible* (JSOTSup, 143; Sheffield: Sheffield Academic Press, 1993), pp. 91-113. Reprinted in J.C. Exum, *Fragmented Women: Feminist (Sub)versions of Biblical Narratives* (JSOTSup, 163; Sheffield: Sheffield Academic Press, 1993), pp. 148-69.

Hans Frei, *The Eclipse of Biblical Narrative* (New Haven/London: Yale University Press, 1974).

James K. Hoffmeier, *Israel in Egypt: The Evidence for the Authenticity of the Exodus Tradition* (Oxford: Oxford University Press, 1997).

Thomas Kuhn, *The Structure of Scientific Revolutions* (Chicago: University of Chicago, 3rd edn, 1996).

R. Walter L. Moberly, *The Old Testament of the Old Testament* (Overtures to Biblical Theology; Philadelphia: Fortress Press, 1992).

Augustine Pagolu, *The Religion of the Patriarchs* (JSOTSup, 277; Sheffield: Sheffield Academic Press, 1998).

Part I

GENESIS 1–11

John W. Rogerson

Chapter One

GENESIS 1–11 IN CONTEXT

A hundred years ago, the main concern of biblical scholarship was to reconcile Genesis 1–11 with the scientific discoveries of the nineteenth century. In the 1970s and 1980s its main concern has been to interpret Genesis 1–11 in the light of liberation theology, feminist theology and the ecological crisis.

This statement may surprise readers for several reasons. First, many church-goers, while not taking Genesis literally, believe that the Bible gives us information about the origin and purpose of the universe. Does modern scholarship have nothing to say about this? Many schools and college courses, not to mention their textbooks, interpret Genesis 1–11 in the light of the ancient Near Eastern background. They study the meaning of 'myth' and they compare Genesis 1–11 with parallel texts from ancient Mesopotamia. What has happened to this approach in recent academic study? Some readers will find it hard to believe that academic biblical scholars are being influenced by such things as liberation theology or the ecological crisis. They may go further and say that for scholars to have such interests is to betray the integrity of academic study.

The purpose of this first chapter is to sketch the movement of interpretation from its concern with science a hundred years ago, through its attention to the ancient Near Eastern background, to the present engagement with contemporary issues. This will introduce the very complex situation that exists at present in the interpretation of Genesis 1–11, and it will also show that, basically, scholars today are doing what all scholars have done in the past hundred years: they are interpreting the text from their own situation or context.

Genesis 1–11 and Science
The exploration of the world by sailors in the fifteenth to eighteenth centuries indicated that Genesis 10 could no longer be regarded as an authoritative account of the geographical disposition of the world and its peoples. However, at the beginning of the nineteenth century it

was still generally believed that Genesis 1 could be shown to be in perfect harmony with scientific discoveries, and that Genesis 2–3 was a true story about the earliest ancestors of the human race. Calvin's view, that Genesis 1 was an account of the creation from the standpoint of a Hebrew observer and not a modern scientific account (*Genesis*, pp. 79, 86), was overlooked.

Scientific discoveries in the form of the geology of the 1820s and 1830s and Darwin's theory of natural selection (1859 and 1870) challenged the early chapters of Genesis on two points. First, the world was seen to be many thousands (*sic*) of years old, as against one influential reconstruction of the biblical chronology which yielded a figure of 4004 BCE for the creation of the world. However, this was not too damaging. It was possible to understand the six days of creation as six eras, as had been done by interpreters for many centuries. The implications of Darwin's theories were more disturbing, for they directly contradicted the biblical account. Whereas the latter told the story of the creation of the first human beings by God, and of their fall from a state of paradise to the hard conditions of the ancient world, the theory of evolution required that the human race had developed from lower forms of life, and that its history was one of uninterrupted progress. As the nineteenth century came to an end, the attempt of critical, theological scholarship to interpret Genesis in the light of scientific discovery was exemplified by S.R. Driver (cf. Rogerson, *Criticism*, pp. 282-23). He put forward the proposal that the Bible has an outer and an inner sense. Its outer sense was its narrative form, expressed in terms of the ideas and language of the ancient world. Its inner sense was a revealed truth which criticism of the outer sense could in no way affect. Driver reconciled Genesis 3 to the theory of evolution by assuming that the human race or its separate branches had been faced with a moral choice that would affect its future, and that the wrong choice was made (Driver, *Genesis*, pp. 56-57).

Genesis 1–11 and the Ancient Near East
Driver was interpreting Genesis 1–11 from his standpoint as a churchman and a critical scholar; we may call this standpoint his context. Even as he worked, the context for the study of Genesis 1–11 was changing. The change resulted from the discovery and decipherment of original texts from ancient Mesopotamia beginning from the late 1840s.

Biblical scholars had long known from writers of Greek antiquity that the Babylonians possessed creation stories similar in some respects to that in Genesis 1. They regarded these stories as dependent on that found in Genesis. But from 1876 newly discovered Babylonian accounts of creation began to be published (see Delano, 'Genesis 1', pp. 52ff.), and the view began to emerge that Genesis 1 was dependent on the Babylonian accounts and not *vice versa*. Further, in 1872 the discovery of a Babylonian version of the flood had been announced.

A new context for the interpretation of Genesis 1–11 began to emerge, a context in which these chapters were no longer seen as the beginning of a sacred, inspired book, the Bible. Instead, they were seen as ancient Hebrew narratives similar to other narratives from the ancient world about cosmic and human origins. If the task of Driver had been to interpret Genesis 1–11 for Christian faith, the task of interpretation in the new context was to discover how ancient Israel had used traditions from the ancient world to express its distinctive faith. Thus in the new context the concern was with the *beliefs* of Israel's official religion. It remained for theologians to make of this what they could for contemporary Christian belief.

Within the context of the view that the stories of Genesis 1–11 were Israelite versions of ancient traditions, several positions emerged. Three of these may be mentioned. At one extreme, it was argued that the alleged dependence of Genesis on Babylonian traditions robbed Genesis of any claim to authority for Christian believers (Delitzsch, *Babel*). At the other extreme, some scholars in Britain and Scandinavia found in Genesis 1 a link with the New Testament teaching about death and resurrection, arguing that it was a liturgy used at the New Year festival when the Israelite kings suffered ritual death and resurrection. This pattern of death and resurrection was also held to be present in the Psalms and in Isa. 52.13–53.12, making possible a link between the suffering, royal Messiah of the Old Testament and the crucified and risen Messiah of the New Testament (Bentzen, *King*). A different viewpoint was that exemplified by the German scholar von Rad (in Anderson, *Creation*, pp. 53-64). Von Rad held that Israel took over the idea of creation from its neighbours in the ancient world quite late in its religious development, and that the salvation of Israel in the exodus event was more fundamental to Israelite belief than faith in creation. The effect of this position was to shift attention away from Genesis 1–11 and to emphasize the traditions about God's election and salvation of Israel. Israel knew its God first as redeemer and only later came to confess that he was Lord of the universe.

A New Context

A feature of Old Testament studies in the last twenty years has been a growth in the number of methods applied to its interpretation. Many of these methods have come from other disciplines. Old Testament scholars have, for example, taken over from modern literary theory, sociology and social anthropology such approaches as structuralism, close reading and a renewed interest in the social background to the Bible.

Some of these methods have been applied to Genesis 1–11. At the same time, there has been a new regard for the authority of Genesis 1–11, even if this has sometimes been in a backhanded sort of way. For example, some feminist theologians have argued that the interpretation of Genesis 3 in terms of female subordination to males is a distortion of the true meaning of the text. As will be outlined later, they have argued for an interpretation that stresses the equality or complementarity of the sexes; and in so doing they have implicitly asserted the authority of Genesis 3 for Christian practice. On the other hand, more radical feminists have used the biblical text in order to penetrate behind it to discover a suppressed women's history with which they can identify themselves. This rejection of the surface meaning of the text has been a back-handed acknowledgment of its authority, at least for a male-oriented Church and society. Similarly, liberation theology has either re-asserted the authority of the text looked at it from a liberation perspective, or has rejected its surface meaning in a search for the history of the oppressed.

The present context in which Genesis 1–11 is being interpreted is thus characterized by two features: a growth in the number of methods applied to the study of these chapters, and a renewed interest in the relevance of Genesis 1–11 for such questions as the rights of the oppressed and poor, the status of women and the ecological crisis. In the case of the last of these, Old Testament study has been responding to those ecologists who have argued that the command to humanity in Gen. 1.26ff. to subdue the earth is the cause of the crisis that we face. In becoming sensitive to some or all of these issues, academic biblical studies have been moving into a new context, a context that has affected the interpretation of Genesis 1–11 as profoundly as the discovery of Babylonian texts affected interpretation at the end of the nineteenth century.

One difference between the present context and previous contexts is the greater diversity of methods and approaches that characterizes the present situation. To conclude this chapter, an attempt will be made to summarize these. This summary will then form the basis for a more detailed exposition in the next chapter. Full references are given in the next chapter to the works briefly mentioned here.

1. *Literary-Critical Readings with Contemporary Implications*

The work of Catholic scholars such as Lohfink, Beauchamp and Zenger has concentrated upon those parts of Genesis 1–11 traditionally assigned to the Priestly source of the Pentateuch. The conclusions of these scholars have, however, been of greatest interest in the light of the current concern with ecological matters. Lohfink, taking up a suggestion first made by McEvenue, has argued that P is written from a 'pacifist' standpoint, and that this must affect the interpretation of passages such as Gen. 1.26ff. regarding the human domination of the world. Lohfink argues that Gen. 1.26ff. gives no sanction to domination and exploitation. Beauchamp's discussion deals with human relations with the animal creation, while Zenger, in his discussion of the 'bow' in Gen. 9.13 explicitly addresses ecological questions in a work which is a detailed example of traditional literary criticism.

2. *Literary Readings*

Literary readings are of various kinds. They may be concerned with the whole of Genesis 1–11 or only with parts of it; and they may be either thematic or structuralist. Clines applies the concept of 'theme' to Genesis 1–11, arguing that the content of the chapters can be described in two ways: (a) humankind's tendency to destroy what God has made good, (b) God's ability to overcome humanity's destructive tendencies. He opts for the latter theme in the light of the Pentateuch as a whole. Structuralist readings of Genesis 2–3 occupied a whole issue of *Semeia* in 1980 (Patte, *Genesis 2 and 3*). The various contributors were agreed in regarding the text as mysterious and multilayered, and their aim was to make some of this depth apparent. Jobling used the opposing categories of inside/outside to illumine the text.

   Literary readings differ from other approaches in being a-historical. Whereas Lohfink, for example, locates the P source in a specific historical setting, literary interpreters are concerned with the inner dynamics of the text itself, and not necessarily with reference to reality outside the text.

3. *Liberation Readings*

At least three approaches can be distinguished here. The first, exemplified by scholars such as Louise Schottroff and Wittenberg, is essentially historical-critical, but with a different emphasis from that of Lohfink and his colleagues. The latter deal much more closely with the details of the text. Schottroff and Wittenberg gain their impetus more from what they presume the social background to have been than from the text itself. Thus Wittenberg regards the Yahwist source (J) as anti-Solomonic propaganda and sees in Genesis 3 and in Genesis 11 a condemnation of Solomon's wisdom and of his building activities. Mosala also sets out from historical-critical reconstructions of the setting of texts, but is more interested in what the text conceals than in what it says. Historical criticism is used by Mosala to recover a lost history of the oppressed. Boesak's liberation reading of Genesis 4 is an existential reading that takes the narrative about Cain and Abel as a story with universal application.

4. *Feminist Readings*

Two different approaches can be noted here. Trible, in her classic *God and the Rhetoric of Sexuality*, uses an essentially literary approach; yet this has a specific purpose, which is not simply to explore the dimensions of Genesis 2–3 for their own sake, but to argue a feminist case. Meyers uses the latest research on the sociology of women in Israelite highland agriculture as the key to understanding Genesis 2–3.

5. *Genesis 1–11 and Ancient Near Eastern Texts*

This section comes last deliberately. It would be wrong to suggest that scholars no longer interpret Genesis 1–11 against the ancient Near Eastern background. On the other hand, this has become only one of many possible approaches, and it is sometimes used by writers who fall into the categories earlier mentioned in this chapter. While it is valuable in providing a contrast between the faith of Israel and that of Israel's neighbours, it does not provide an obvious link with contemporary problems.

The approaches just outlined will now receive detailed attention.

Chapter Two

APPROACHES TO GENESIS 1–11

1. *Literary-Critical Readings with Contemporary Implications*

In a series of detailed studies of the Priestly source of the Pentateuch or, more exactly, what he calls P^g (the Priestly historical narrative: the 'g' stands for the German *Geschichtserzählung*, which means historical narrative), N. Lohfink has suggested some striking interpretations of parts of Genesis 1–11. He believes that P^g was composed toward the end of the exile, and was intended to present an account of Israel's history deliberately different from the Yahwist's history and the Deuteronomic history (Lohfink, 'Pentateuch', pp. 55-56). The writer of P^g wished Israel to be a temple-based community centred upon the presence of God and governed by sacred rituals and sacrifices in such a way that no one would exercise power over others. The frictions and stresses within the society that would normally lead to bloodshed were to be removed by the use of sacrifice to restore the broken relationships. P^g rejected the notion of war, a fact indicated, according to Lohfink, by its treatment of the exodus and of the mode of possession by the Israelites of the land of Canaan. Whereas J and D indicate a military defeat of Egypt and a warlike occupation of Canaan, P^g has no account of Egypt's military demise at the exodus, describes Israel as a sacral and not a military body in the wilderness, and represents the occupation of Canaan as the peaceful setting up of God's sanctuary in the land. (See Lohfink, 'Die Schichten', pp. 194-99 for an account in English of some of these points.)

Seen in the light of the whole of P^g, those parts of this source that are found in Genesis 1–11 have a clear message. It is noteworthy, first, that in Gen. 1.26-30 humankind is not given permission to eat meat. This permission comes only after the flood, at Gen. 9.3-4. According to Lohfink the ideal implied in Gen. 1.26-30 is that humans will not exercise force over the animal creation. However, in the view of P^g, humankind did not hold to this ideal, and this was why God brought the flood upon the earth. The situation after the flood is a compromise. Humans are given permission to eat meat; but this is not a mandate for the exploitation of animals. The reason for the permission to eat meat is that Israel can offer to God the sacrifices that will enable order to be maintained in a sacral, oppression-free community.

Lohfink also argues strongly that the Hebrew verb *rādâ* in Gen. 1.28, usually rendered 'to have dominion over', has the basic sense of 'to wander around'. Its semantic field includes 'accompany', 'pasture', 'guide', 'lead', 'rule' and 'command', from which it is clear that its meaning of 'to rule' has to be understood in the context of shepherding. Thus the task given to humanity in Gen. 1.28 in relation to the rest of the created order is to be a shepherd (Lohfink, *Themen*, pp. 167-68; English in Lohfink, *Great Themes*, pp. 178-79). With regard to the command to be fruitful and multiply, Lohfink argues that in the light of P^g as a whole this must be taken as a command limited to the establishment of the families of the earth and of their possession of their own lands. The command has nothing to do with the modern notion of continuous growth:

> There was once growth; not, there must always be growth. The goal of growth was simply that the nations would come from the original families. They now exist; and as a result the blessing of growth has achieved its goal (Lohfink, *Themen*, p. 185 my translation; see also Lohfink, *Great Themes*, p. 196 for an English version).

Lohfink's treatment of parts of Genesis 1–11 anchors these texts firmly in the situation of postexilic Israel. Genesis 1 becomes a prophetic text, depicting an ideal which no longer exists: an ideal of human society in which there is no war, and no exploitation of the created order, and in which human responsibility is to act as a shepherd to the created order.

However, the picture presented by P^g, although a compromise with the violent realities of human nature, is nonetheless an attempt to create an oppression-free society based upon sacral institutions. Although Lohfink does not draw conclusions from this about how we should order the world today, his exegesis rules out interpretations which are commonly heard today: e.g. that Genesis 1–11 teaches us that we live in a world created by God which he has described as 'good'; or that Genesis 1 is responsible for the human exploitation of the natural world. (This last charge could be true, of course, if misinterpretations of Gen. 1.28 had been responsible.)

It is likely that Lohfink's suggestions will strike a chord with many modern readers; and the implications of this will be discussed elsewhere in this book. For the moment, it is sufficient to observe that the questions to which Lohfink is sensitive are questions relevant to

the end of the twentieth century, and indicate how the contemporary
situation can interact with work of a rigorous literary-critical nature.

Beauchamp ('Création', pp. 139-82), in a complex and subtle essay,
follows Lohfink in some respects; but his essay concentrates upon the
tension between Gen. 1.26-30 and Gen. 9.1-7; and to that extent it
avoids the criticism that he is interpreting not the text of Genesis 1–11
but sources that have been hypothetically isolated by scholars. The
differences between Gen. 1.26-30 and Gen. 9.1-7 are that, in the
former, humans are not permitted to eat animals, whereas in the
latter, not only is this permission given, but language is used about
the relation between humans and animals that implies a significant
increase in human domination. Gen. 9.2 says that the fear of humankind shall be upon every beast of the earth, etc., and that they will be
delivered into the hand (or power) of human beings. This last phrase is
one which is used elsewhere in the Old Testament to describe God's
giving victory over his enemies. But not only does Gen. 9.1-7 envisage
the human consumption of animals; it envisages the killing of human
beings by human beings, and it seeks to restrict such killing by allowing the execution of murderers, on the grounds that humankind is
made in God's image.

Beauchamp argues that in these two texts (and elsewhere in the Old
Testament) the animals act as a sign indicating the nature of humanity, and humankind's relationship to the created order. The regime of
Gen. 1.26-30 does not propose vegetarianism for its own sake. The
vegetarianism helps to define what it means to say that humanity is
made in God's image; for this language is about relationships with the
animals, as is evident from Gen. 1.26, 'Let us make...in our image...
and let them have dominion...' This dominion is characterized by
tenderness towards the animals, and since no animal blood is to be
shed by human beings, it is also implied that humans do not shed
each other's blood and that animals do not shed that of other animals
(cf. 1.30). What is implied in Gen. 1.26-30 is elaborated in Gen. 9.1-7,
in the changed circumstances of the post-flood world. In place of
tenderness towards animals on the part of humanity there is now
warlike domination. If the animals experienced tenderness in Gen.
1.26-30 they now experience fear and dread (9.2). It is implied that
animals will seek to kill human beings (v. 5b) and so each other, and
that human beings will be like animals in that regard. The only
difference will be that the extent of human beings' killing each other
will be limited by the right of execution of murderers. This is because
humankind is created in God's image.

From the contrast between Gen. 1.26-30 and 9.1-7 it is clear, in

Beauchamp's view, that mankind is no longer in the image of God as defined in Genesis 1. Humanity's relationship to animals has changed from that of tenderness to that of domination; from that of the shepherd to the hunter. Humans have become more like the animals, not only through murders and war, but through the enslavement of human by human. Thus Gen. 1.26-30 is a text expressing an ideal:

> It is able to believe that a mastery over the earth is possible without exercising a mastery over the other beings, who are intermediate beings between the master and the earth. Genesis 1 teaches us that there is only true mastery over the earth if mankind does not enslave itself by enslaving its fellows (p. 170).

As such, it has much in common with prophetic texts that see a new creation as including peace between the animals and between the animals and humanity (see Isa. 65.17-25).

The Bible does not think of peace between human beings without peace between human and animal (p. 180).

Beauchamp's stress on human relations with animals as an important sign enables him to make other illuminating comparisons. For example, in Lev. 26.21-22 one of the penalties for disobedience on the part of Israel is that God will bring wild animals to devour their crops and their children. Thus, animals will be a sign of disobedience and judgment. In Genesis 10, those parts belonging to P^g and containing the words, 'by their families, languages, their lands and their nations' (vv. 5, 20, 31), suggest a differentiation of the human race into an equivalent of the species (kinds) that characterize the animals; if so, the greater stress on the (violent) animal constituent of humankind after the flood is indicated.

Like that of Lohfink, Beauchamp's exposition is firmly anchored in what he believes parts of Genesis 1–11 meant to the Priestly circles who were revising the outlook of Israel's earlier traditions; and again, it is one which is bound to be read with sympathy in our contemporary world. For while there is no reason why we should give precedence to the viewpoint of P^g over against that of other strands of the Old Testament, we are strongly tempted to do so by our modern concerns, and we are once again entitled to conclude that these concerns have not been without influence upon Beauchamp's work.

An interesting feature of Zenger's detailed and subtle monograph (*Untersuchungen*) is the fact that he mentions the current ecological crisis several times at the beginning of his work, and devotes a brief concluding section to 'some ecological-theological implications' (pp. 179–83). Here is another work of traditional literary-critical study which is explicitly sensitive to an important modern issue.

There are many similarities between Zenger's approach and those of Lohfink and Beauchamp. Like Lohfink, Zenger assigns parts of Genesis 1–11 to the Priestly narrative (P^g) and interprets these in the light of his view of the narrative as a whole. Like Beauchamp, he sees the relation between Gen. 1.26-30 and 9.1-3, 7 as a crucial issue in interpretation. However, he disagrees with Lohfink about the extent of P^g and, against Beauchamp, regards 9.4-6 as a later addition to P^g.

Zenger accepts the view proposed by Wellhausen, and supported by 'the majority of recent publications' (p. 41) that P^g ends at Deut. 34.7-9, that is, with the death of Moses. This enables him to argue that three figures are crucial in P^g — Adam, Abraham and Moses — and that P^g is to be divided into two main parts, Gen. 1.1 to Exod. 1.7 and Exod. 1.13 to Deut. 34.9. Although he has a different view from Lohfink and others about the importance of the occupation of the land of Canaan in P^g (Lohfink sees Josh. 19.41 as the ending of P^g), Zenger's conclusions have much in common with those of Lohfink:

> P^g is the programmatic outline for a non-political Israel, which regards the gift of a communal experience of God's nearness as the most important of all benefits, rather than being a state and having its own land. As such, P^g does not attempt to present a detailed and realizable constitution, such as is found in Ezekiel 40–48. It is a basic reflection on the presupposition and purpose of a new manifestation of Israel, that is to become the medium of the mighty activity of the creator God who gives life (pp. 45-46).

Written towards the end of the sixth century, probably in Babylon (although Jerusalem remains a possibility), P^g offers to the community the chance to realize, in its religious life, its status as a community fulfilling the purpose of the creation. This was once upon a time achieved in the period from Abraham to Sinai, and the status of the community, as being in life-giving relationship to Yahweh, was embodied in the Sinai covenant. Thereafter, the history of Israel was a history of failure to become, in the promised land, what it had been. However, this history of sin and failure did not threaten the creation, because God had already made the created order so secure that it could not be threatened.

This view of the purpose of P^g brings us to one of the central claims that Zenger makes about those parts of Genesis 1–11 that belong to P^g. Discussing the relation between the creation and flood stories and between Gen. 1.26-30 and 9.1-3, 7, he argues that both, taken together, constitute the account of creation as it impinged upon the world of P^g. He does not deny that there are differences between these passages.

Gen. 1.26 describes a shepherd-like function for humankind which is strengthened after the flood. Also, the flood to some extent damages the earth as long as the waters remain. There is a new 'realism' after the flood, one which recognizes that the world contains violence and injustice.

Yet, when all this has been allowed, Zenger's emphasis is more upon continuity than discontinuity. Even if the world implied in Gen. 1.26-30 alone no longer exists, if it ever did, the world implied in Genesis 1 and Gen. 9.1-3, 7 taken together does exist, and offers to Israel the hope of life lived in close relationship with the creator God. After the flood, there is not a new creation of the world, but rather, the beginning of a new era for a purified world. It is at this point that we must consider Zenger's treatment of Gen. 9.1-3, 7 and of the bow in the clouds which God promises to set (9.13). He begins by noting that the language of 9.2—'the fear of you and the dread of you shall be upon every beast of the earth'—is not the language of war, but that of God's gift of the land of Canaan to his people (Exod. 23.27ff., 'I will send my terror before you...I will drive them out from before you'). Gen. 9.1-3 therefore adds to the idea of Gen. 1.26ff. the idea that humankind must shepherd the animals: that is, it imposes the additional charge to be the lord of the created order, in other words, so to rule over it that the weaker and threatened animals will be protected. Gen. 9.13, then, does not abolish Gen. 1.26ff. but strengthens it.

The bow in the clouds is not a sign of peace and reconciliation but a sign that over and above humanity stands the protector of the created order: the creator God who will protect his creation from all that would destroy it. Zenger points out that, in the Old Testament, it is a broken bow that is the sign of peace (Ps. 46.9; Zech. 9.10). This does not compromise the 'pacifist' nature of P^g. The bow is not a summons to war or a justification of it. Rather, it is a call to trust in the determination and ability of God to safeguard his creation.

In the concluding section on ecological implications, Zenger makes the following points. For P^g the history of Israel is inseparable from the story of creation, as is also the history of the Church. What God does in order to redeem his people is part of what he is doing to preserve the life of his creation. Thus humanity is an integral part of creation in the sense that humankind 'either survives with the created order by living in harmony with it, or goes under with the created order by living against it' (p. 179). Second, humanity is given responsibility for the created order and is answerable to the creator God. This answerability, according to P^g, is to be established by Israel's building of a sanctuary where the creator God will reveal himself to humankind. The people of God is called to live an exemplary life in this regard, so that the earth will be a place of life for all that lives.

To the extent that humans destroy the earth as a place of life, they lose their humanity:

A human race that regards the earth as material for satisfying its own needs, that uses animals as creatures without rights, that makes power the criterion for decisions (and only reflects later on the morality of what has been done), that produces weapons that can destroy the ecological balance of the world completely—such a human race is acting contrary to creation and is on the way to becoming the 'all flesh' (which had 'corrupted its way') of which Gen. 6.12 speaks (p. 180).

The bow in the sky, then, is a sign of hope to a suffering world, witnessing to the royal sovereignty over the earth of the creator God.

Zenger's final point stems from his views about the tent sanctuary whose construction P^g describes (Exod. 25ff.) as a place where God meets his people in their worship on the seventh day. The stone-built temples of Solomon and the ancient world were symbols of political might and of the oppression of the poorer classes. The cult to be celebrated in the tent (Lev. 9) is neither the state cult of Solomon, which legitimized power, nor the priestly dominated orgiastic cult of Canaan and Egypt. In both cases, the priestly cult degraded the participation of the people. What is envisaged by P^g is a cult for the whole community, whose sacrificial offerings are a thankful rendering to the creator God of what he has given to his people. For the modern world, this indicates responsibility for creation flowing from a common life rooted in worship and centred on the meaning of creation, which consideration becomes the criterion for the ordering of daily life. We shall return to Zenger's rich monograph in other sections of the book. This summary has been restricted to the treatment of Genesis 1–11 and to the ecological implications.

2. *Literary Readings*

Literary readings of Genesis 1–11 differ from the literary-critical readings that we have been considering in at least two ways. First, they ignore the sources that are presupposed by literary-critical approaches; second, they hold that the important thing about the narratives is not their presumed setting in a particular period of Israelite history, but their internal dynamics of plot, characterization and theme.

Although doubt continues to be expressed about the possibility or propriety of dividing Genesis 1–11 into sources, the attempt to do so is not without good grounds. Leaving aside the striking differences between the use of the divine name in Gen. 1.1–2.4a and 2.4b–3.24 we may note two apparent contradictions. If Gen. 1.26-30 does not allow human beings to kill animals, why does Abel offer sheep as a sacrifice to God, and why does God accept the sacrifice (4.4)? If the human race was not divided into nations and scattered abroad speaking different languages until after the building of the tower of Babel (11.19), why do 10.5, 20 and 31 speak of the languages and lands of the various peoples listed? Two possible answers can be given by those reading the final form of the text in a literary way. First, Gen. 1.26-30 may have to be read in the light of 4.4, with the conclusion that the former text does not, at the very least, exclude killing animals in order to sacrifice them. Second, the apparently contradictory arrangement of Genesis 10–11 may be of significance for the interpretation of the whole (see below). The strength of the second answer, which gives preference to the text as a whole as opposed to trying to divide it into sources in order to remove contradictions, is that source division is always bound to be hypothetical, whereas the final form of the text is a reality.

Of the various possible literary readings this section will deal with those of Clines (*Theme*) and Jobling ('Semantics'). In the course of his study of the 'theme' of the Pentateuch, Clines considers the question of what might be said to be the 'theme' of Genesis 1–11. Drawing upon the work of standard commentators such as von Rad and Westermann, Clines considers several possible themes. The first is a sin–speech–mitigation–punishment theme. He shows that in each of five episodes, those of the fall (ch. 3), Cain and Abel (ch. 4), the sons of God (6.1-4), the flood (6.5–7.24) and the tower of Babel (11.1-9), before God punishes the evildoers there is a divine speech and a mitigation of the punishment *before* the punishment is administered. Thus, in 3.21 God clothes the humans with skins following his speech in 3.14-19 and prior to driving Adam and Eve from the garden in 3.22-24. In ch. 4, God puts a protecting mark upon Cain (v. 15) following his speech in vv. 10-11 and Cain's departure to the land of Nod in v. 16. In the flood story we are told that Noah found favour in God's eyes (6.8) following God's speech announcing judgment in 6.6-7.

The tower of Babel is an interesting case, because Clines implies that the mitigation is in 10.1-32, that is, that it precedes the tower of Babel story (p. 63); and later (p. 68) he argues that, if 10.1-32 were placed after 11.1-9, the passage would have to be read under the sign of judgment rather than as a fulfilment of the renewed command of

9.1 to be fruitful and multiply. This illustrates how a literary approach deals with the problem on which source critics base their detection of sources.

Clines rejects the sin–speech–mitigation–punishment scheme as the overall 'theme' of Genesis 1–11, because it cannot include the creation or the genealogies. Rather Clines accepts that it is a recurrent *motif*. He next tries a spread of sin, spread of grace theme. This draws attention to the way in which wrongdoing escalates from the sin of Adam and Eve through the violence of Cain and Lamech to the generation destroyed by the flood; and after the flood there is an escalation from Noah's family to the building of the tower of Babel. In each case, God responds graciously. God does not kill Adam and Eve, he puts a protecting mark upon Cain and he commands Noah to build an ark. The sequel to the tower of Babel is the growth of the nations (10.1-32), which account comes before the tower of Babel story so as to be seen as a sign of grace. Clines also incorporates the creation narrative and the genealogies by arguing that the former expresses a series of gracious acts which balance the pessimism of some of the subsequent narratives; and that the genealogies, by emphasizing the continual presence of death, imply also God's grace which enables life to continue.

Clines then explores a further possible theme, that of creation–uncreation–recreation. He notes that, in the flood story, some of the boundaries fixed in Genesis 1 are removed in order to allow the waters to cover the earth. The flood is finally restrained by the re-imposition of the boundaries. This approach then yields the suggestion that the flood story is only the culmination of a process of undoing of the creation which is discernible in chs. 3–6. After the flood, the process of uncreation begins again, as the narrative moves through the strife within Noah's family to the dispersion of the human race after the building of the tower of Babel. The combination of the sin and grace theme with the creation, uncreation theme enables Clines to propose as the most comprehensive theme that of the unfailing grace of God in the face of human sin, even when that sin brings the creation to the brink of uncreation.

Clines's literary reading yields many insights. It is also noteworthy that it is explicitly theological and not related to modern problems as are the modern readings outlined in the previous section. Indeed, Clines goes out of his way to emphasize that a literary reading offers the text as story:

What is offered in the story is a 'world'—make-believe or real, familiar or unfamiliar. To the degree that the hearer or reader of the story is imaginatively seized by the story, to that degree he or she 'enters' the world of the story. That means that the reader of the story, when powerfully affected by it, becomes a participant of its world. One learns, by familiarity with the story, one's way about its world until it becomes one's own world too (p. 102).

And again:

The Pentateuch becomes…a source of life, not by being fed through some hermeneutical machine that prints out contemporary answers to contemporary questions, but through the reader's patient engagement with the text and openness to being seized, challenged, or threatened by the 'world' it lays bare (p. 118).

Clines discusses motifs that are apparent on the surface of the text of Genesis 1–11, and seeks to find an organizing principle that would encompass their interrelation and their potential for development. Structuralist readings are more concerned with levels of meaning below the surface; however, when these levels are described, they inevitably affect our appreciation of what is going on at the surface level.

In the 1980 *Semeia* symposium on Genesis 2–3, Jobling proposes the opposition of inside/outside as a clue to the semantics of the passage. The story begins with God's introducing the man (from outside) into the garden, and ends with the human beings outside the garden. The story takes place inside the garden, but to be inside the garden is to be in an almost dangerous situation. It contains a serpent who is a source of temptation as well as trees whose prohibition is a potential source of danger. Life inside the garden differs greatly from that outside. Inside the garden, agriculture is easy, but it is the only occupation. If the garden contains animals, these are not bred or used by the man. Although he has a female companion there is no other society; neither is there sexual awareness or sexual reproduction. Although inside there is immortality, it is an immortality of a non-societal monochrome variety.

All this is in contrast with the outside, the world familiar to human beings, with difficult agriculture, but with husbandry and hunting in addition to agriculture and a larger society based upon sexual awareness and procreation.

According to this reading the story functions to enable men to cope with women and with the harshness of agricultural life. Men may face hard work and death and may yearn for immortality and ease. But these latter ideals, when available to the first man in the garden of

Eden, were not without danger and disadvantage. Woman plays a complex role in the story. Created out of the man's rib to provide the companionship no animal could provide, she nonetheless pursues independent action, until she becomes largely responsible for man's being outside the garden. She is thus part of man, but enables man to argue that expulsion from the garden was not his fault. The story enables man both to long for the lost life of the garden, and to prefer the realities of his present existence.

Although this type of analysis is based wholly upon the text, it does refer to realities outside the text, namely, human awareness of the contradiction between dream and reality. It assumes a setting in a non-specified Israelite or even universal human situation, it does not provide theological truths and it is male-orientated as are some of the other structuralist readings, although this does not mean that such approaches are necessarily sexist. Yet it enables readers to see the text in new ways, and indicates how difficult it is to exhaust a text of its possibilities of meaning.

3. *Liberation Readings*

Liberation readings of the Bible take a number of forms. Some are literary-critical readings which describe situations in the life of ancient Israel, but which attempt an application to modern situations. Others simply use the historical situation in Israel to establish common ground between the Old Testament situations and modern conditions, and assume that the biblical text can then address the modern conditions directly. Another approach assumes the unitariness of human nature, so that the biblical narrative has universal application. Finally, there is the approach that goes behind the text to discover a suppressed history of oppressed people.

Wittenberg (*Solomon*) dates the J parts of Genesis 2–11 to the Solomonic era, and sees the J work as part of a theological critique of Solomon's reign. He notes that various scholars have detected royal motifs in Genesis 2–3, and he suggests that the garden of Eden was reminiscent of the Solomonic royal park, that the serpent could be connected with a serpent cult in Jerusalem which was later abolished by Hezekiah (2 Kgs 18.4), and that the cherubim guarding the garden of Eden could be an allusion to the cherubim in the temple which protected the ark. We could add that the tradition in Ezek. 28.11-19, which in many respects is so similar to Genesis 3, is also concerned with a royal figure.

Given these royal allusions, Wittenberg reads Genesis 2–3 as an attack upon the reign of Solomon. Adam is a royal figure whose undoing results from his desire to know good and evil apart from God. The reign of Solomon resulted in a royal reorganization of the whole society, which brought great hardship upon the people and the break-down of society as it had been previously organized. Just as in Genesis 2–11 the 'fall' of Adam had brought about an increase in violence, with Cain killing Abel and Lamech exacting vengeance far in excess of his grievance, so the desire of Solomon to determine what was right led to violence and to the loss of social cohesion.

Wittenberg argues further that the genealogies in Genesis 10 emphasize socio-economic differences between prosperous cities such as Erech (Uruk), Accad (Agade) and Nineveh, cities that belonged to the list of Ham, and the tribal societies that belonged to the list of Shem. Thus the lists contrast the centralized city states with the decentralized tribal peoples. The standpoint of the J writer is that of the tribal peoples, whereas Solomon, contrary to the traditions of his people, created a centralized state. The story of the tower of Babel is an attack upon the building activity of Solomon, with the king wanting to create a reputation by his great building works. The only result of this was to place such a strain upon his kingdom that it divided after his death in the same way that the building of the tower of Babel resulted in the division of the people.

Wittenberg isolates a strand in Genesis 1–11 which is critical of the centralization and the misuse of power. He assigns special importance to this strand for Christian usage by claiming that, 'in the crucified Jesus the resistance theology of the Solomonic age received its ultimate vindication' (p. 17). Louise Schottroff ('Schöpfungsgeschichte', pp. 8-26) gives a social-historical reading of Gen. 1.1–2.4a, placing the account in the presumed situation of the deported Jewish farmers and craftsmen living in exile in Babylon after the fall of Jerusalem in 587 BCE. She assumes the correctness of the account of the circumstances of the Jews as worked out by W. Schottroff ('Arbeit', pp. 122-28), according to which the deported craftsmen had no chance to pass on their skills to their families, and where some Jews were enslaved to rich families. Believing that the social setting of the text is a clue to its meaning, she notes that Genesis 1 describes God as a craftsman fashioning the world. She also notes that God is depicted both as a mother bird and as a sovereign king. Schottroff next contrasts the beauty of the original creation with the polluted and threatened world we live in today. She contrasts our experience of the creation story with that of its original readers. For them, in their oppression and hopelessness, the story of creation gave them faith in their God who had created so much beauty. No one could take from them the contemplation of that beauty.

The verses about humankind's being created in the image of God (Gen. 1.26-27) produce two comments. For the original readers, the exiled Jews, these verses gave hope. In their exile they had no value in the eyes of their overlords other than their economic value. But their sacred traditions assured them that they were made in God's image, and that gave them incomparable value. Schottroff illustrates this with a charming story about Hillel, who, in going to bathe, noted that, since the statues (images) of the Caesars were regularly washed, he also needed to wash. He was greater than a Caesar because he was made in the image of God. For contemporary readers, the question provoked by Gen. 1.26-30 is 'are we going to live as those made in the image of God, or as a race of superhumans?' If the answer is in favour of the former, this will require more than the banishing of environ-mentally harmful products from our kitchens!

Schottroff's exposition of the relation between man and woman in Gen. 1.26-30 brings us close to a hermeneutics of rejection, that is, a reading which questions the assumptions of the text. She argues that, among the exiles, to have many children was an aspect of liberation by ensuring the continuance of the people and increasing their eco-nomic strength. She rejects interpretations of humankind's being made in God's image such as that in 1 Cor. 11.7 according to which only man is the image and glory of God and the woman is related to God only via man. She is also critical of Barth's views that man and woman constitute the divine image in their relationship to each other. This simply sanctions male views of marriage together with their dis-advantages to women. Schottroff prefers to interpret language about the image of God as a summons to men and women to work together in equality and justice. But she also feels that the female experience of oppression that this text has caused and sanctioned will enable women to work all the more effectively for the alleviation of every kind of injustice. It is here that we are close to a hermeneutics of rejection, in the sense that the negative effect of the text upon women can be put to positive use. Because the text has been misused in the past to the detriment of women, it needs to be women who assist to understand and use the text appropriately today.

The third example of a liberation reading of part of Genesis 1–11 is Boesak's treatment of Genesis 4, as presented by West ('Reading', pp. 279-99). Boesak is well known in the West as a leading South African churchman who is engaged in the struggle against apartheid. His reading of Genesis 4 is thus deeply affected by the situation in which he works, and by his belief that the text tells a universal story applicable to all ages:

> The story of Cain and Abel is a story about two types or kinds of people. It is a very human story that is still being enacted today. This story does not tell us in the first place what happened once upon a time; rather, it tells us about something that happens today. Because this story is a human story, we find very human elements in it and elements from our own human history (West, 'Reading', p. 285).

From this standpoint Boesak gives an essentially literary reading of Genesis 4. He notes the repetiton of the word 'brother' in the story of Cain and Abel (vv. 2, 8 [twice], 9 [twice], 10 and 11) as a way of emphasizing the wickedness of Cain's actions. He has killed the human being closest to him and has thereby essentially denied his own humanity, since humanity is a co-operative venture. Cain's punishment is that he is alienated from the land on which he relied for a living (he was a tiller of the ground) and is forced to wander without rest and without a goal.

The continuation of the story in vv. 23-24, where Lamech, Cain's descendant, boasts that he has killed a man for wounding him, shows that as history moves on humans learn nothing, and things do not change. We can add that this might be a justification for the way in which Boesak applies the story universally.

However, the story does not end in complete darkness. Gen. 4.25-26 records the birth of a son to Adam and Eve to replace the murdered Abel, and the chapter ends with the words, 'At that time men began to call upon the name of the Lord'. Boesak comments: 'After murder, after death, after annihilation and inhumanity, God begins again' (West, 'Reading', p. 284).

I shall not comment on the way in which Boesak draws parallels between the anxieties experienced by Cain after he has murdered Abel and the anxieties Boesak believes are experienced by those he regards as oppressors in our contemporary world. Whatever one's views on this matter, it is not difficult to see how Boesak's reading can bring hope to people who are being oppressed. The text makes it clear that the oppression of human beings by other human beings is not God's plan for the world, that God pronounces judgment against it, but that he is also at work to bring hope through those who honour his name. Whereas Clines's literary reading is concerned to bring readers into 'the world of the text', there to find the values of their own world challenged, Boesak sees the text as referring to concrete situations in our own world, and is saying to his own people that the oppression they suffer is condemned by God, but that he is even now at work to make things new.

Mosala's reading of the story of Cain and Abel (West, 'Reading', pp. 287ff.) is very different from that of Boesak. He begins from a hermeneutics of suspicion, that is, he does not take the text at its face value but looks behind it to discover its origins within the class struggle in ancient Israel. Such research indicates that Genesis 4 comes from the hand of the ruling class, and that its historical background is the Davidic monarchy, during which there was a relentless dispossession of Israelite village peasants from their lands. Given this setting, the text seeks to justify this dispossession by identifying the peasants with Cain, whose offering God rejected. The idea of the offering to God is a reminder that the village peasants were required to pay crippling tribute to the ruling classes. The death of Abel may well mask a case of successful resistance by a peasant against an attempt of a more wealthy man to appropriate his family lands. That such attempts at appropriation were made is clear from the story of Naboth's vineyard (1 Kgs 21).

Mosala admits that his reading is

> not immediately obvious to the reader. It requires a reading that issues out of a firm grounding in the struggle for liberation, as well as a basis in critical theoretical perspectives which can expose the deep structure of the text (cited by West, 'Reading', p. 288).

Basic to his position is his belief that texts which originate from the class of the oppressors cannot be used in the struggle for liberation. If they are, they may undergird the interests of the oppressors even though they are being used by the oppressed. 'Oppressive texts cannot be totally tamed or subverted into liberative texts' (West, 'Reading', p. 293).

Thus read, the biblical text ceases to be an end in itself. It becomes a means to an end, which is to help to reconstruct a history of class struggle with which the oppressed can identify. Further, it makes possible the necessary unmasking both of the oppressive nature of biblical texts and of their interpretation within a Church and an academic community which have represented, and still represent, the interests of élites rather than of oppressed people. While this may sound very strange to those of us who are indeed students of the Bible from within a privileged rather than an oppressed situation, we cannot overlook the intense sincerity of Mosala's position, and reflect that, if we were in the same position, what he is saying might not sound quite so strange.

4. *Feminist Readings*

Feminist readings of the Bible are as diverse as liberation readings. They can range from readings designed to bring out hitherto unnoticed facets of the text, to readings which are similar in their aims and execution to the hermeneutics of suspicion or rejection which we noted above in the work of Mosala and Schottroff (see further Collins, *Perspectives*).

A feminist reading of Genesis 2–3 that has become a classic is that of Trible (*Rhetoric*). It is essentially a literary reading with structuralist undertones and it is executed with skill and sensitivity that cannot be adequately conveyed in a brief summary. From a feminist standpoint, its aim is to combat a number of misogynist readings which have 'acquired the status of canonicity', including the view that man is superior to woman for the following reasons: he is created first, the woman is made from the man's rib to be his helper, she is named by the man, is responsible for his downfall, is punished by childbirth because of her greater sin, and in her desire for her husband is to be submissive to him. Trible's strategy is to provide a reading which rebuts all of these arguments; the following summary will concentrate upon the alternative reading which she offers.

Genesis 2.5 states, in the standard translations, that there was no man to till the ground. On the basis of the pun in v. 7 on the Hebrew words *'ādām* (man) and *"dāmâ* (earth), Trible renders the Hebrew *'ādām* as 'earth-creature' and maintains that it is 'neither male or female nor a combination of both' (p. 98). It is God who, unilaterally, decides that the earth-creature needs an *'ēzer*, a Hebrew word that here denotes a companion 'who is neither subordinate or superior; one who alleviates isolation through identity' (p. 90). Whereas birds and animals were created from the dust of the earth (2.19), the *'ēzer* is made from the earth-creature and is thus unique. When she is brought to the man he does not name her, as he had named the animals and thus had assumed power over them. Rather, he recognizes the existence of sexuality.

With the creation of the companion from the material of its body, the earth-creature becomes a different being: it 'is no longer identical with its past, so that when next it speaks [when the companion is brought to it] a different creature is speaking' (p. 97). This different creature is a male; and it was not created prior to the female. Both were created simultaneously from the earth-creature. 'His sexual identity depends upon her even as hers depends upon him. For both of them sexuality originates in the one flesh of humanity' (p. 99).

The scene of the temptation of the woman by the serpent (Gen. 3.1-7) indicates a continuity between the earth-creature and the human couple, since the order not to eat from a certain tree was given to the former (2.17). Trible notes that the serpent uses the second person plural in referring to God's command (compare 2.17, literally, 'and of the tree of the knowledge of good and evil *thou* shalt not eat from it', with 3.2, literally, 'Did God say, "*You* may not eat from any tree of the garden?" '). This indicates both the unity and the distinction of the male and female, and although the woman takes the initiative in eating from the forbidden fruit, the husband is at one with her in this act (cf. 3.6, 'and she gave also to her husband with her and he ate'). Trible notes that the man follows the woman 'without question or comment' (p. 113). However, with the act of disobedience and its aftermath the unity of the male and the female is disrupted. Trible shows that there are three moments in the relationship between the man and the woman; before disobedience, with(in) disobedience and after disobedience. In the first, the distinctions combined in fulfilment, in the second they became oppositions. In the third, the unity of the one flesh is shattered. 'The man turns against the woman whom he earlier recognized as bone of bone and flesh of flesh' (p. 119).

In the sentences pronounced upon the serpent, the man and the woman, the woman is the only one who is not cursed. Yet the outcome is bad for her. Commenting on 3.16—'Your desire shall be for your husband, and he shall rule over you'—Trible says that the woman desires the original unity between male and female but that the man will not reciprocate. He wishes to rule over her, and in so doing corrupts himself and his wife: 'His supremacy is neither a divine right nor a male prerogative. Her subordination is neither a divine decree nor the female destiny. Both their positions result from shared disobedience. God describes this consequence but does not prescribe it as punishment' (p. 128).

However, the man complicates the matter by giving his wife a name (3.20), an act that recalls his assumption of power over the animals by giving them names. The woman is, in effect, reduced to the status of an animal: 'The act itself faults the man for corrupting one flesh of equality, for asserting power over the woman, and for violating the companion corresponding to him' (p. 133).

This sketch of Trible's treatment of Genesis 2–3 has concentrated only on her interpretation of texts which have been used to maintain male supremacy, and has omitted much in her treatment which is illuminating. Something that must not be overlooked is her discussion of the relation between the earth-creature and the rest of the created order prior to the disobedience. The earth-creature was placed in a garden in which grew 'every tree which is pleasant to the sight and good for food' (2.9). The world of nature thus provided pleasure for the earth-creature at the level of sight and taste. In return, the earth-creature looked after the garden, preserving its order and beauty. Thus work was a joyful unity between the earth-creature and nature: 'Distinction without opposition, dominion without domination, hierarchy without oppression: to serve and to keep the garden is to live life in harmony and pleasure' (pp. 85-86).

At the same time, the command not to eat of a certain tree showed that freedom, within limits, was assigned to the earth-creature, and it also showed that there were limits to human dominion. 'Nature itself also has God-given independence' (p. 87).

The creation of the animals increases the dominion of the earth-creature. Although they, like it, are formed from the ground, its dominion over them is indicated when it gives them names. God is the 'generous delegator of power who even forfeits the right to reverse human decisions [to give whatever name is appropriate]' (p. 93). The animals do not satisfy the earth-creature (this is God's viewpoint), and their creation paves the way for the creation of the companion and the disobedience that results.

Whether or not we are convinced by Trible's reading it can be said, without reservation, that our appreciation of Genesis 2–3 would be very much the poorer without it.

The chapters by Meyers (*Eve*) on Genesis 2–3 acknowledge the work of Trible, and occasionally draw upon her analysis. However, the methodology is quite different. Meyers holds that Genesis 2–3 must be recognized as containing myth, aetiology and wisdom teaching, and must be understood from their social and historical setting in ancient Israel. She accepts that the two chapters are part of the J document for which she also accepts a tenth-century dating, and she suggests in addition that parts of the story may be even earlier. Their social setting is that of Israelite agriculture in the highlands of Canaan at the beginning of the monarchy.

In this setting, women were required to do very hard work as they helped to grow food in a far-from-helpful environment. This was a labour-intensive activity, which also involved the building and maintenance of terraces. Viewed from this standpoint of harsh reality, the position of the earth-creature in Genesis 2 was indeed to be envied. Its food came from succulent fruit trees provided by God (2.9). In 3.7-18, however ('in toil you shall eat of it [the land]...in the sweat of your

face you shall eat bread...'), the text speaks of the harsh realities of
agricultural life in highland Canaan; its purpose was to help the
Israelite settlers there to cope with these harsh realities. Such an
approach also sheds light on the incident of eating the forbidden fruit.
To the people for whom Genesis 2–3 was composed, eating and providing food to eat constituted the difference between life and death.
Behind the narrative of Genesis 3 are folk explanations of the human
abhorrence of snakes, and of the vital connection between food
(eating) and life.

Meyers also devotes a chapter to Gen. 3.16, whose detailed
argument about the correct translation of the verse cannot be
reproduced here. With some support from some of the ancient
versions she renders the verse:

> I will greatly increase your toil and your pregnancies;
> (Along) with travail shall you beget children.
> For to your man is your desire,
> and he shall predominate over you (p. 118),

and she explains the translation thus:

> Women have to work hard and have many children, as lines 1 and 2
> proclaim; their reluctance to conform, which is not explicitly stated but
> can be reconstructed by looking at the biological and socio-economic
> realities of ancient Palestine, had to be overcome. Lines 3 and 4 tell us
> how: female reluctance is overcome by the passion they feel towards
> their men, and that allows them to accede to the males' sexual advances
> even though they realize that undesired pregnancies (with the
> accompanying risks) might be the consequence (p. 117).

For Meyers, then, Gen. 3.16 is addressed to Israelite women living and
working in the Canaanite highlands in the early Iron Age. They lived
during the formative period of ancient Israel when the people had a
newly acquired sense of unity and a common faith in Yahweh. Their
situation demanded intense agricultural labour, together with the
need to increase the population significantly. It is this combination of
hard work and the need to bear many children that is apparent in
3.16, and which is given divine sanction. In interpreting the verse,
Meyers explicitly rejects a canonical reading of the text which would
connect it with the act of disobedience in eating the fruit. The oracles
have an independent etiological force. Hence, the prescriptions in
them become penalties only in their canonical position within the
prose framework' (p. 119).

Meyers's exposition is an interesting use of historical-critical and
ethno-archaeological work, combined with a hermeneutical approach

that is similar to a hermeneutics of suspicion, without a declared intention to mistrust the text. Meyers's mistrust is rather directed against the misuse of the text in its canonical form. Her treatment of the eating of the forbidden fruit prompts one to ask whether, on the view that myths justify alterations to the environmental balance and the effect these alterations have on societies, the narrative derives from a situation in which an increase in population made it necessary to prohibit the products of fruit trees for use as food. If this were so, however, the setting would hardly be the central highlands of Canaan, although the Shephelah might just be a possibility.

A quite different feminist reading of part of Genesis 1–11 is Bird's discussion of 1.26-29 ('Male and Female', pp. 129-59). Her starting point is the rift that has developed between biblical scholars and theologians with the latter, in her opinion, making pronouncements about the 'image of God' which have little or no basis in the biblical text. Bird is feminist in the sense that feminism has provided 'a new socio-theological context, characterized by new questions, perceptions and judgments' (p. 134). It is from this new perspective that she undertakes a fresh look at 1.26-30 from a traditional historical-critical standpoint. A careful examination of the use of the word for 'image' in Hebrew, and in Akkadian texts, leads to the conclusion that, in the latter, a king who is described as the image of God is designated as a special representative of the god, holding a mandate to rule on its behalf. The king so designated is divine in his function as a representative and as a ruler. Against this, Bird argues that, in 1.26, language restricted in Mesopotamia (and possibly Canaan) to the king is applied to humanity as a whole. Humanity in its essential nature stands in a special relationship to the divine world (p. 144).

The statement that God created humanity as male and female (1.27) has nothing to do with the statement that humanity was created in the divine image, according to Bird (pp. 146ff.). Its meaning is limited to the reproduction of the human race, for which both male and female were required. This reproduction will enable humanity to fill and rule the earth:

> There is no message of shared dominion here, no word about the distribution of roles, responsibility and authority between the sexes, no word of sexual equality. What is described is a task for the species...and the position of the species in relation to other orders of creation (p. 151).

Bird summarizes the results of her historical-critical search for the message/intentions of the ancient author(s) as follows: P is not an 'equal rights' theologian, nor does he suggest that the divine nature, as read back from the image, contains male and female. The words about sexual distinction refer only to the reproductive task of the human race. On the other hand, the text allows us to say that, since male and female are both human, then woman 'images the divine as fully as man and...she is consequently as essential as he to an understanding of humanity as God's special sign or representative in the world' (p. 159). Bird adds that this conclusion, while exegetically sound, probably 'exceeds what the Priestly writer intended to say or was able to conceive'.

5. *Genesis 1–11 and Ancient Near Eastern Texts*

That parts of Genesis 1–11 have much in common with the traditions of other peoples of the ancient Near East has become even clearer in the past twenty years than it already was, thanks to the publication of new texts and the publication of improved editions of already known texts. A good example is the edition of the *Atra-Ḫasis* text by Lambert and Millard. The use to which such information has been put has moved away from the attempts of earlier scholarship either to interpret the Old Testament traditions almost wholly in terms of the culture of ancient Babylon or to assert the absolute uniqueness of Israel's use of material shared with its neighbours. Arguments both for similarity with and difference from other traditions of the ancient Near East have continued to be put forward, but in different ways and with a more moderate tone; and more attention than before has been paid, in making the comparisons, to material from Egypt and to ancient Near Eastern art. In a series of studies, Müller has stressed the positive side of the similarities between parts of Genesis 1–11 and ancient Near Eastern parallels ('Mythische'; 'Motif'). He has argued that what he regards as the original form of ch. 2 (vv. 4b-8, [10-14], 15b, 18-24) is mythical in the sense that the narrative serves the same function as similar ancient Near Eastern traditions, which is to explain and to legitimate humanity's position in its world. Faced by forces, especially in the world of nature, that shape and often threaten human life, it is necessary for humanity to name these forces and to tell stories about them in order to make the world more hospitable. The fact that Genesis 1–11 speaks of God rather than gods does not alter this fact. It is not the presence or absence of gods that determines whether texts are mythical: it is their function.

All this is not original to Müller, as he readily indicates; but he develops this view in some interesting directions. In his study of the flood narrative ('Motif'), he points out that the combination of a creation story and a flood story in a single text is not peculiar to the Old Testament, but is found also in *Atra-Ḥasis* and in the Sumerian flood story about Ziusudra. He believes the connection between creation and flood stories to be important, and labels the flood story an anti-myth, a story of the destruction of order. The two stories taken together—creation (myth) and flood (anti-myth)—articulate an understanding of what it means to be human that is essentially paradoxical. The texts describe a situation in which the world is not an ordered whole but an interaction of tensions, in which the incomplete power of God or the gods over the whole of reality is dramatically portrayed ('Motif', p. 308).

From this position, Müller develops two ideas. The first is that the world view expressed in these Old Testament and other traditions is not the product of the thinking of isolated individuals, but arises rather from the collective experience of humanity, and is thus the expression of inter-subjectivity. Yet the texts are also sufficiently open to differing uses and interpretations that they can serve as an expression of human self-awareness in varying situations. Müller compares here the reasons given in Genesis 6 for the flood with the different reasons given in the other texts. We might add that this suggestion may explain the continuing importance of these texts even today.

Müller's second main point is that these traditions must not be explained away as being merely pre-scientific or an expression of humanity's biological needs. They are concerned with the relationship between the human and the non-human in the world, and how this relationship may be brought to expression in speech and thought. In this regard, they have much in common with modern scientific attempts to explain the world, as well as with those of Christian theology employing the mythological language of the incarnation of God. The very fact that these traditions are not peculiar to the Bible, but can be shown to be an expression of human subjectivity, is a reminder to theology that its ultimate task is to understand reality and to do this in dialogue with other scientific disciplines. Thus Müller skilfully uses the similarities between parts of Genesis 1–11 and ancient Near Eastern texts in order to give the passages an almost timeless, existential significance.

The opposite approach has been to contrast Genesis 1–11 and the parallel traditions by showing how Genesis 1–11 has used motifs common to these texts in distinctive ways. Thus Bird, in discussing humankind's creation in the image of God, refers to Egyptian evidence 'where the idea of the king as image of the god is a common one, finding expression in a rich and diverse vocabulary of representation which describes the Pharaoh as image, statue, likeness, picture, etc., of the deity (usually the chief creator god)' ('Male and Female', p. 140). She also refers to similar evidence from Mesopotamia which is closer to P in language, conception and time, before going on to argue that Genesis 1 is unique in using the image language to describe not a king, but humanity as a whole in relation to God.

Other approaches along these lines are as follows. In some texts from the ancient Near East, human beings are created by the gods to perform the hard labour that the gods do not wish to do. In Genesis 2, the man (or earth-creature) is created to tend the garden; but his/its function is not to toil, and food is abundantly provided from fruit trees. When toil becomes the lot of humanity, this is because of human disobedience, not divine arbitrariness. Again, in some texts, humanity is created from the blood of the gods. In Genesis 2, the part of humanity that comes from God is the breath; thus the difference between God and humanity is emphasized. Genesis 1–2 is unique in ancient Near Eastern texts so far known to us in describing the creation of women (see Rogerson and Davies, *World*, pp. 198-208 for the above paragraph).

Zenger, in his monograph on the Priestly parts of Genesis 1–11, makes use of the rich material assembled from ancient Near Eastern art by Othmar Keel, regarding the bow, and the relation between human beings and animals. He also cites an Egyptian text from about the fifteenth century BCE, the myth of the heavenly cow. This describes a time when there was harmony in the created order between the gods and humankind. This was disrupted, however, by a rebellion of the humans, caused by the ageing of the creator god Re. This ideal world could not continue in unaltered existence, but was subject to decay followed by regeneration. The rebellion of human-kind was punished by the creator god by a fire supervised by the goddess Hathor. However, the creator god himself rescued some human beings, and inaugurated a new order far less satisfactory than the former situation. The only access to the former creation is through death, and the creator god effectively withdraws from human affairs.

This story contains some motifs also found in Genesis 1–11. An ideal creation is disrupted by human rebellion against the god, there is a destruction (by fire, not water) and another order emerges, falling short of the original creation. The differences are also striking compared with Genesis 1–11. As Zenger puts it:

> P^g begins with the concept of a complete creation which, left to take care of itself, becomes a corrupted world full of violence. This does not lead, however, to the disappointed withdrawal of the Creator God, but to the

acknowledgment of his active involvement by means of the 'sign of the cloud', which indicates his residence not in a remote heavenly palace, but among his people (*Untersuchungen*, p. 134).

Comparison with ancient Near Eastern texts, therefore, continues to be a fruitful part of the study of Genesis 1–11, but with new emphases.

6. *Discussion and Evaluation*

Faced with the great variety of approaches and conclusions that have been mentioned in this chapter, readers can be forgiven for feeling bewildered. They may find themselves thinking that however interesting many of the individual insights of these approaches may be, they surely cannot all be correct or equally valid, and that means that we have no certain way of discovering what Genesis 1–11 is saying.

In reply to this natural reaction we can say that the history of interpretation shows that there probably never has been a time when all interpreters were agreed about the meaning of Genesis 1–11, and that each generation of interpreters has been influenced by what they have found in the text in relation to the situation in which they worked (for some examples see Rogerson, 'The Old Testament'). If the present state of affairs is different from what previously was the case, it is a difference of degree. The diversity of modern readings of Genesis 1–11 arises from a greater diversity of situations in which the text is being read. Yet, as will be argued, this greater diversity can be reduced to an underlying unity. This will not mean that we shall then get an agreed answer to the question, 'What is Genesis 1–11 saying?' It will mean that we shall be in a better position to understand the reasons why we are studying the text and what it is that we want from it. This self-discovery will assist each of us as we study Genesis 1–11. Underlying all of the approaches outlined in this chapter is a decision or decisions taken by the interpreters either deliberately or unawares. These will now be stated and discussed, but not in any particular order of importance.

a. *Sources versus Final Form*
This book will not argue for or against dividing Genesis 1–11 into the sources J and P. In Chapter 3 below, some sections will give reasons why certain parts of Genesis 1–11 have been divided into sources, and there will also be references to literature that advocates or rejects source division. The task here will simply be to discuss the implications of choosing or rejecting the sources theory in interpreting Genesis 1–11.

The first issue that arises is whether the Bible is to be interpreted as a whole (although this is not as simple as it seems, as will be explained) or whether certain traditions are to be set over against other traditions. The setting of traditions in opposition is most clearly seen in the work of Lohfink, where P^g is held to be giving a different view of the meaning of Israelite history compared with J or D. Meyers sets traditions in opposition in a slightly different way when she interprets Gen. 3.16 in its presumed historical and sociological context, and deliberately rejects the link between this passage and the act of disobedience in ch. 3. As I understand her, she is rejecting a reading of 3.16 that the final form of the text makes possible, and is opposing to that reading an interpreting of 3.16 regarded as an original, isolated unit.

It must be stressed that putting traditions in opposition is not a necessary consequence of accepting source criticism or of breaking the sources into smaller, prior units. It is possible to accept the existence of the distinct sources J and P and nevertheless to interpret them harmoniously. One can argue, for example, that it was the P writer who composed Genesis 1–11 by incorporating J into his own account, and who thereby stamped his own intentionality upon the whole, regardless of what the J material might have meant in isolation.

Readings of the final form of Genesis 1–11 are of various types. They can be literary, structuralist or historical-critical. An excellent example of the first type is that of Clines. He decides to make no attempt to appeal to sources or to historical background (although he discusses these matters carefully) in his attempt to find a 'theme' that will do the greatest possible justice to the literary features of Genesis 1–11. No structuralist reading of the text as a whole was discussed in this chapter, but such a reading would eschew sources (though not necessarily historical setting) in an attempt to detect beneath the literary surface of the text various oppositions or distinctions that suggest themselves as part of the underlying structure. An historical-critical reading of the final form of Genesis 1–11, such as would be implied in the canonical approach of Childs (*Introduction*, pp. 148-50), would not reject the existence of sources nor rule out a long process of composition. It would, nevertheless, maintain that however Genesis 1–11 reached its final form, and whatever may have been the sources used, the final form has an intentionality that scholarship must try to discover by historical-critical rather than by formal literary methods.

It is possible to combine some of the underlying decisions mentioned above. There is no reason why a scholar should not accept J and P, accept that, in isolation, they express different ideologies, and yet also accept that, in combining them, their redactor or editor understood them as expressing yet a third viewpoint. This, however, raises the issue that is discussed in the next section. In a case such as that immediately above, where a scholar is accepting three intention-alities of Genesis 1–11 — that of J, that of P and that of the editor — is one of these to be preferred as more 'authoritative'? This issue does not arise, of course, for those who reject sources; and one reason why some scholars reject sources may be that it relieves them from pre-cisely this question.

b. *Intentions, Motives and Authority*

Brett ('Motives') has recently suggested that we should distinguish between intentions and motives when we interpret texts. By an inten-tion he means that which we can infer from a text itself about what it is trying to convey. By a motive he means a judgment, based on con-siderations other than the text itself, about the reason why a text was written. An example of intention would be the significance of Gen. 1.26-30 and 9.1-3, (4-6), 7. The similarities and differences between these texts are the major clue to what they are seeking to convey. An example of motive would be Wittenberg's claim that the purpose of the J material was to oppose the political and social effects of the reign of Solomon. There is nothing in the text itself to suggest this, and Wittenberg bases his claim upon other considerations such as his view of the date of J and the circles that produced it.

Brett also uses the term 'indirect intention'. By this he means the interpretation of a text against the background of other texts, such as those from the ancient Near East. There is no direct evidence in Genesis 1–11 that these chapters are referring to creation and flood stories known from ancient Mesopotamia, or to Egyptian and Assyr-ian notions of the king as the image of the god. However, there is no doubt that certain parts of Genesis 1–11 appear to us in a new light if we assume that their writer(s) knew some or all of these extrabiblical traditions.

Brett's suggestions enable us to distinguish between three types of operation, although it can be conceded that, in practice, they may merge and overlap. First, there is the attempt to establish from the text itself what it is trying to convey. Second, there is the study of the text primarily from the point of view of its motivation within a pre-sumed political and social setting. Third, there is an attempt to put the text in the wider context of ideas known from extrabiblical material to have existed in the ancient Near East.

Even if some of these operations overlap, a weighting towards one or the other may produce differing interpretations. For example, Bird comes to a different conclusion from Beauchamp about the meaning of humankind's creation in the divine image. This is because she interprets 1.26ff. partly in the light of Egyptian and Assyrian texts, whereas Beauchamp is concerned to work out the exegetical problems provoked by the contrast between Gen. 1.26-30 and 9.1-7. Again, Boesak's reading of Genesis 4 pays very close attention to the text of that chapter and the meaning suggested by its literary features, whereas Mosala's interpretation of the same passage is far from obvious because he is concerned with the motives behind the text's production.

What is the 'authority' of these various decisions and their resulting interpretations? Strictly speaking, this is a religious question generated by the fact that Christians have believed that the Bible is in some sense a communication from God to humanity—a proposition to which the present author is committed. But can a text be a communication from God if a diversity of ways of reading it gives rise to so many interpretations? The same difficulty may be felt by non-believers who expect, perhaps without having asked themselves why, that Genesis 1–11 should have at least one interpretation that can be regarded as 'authoritative'.

In an attempt to resolve these matters several strategies could be employed. It could be argued, for example, that a reading is more likely to be 'authoritative' if it eliminates uncertainties. For example, the final form of the text exists, whereas the discerning of sources is theoretical. Again, suggestions about the motivation of the writer(s) are theoretical, since we actually know so little about how and when the texts were produced. Again, we do not actually know whether the writer(s) of Genesis 1–11 were familiar with other creation and flood stories from the ancient world. The result of this kind of argument would be that an interpretation whose aim was to discover the intentionality of the final form of Genesis 1–11 from the inner dynamics of the text was more 'authoritative' than readings which resulted from assumptions that were no more than plausible.

This kind of argument is given only as an example; and it is not the purpose of this guide either to reject or to endorse it. It must also be stated that there are scholars who are absolutely convinced that the only way to discover the meaning of the text is to isolate the sources of which it is believed to be composed and to see how these sources have been used in the final composition.

Another crucial question that has to be addressed is that of the relationship between the meaning of a text and what we take to be its intentionality or motive. The meaning cannot be confined to intentionality or motive, from which it follows that 'authority' cannot be confined to intentionality or motive either. This can be illustrated as follows. According to Wittenberg, the motive for writing Genesis 11 was to criticize the building schemes of Solomon. Let us assume that he is correct. Does it follow from this that any other interpretation of the tower of Babel story is incorrect, or to be ruled out? Are we wrong to see it as a story of humankind in general, wrongly and vainly trying to enter those realms that probably belong to God alone? Surely not. Again (and this is a personal view) I doubt very much that the writer of Genesis 2 thought that the *'ādām* that God placed in the garden of Eden was an earth-creature that was neither male nor female. This does not mean, however, that I reject out of hand Trible's reading of this passage in those terms. On the contrary, she has enriched these chapters by the suggestions that she has made. This brings me to the point where I must try to state what I believe to be a unity underlying the diversities that have been outlined in this chapter. It can be summarized in the following statement: What is common to all these approaches is that they are the work of interpretative communities and that these communities have an implicit view of what it means to be a human being.

At the end of the nineteenth century, the churches and universities and colleges constituted a single interpretative community, whose main concern was to answer the questions arising from the natural sciences, especially Darwinism. The implied view of what it means to be human was that humans were essentially thinking creatures whose intellectual questions needed to be answered. The twentieth century saw a growing apart of the churches and the universities. The need to understand Genesis 1–11 in the light of newly discovered Babylonian texts was an academic rather than an ecclesiastical concern. What has happened in the past twenty years is that there has been an increase in the number of interpretative communities, and that some of these have become established within universities.

The most obvious new interpretative communities have been those concerned with liberation and feminism. It will be clear from what was said earlier in the chapter that liberation and feminist standpoints can vary and even disagree among themselves. What is distinctive about liberation interpretative communities, however, is that they do not view human beings as simply thinking creatures with primarily intellectual concerns. Human beings are social beings embedded in political and economic structures; and where these structures oppress, discriminate and de-humanize, they must be resisted. In such situations the biblical text becomes a partner in the struggle to achieve conditions worthy of the dignity which belongs to human beings.

Similar things can be said about feminist interpretative communities. Their concern is to make the biblical text a partner in the struggle against sexism, so that a new and appropriate understanding can emerge of the respective contributions of males and females to the business of living as human beings.

In academic circles twenty years ago there was probably still only one principal interpretative community, even though its interests were many and varied. This was the community that believed in study for its own sake, and which therefore implicitly understood humans to be essentially thinking and rational creatures. The situation today in academic circles is that, increasingly, there is a willingness to entertain the possibility of other interpretative communities having a legitimate place alongside that which believes in study for its own sake. This chapter has indicated the results of this new diversity. Of course, what I have just written gives too rigid a picture, as though people belong to different interpretative communities that exist in watertight compartments. In fact, many people belong to more than one such community. It is possible, for example, for an individual to be committed to one of the churches, to work in a university and to be a feminist. But it is also likely that one of these interpretative communities will be considered to be the most important, and will influence that person's work more strongly than the rest.

It is within the interpretative communities that the standards for acceptable readings are established. If the main interpretative community is a church, that body's beliefs and concepts of mission will ultimately decide what is and is not an acceptable reading of Genesis 1–11. For example, a church that is doctrinally committed to the subordinate role of women is not likely to approve of interpretations that seek to establish female equality with males. If the main interpretative community is a university, sympathy with other approaches will be difficult to obtain if their readings of Genesis 1–11 rely on impossible translations of the Hebrew or implausible reconstructions of the social and historical background to the text. If the main interpretative community is one actively engaged in the struggle against injustice, there will probably be little enthusiasm for readings of Genesis 1–11 that are mainly interested in relating the flood story to the *Atra-Ḥasis* narrative.

All this implies that, as well as taking the academic decisions mentioned earlier, such as opting for the final form as against interpreting

J and P, readers need to reflect upon their membership of interpretative communities and what are the considerations that are the most influential in determining how they prefer to interpret Genesis 1–11. It is very much to be hoped that members of differing interpretative communities will be prepared to listen to each other and to learn from each other. The current great diversity of approaches to reading Genesis 1–11 should be seen not as a threat but as an opportunity. They all represent the activity of that human race whose origins and nature are the subject of Genesis 1–11.

One final consideration is that, as time progresses, some readings of texts stand the test of time, whereas others are quickly forgotten. This will surely be the case with regard to some of the interpretations discussed in this chapter. At the same time, the history of interpretation shows that in every generation, differing interpretations are part of a continuing struggle to hear the text of the Bible addressing communities as the Word of God. Even if there are many voices, and they sound confusing, their existence is a testimony to the fact that the biblical text is alive and not simply a dead letter.

Chapter Three

CRITICAL ISSUES

1. *Myth*

At various times in the past two hundred years, and for various reasons, it has been suggested that parts or all of Genesis 1–11 are myths or mythical (see Rogerson, *Myth*, for an extensive survey). Two separate questions will be dealt with here: How did the presumed Israelite readers of Genesis 1–11 understand these passages? What do we mean when we classify Genesis 1–11 or parts thereof as myths or mythical?

There can be no doubt that when Israelites read Genesis 1–11 they believed that these stories belonged to an age that was different from their own times. Yet this past age was in continuity with their own times, and what had happened then determined what the world was like now. We find in Genesis 1–11 a series of phrases which mark off the narratives as belonging to a different age. They are:

1.1 When God began to create (if this is the correct rendering; see below, §2).
2.4b In the day that the LORD made the earth and the heavens...
2.25 and the man and his wife were both naked and were not ashamed...
3.1 now the serpent was more subtle...
6.1 When men began to multiply on the face of the ground...
6.4 Nephilim (giants) were on the earth in those days.
11.1 Now the whole earth had one language and few words...

Müller ('Mythische', p. 265 n. 22) gives some parallels from the ancient world. To these phrases must be added the fact that ancient Israelites did not expect snakes to speak (in Hebrew?) or to propel themselves in an upright position, did not expect people to live to be over 900 years, and were aware that Hebrew was only one of a number of languages spoken in the ancient Near East.

We must also not overlook the fact that the narratives themselves clearly describe 'before' and 'after' situations, making it explicitly clear that there can be no return to the 'before' situations. Thus, humanity is forever banished from the garden of Eden, and the earth is no longer benign when it comes to producing food. The possibility is excluded that there will ever again be a flood that totally destroys the earth and its inhabitants. Humankind remains separated by the barriers of language.

On the other hand, the age that is described by Genesis 1–11 has continuity with that of the Israelite readers. This is indicated by the genealogies that form a chain of descendants from Adam to Abraham: ten generations from Adam to Noah and ten from Noah to Abraham, with the first series characterized by the very long ages lived by the men of those generations. Other links are provided by the explanations (aetiologies) that begin from the world as known by the Israelite readers and refer back to the world of Genesis 1–11 as though to say: you know that the stories of this past age are true because of what is true in your own world. For example, the fact that when a man and a woman marry they enter into a deeper relationship than they had with their parents (2.24) indicates the truth of the story of the woman being first made from the man's rib. Again, the fact that a rainbow appears in the sky only when it has been raining is a confirmation of the story that the world was once destroyed by a flood (van Dyck, 'Function').

For Israelites, then, the narratives of Genesis 1–11 were factually true, but Israelites did not expect to experience the things that they describe. Adam and Eve were accepted as real human beings, but any Israelite woman who claimed that she had had a conversation with a snake would have been dismissed as a crank. The stories in Genesis 1–11, compiled from ancient traditions about origins which the Israelite shared with other ancient Near Eastern peoples, and enriched with folk tale motifs (see Rogerson, *Anthropology*, pp. 66-85), expressed Israel's understanding of how the world of their experience had been brought into being by the God of Israel, and how it had been shaped by the response of their forefathers.

So far, we have been considering what the narratives meant to the Israelites. A quite different matter arises when we today designate Genesis 1–11 as myth. We are using a classification which is based upon the comparative study of the literatures of ancient and modern underdeveloped peoples. Although the terms 'myths' and 'mythical' have been used in many ways, three can be selected for brief mention. The first is a literary definition of 'myths' which goes back to the work of the brothers J. and W. Grimm in the nineteenth century (Rogerson, *Myth*, pp. 27-28). According to this view, myths are stories about the gods, from which it has often been concluded, rightly or wrongly, that Genesis 1–11 contains no myths except, perhaps, for 6.4, where the 'sons of God' marry human wives. Another view, which became widespread in the present century, is the ritual theory of myth, according to which myths are the liturgies that accompany rituals. On the face of it, this removes Genesis 1–11 from the category of myth since we have no evidence that any of its material was used in ritual; and in any case the ritual theory itself has been largely rejected (pp. 66-84). The third view is that of Müller, mentioned in Chapter 2. Müller has argued convincingly that, with regard to their general function in articulating an understanding of the world, the narratives of Genesis 1–11 cannot be treated differently from similar traditions from the ancient Near East, even if the latter are polytheistic and Genesis is monotheistic. Müller's view has the advantage of linking Genesis 1–11 with similar ancient material, and of seeing it as a fundamental expression of the human striving to discover truth, while leaving open the need to interpret the actual content of Genesis 1–11 in its own terms. Müller's approach to myth is, in my view, the best option for modern interpretation of Genesis 1–11.

2. *Genesis 1.1-3*

A glance at recent translations of the Bible indicates that the rendering of the opening of Genesis is not without problems. The RSV opens with 'In the beginning God created' but has a small (a) after 'created' and a footnote giving as an alternative translation 'When God began to create...' The NEB has something like the RSV footnote as its main text, with the traditional words relegated to a footnote. In the REB the situation found in the RSV has been restored.

The main problem is that in the traditional vocalized Hebrew text, the phrase b^e'*rēšît* (traditionally rendered as 'In the beginning'), means either 'in a beginning' or, if it is to be translated 'in the beginning' it must introduce a subordinate clause such as 'of God's creating...' Unfortunately, the immediately following words in the traditional vocalized Hebrew text cannot be rendered 'of God's creating'. Therefore both the traditional translation, 'In the beginning God created', and the alternative, 'When God began to create', imply an alteration to the vocalization of the Hebrew. The former implies reading *bā'rēšît* for b^a'*rēšît* and the second implies reading $b^e r\bar{o}$' (infinitive construct) for *bārā'* (3rd masculine singular perfect). These and other problems have led to three main suggestions about the translation of the syntax of 1.1-3.

(1) The traditional translation in which each of verses 1, 2 and 3 is a statement:

> In the beginning God created the heavens and the earth (v. 1).
> The earth was without form and void (v. 2).
> And God said, 'Let there be light' (v. 3).

(2) The rendering 'When God began to create the heavens and the earth, the earth was without form and void... Then God said, "Let there be light..."'

(3) The rendering 'When God began to create the heavens and the earth— now the earth was without form and void...—God said, "Let there be light..."'

In trying to decide between these alternatives, one view must be rejected, namely that which prefers (1) on the ground that it implies the doctrine that God created the world out of nothing (*creatio ex nihilo*), whereas (2) and (3) imply creation out of pre-existing matter. For a careful look at (1) will indicate that it, too, implies creation out of pre-existing matter. In Genesis 1 the creative acts result from the divine word, 'And God said...' Gen. 1.1 is a statement and not a creative word, and it is followed by the information that 'The earth was without form and void'. Since order and ordering are an essential part of the Old Testament view of creation (see below), the earth had not been created if it was 'without form and void'. It was an undifferentiated mass waiting to be formed into shape.

A stronger argument in favour of (1) is that, whereas v. 1 says that God created the heavens, there is no mention of the creation of the heavens later in the passage (in v. 2). Gen. 1.1 is probably to be understood as follows: 'In the beginning God created the heavens and the earth'. This is a summary statement of what God had done, in which no elaboration is needed of how he brought into being the heavens, which are his own abode. The earth that had been brought into being was, however, an undifferentiated mass, and the purpose of the remainder of the chapter is to describe how this was ordered into a whole for the prime benefit of humankind among the created things.

In v. 2 the words 'without form and void', 'darkness' and 'deep' suggest something sinister about the unformed earth and its waters, and this has led scholars to compare this verse with descriptions of chaos prior to creation in ancient Near Eastern texts (cf. *ANET*, pp. 60-61). The Hebrew word for 'deep', *t⁽e⁾hôm*, has been compared with the name of the goddess Tiamat, out of whose carcass the victorious god Marduk made the world in the Babylonian epic of creation, *Enuma elish* (*ANET*, p. 67), although philologically the two words cannot be connected. It has further been maintained that the phrase translated in the RSV as 'The Spirit of God was moving over the face of the waters' should be rendered as 'a mighty wind was swirling across the face of the waters'. This would mean that the phrase was a description of chaos prior to creation and nothing to do with the Spirit of God.

These are difficult questions to decide. We do not know whether the writer of Genesis 1 was familiar with other creation stories or their motifs or whether, if he was, how he intended references to them in his text to be taken (if there were such references). It is probably unwise to look for allusions to other ancient Near Eastern texts or motifs in order to provide the clue to the understanding of these verses. If Gen. 1.1 asserts that God created the heavens and the earth it is most likely that the phrase about the Spirit of God should be understood in its traditional sense. Thus, although there may be something sinister about the as yet unordered earth, even this is under the divine influence as the Spirit of God hovers bird-like (cf. Deut. 32.11) over the unformed matter.

3. 'Word' and 'Deed' Accounts and the Translation of Genesis 1

In Genesis 1, two types of creative activity can be found: creation by word and creation by deed. An example of the former is 1.3, 'Let there be light', and an example of the latter is 1.7, 'God made the firmament'. However, in the case of the creation of the firmament we also have the words, 'God said, "Let there be a firmament..."' (v. 6). Does this imply that the firmament is created twice, once by word and once by deed? This possible double creation led Schmidt (*Schöpferungsgeschichte*) to argue in an influential monograph that Genesis 1 in its final form was a combination of two accounts, a word account and a deed account. This view has since been challenged by Steck (*Der Schöpfungsbericht*). The most important thing about the discussion, however, is how it affects the translation of Genesis 1. The view that there is a word account and a deed account depends partly on a particular understanding of the phrase 'And it was so' in vv. 9, 11, 15 and 24. If we take vv. 24-25 we seem to have the following elements:

Word account

24   God said 'Let the earth bring forth living creatures...' And it was so
     (i.e. it happened in accordance with God's command).

Deed account

25   God made the beasts of the earth.

However, it is possible to render vv. 24-25 as follows:

24 God said, 'The earth shall bring forth living creatures...'
    And it was so (i.e. in accordance with what God had said):
25 God made the beasts of the earth.

On this view the 'Let there be' statements in vv. 6, 9 not in the Hebrew text, but in the ancient Greek translation known as the Septuagint or LXX), 14, 20 and 24 are not words that create, but statements that declare how God intends the world to be ordered. These declarations are then put into effect by God. In fact, a translation such as the RSV could be read in the way that is being suggested here. In vv. 14-19, for example, the words 'Let there be light in the firmament of the heavens' can be read as a declaration of intent, and the words in v. 16, 'God made the two great lights...', can be regarded as the actual creation. The GNB on the other hand, goes a long way towards supporting the word and deed accounts theory by rendering 'And it was so' as 'So it was done'.

If we pursue the matter further, we notice some interesting variations in the structure of the accounts in Genesis 1.

(1) Creation of light (v. 3)
     God said...
     (no 'it was so')
     (no 'God created the light')
(2) Creation of the firmament (vv. 6-7)
     God said...
     God made the firmament
     'It was so' (*after* God made the firmament!)
(3) Creation of the dry land (v. 9)
     God said...
     It was so
     (no 'God made' — but this is found in the LXX)
(4) Creation of plants and trees (vv. 11-12)
     God said...
     It was so
     The earth brought forth
(5) Creation of luminaries (vv. 14-16)
     God said...
     It was so
     God made...
(6) Creation of sea creatures and birds (vv. 20-21)
     God said...
     (no 'It was so')
     God made
(7) Creation of beasts of the earth (vv. 24–25)
     God said...
     It was so
     God made

(8)   Creation of human beings (vv. 26–27)
      God said
      (no 'It was so')
      God made...

This indicates that the pattern

      God said
      It was so
      God made...

occurs only twice, for acts (5) and (7), and three times if we include (3). (4) is close to the formula, except that it is the earth that produces the plants and trees, and not God that makes them. Indeed, (4) seems to be evidence against a separate 'word' account and to support the view that 'Let there be' is a declaration of intended order:

> God said, 'The earth shall put forth vegetation...' It happened (in accordance with God's command): The earth brought forth vegetation...

If this approach is correct, then we need to understand the 'Let there be' statements in Genesis 1 to refer not only to what God meant to happen at creation: we need to understand them as statements laying down an eternal ordering of the world, an ordering that was begun at creation and which the biblical writer believed to endure to his own day.

4. *The Creation as 'Good'*

A recurrent feature of Genesis 1 is the statement 'God saw that it was good'. This occurs in vv. 9, 12, 18, 21 and 25. It is not found in vv. 6-8 (the creation of the firmament) and in v. 4 there is the variant 'God saw that the light was good'. At v. 31 this motif is summed up 'God saw everything that he had made, and behold it was very good'. This is clearly an important motif. What does it mean?

One often hears it said, on the basis of Genesis 1, that the created order is good in the sense of being a perfect expression of God's will. This must, however, be regarded as dubious. Even if this is what Genesis 1 means, we cannot ignore the cursing of the ground in Genesis 3 (if we are doing a final form reading) nor the qualification of 1.26-30 in 9.1-7 following the flood (if we are reading the final form or interpreting P^g).

These passages indicate that the creation as it was in Genesis 1 no longer exists in the precise form that it did then. This is further borne out by passages such as Isa. 11.6-9 and 65.17-25 in which a new creation is envisaged in which there is no enmity between humans and animals nor between animals and animals.

Zenger (pp. 59-62) has an interesting discussion of the matter on the basis of which it could be suggested that by 'good' the passage means 'good for achieving its purpose'. The structure of most of the works of creation will then be:

Declaration of intent: Let there be...
Creative work: God made...
Acknowledgment: that what has been made meets the intention.
God saw that it was good.

This understanding of 'good' in a weakened sense then enables us to say that, in spite of the curse, the flood and the compromise (9.1-7), the creation is still 'good' in that it provides the order and stability in which the life given by God can be lived out. It is doubtful whether the creation any longer expresses the ideal will of God; but this does not rule out its 'goodness' as providing a viable setting for human and animal life.

5. *Creation as Order*

The previous section leads on to the idea of creation as order, in that it has been suggested that the description of the creation as 'good' means that it achieves its purpose of providing a stable and viable setting for human life. The idea of creation as order can be paralleled from outside Israel in the ancient world (see Schmid, 'Creation', pp. 102-17), and it can also be illustrated from the Old Testament itself, and with some important consequences.

In Genesis 1, the process of creation involves distinguishing, setting boundaries and assigning positions. Light is distinguished from darkness (v. 4), waters above the firmament are distinguished from those below it (v. 7), water is distinguished from dry land (v. 10), and luminaries distinguish day from night (vv. 14-15). The firmament sets a boundary between the upper and lower waters (v. 6), and the luminaries set the limits to days, nights, seasons and years (vv. 14-15). To the earth are assigned trees, plants and living creatures, to the heavens are assigned birds, and to the waters are assigned the sea and water creatures.

What is implicit in Genesis 1 is more explicitly stated elsewhere. Thus in Gen. 6.11, the flood is brought about when the waters above the firmament and the waters below the earth and the seas are allowed to burst their bounds and to cover the whole earth. The bounds, or boundaries, receive an even more explicit mention in Job 38.8-11:

> Who shut in the sea with doors, when it burst forth from the womb…
> and [I] prescribed bounds for it, and set bars and doors, and said, 'Thus
> far shall you come and no further…'?

Indeed, the book of Job has some charming touches when it comes to the idea of creation as order. It suggests (in poetry, of course) that there are storehouses where God keeps the snow and the hail (38.22) and that even light and darkness have their appropriate storage areas (38.19, 24).

There is an important link between creation as order and human moral behaviour, such that the latter can affect the former. This is clear from Genesis 1–11 itself. It is human disobedience that leads to the cursing of the ground (3.17-19), and human wickedness that makes God decide to bring about the flood. But there are other passages in the Old Testament that address this theme. An example is Leviticus 26 where the Israelites are promised that

> If you walk in my statutes and observe my commandments to do them,
> then I will give you your rains in their season, and the land shall yield
> its increase, and the trees of the field shall yield their fruit (Lev. 26.3-4).

The opposite is that

> if you will not hearken to me…your strength shall be spent in vain, for
> your land shall not yield its increase, and the trees of the field shall not
> yield their fruit (vv. 14, 20).

The connection between obeying God and being prosperous will strike many modern readers as naive, and certainly out of keeping with the New Testament paradox that the first followers of Jesus were called to self-denial and suffering. Others might see here a justification for supporting ecology movements, pointing out that human exploitation of natural resources (i.e. disobeying God) does eventually lead to economic disasters. However, the most important point is the following: if creation implies order, then that order is not restricted simply to the non-human world. If creation is order, that order must include ordered human relationships; and if God only guaranteed the stability of the physical universe, but was unconcerned about inter-human relationships, then the creation would be fundamentally immoral. The same would be true of any form of religion that emphasized the spiritual attainments of the individual while remaining indifferent to disordered human relationships resulting from the evil structures of oppression, poverty and injustice.

6. *One Creation Story or Two?*

On the basis of source division, it is often asserted that there are two accounts of creation, one in Gen. 1.1–2.4a, the other in 2.4b-25. Opponents of source division labour to deny this, sometimes rendering the Hebrew verbs in 2.21 as pluperfects

> The LORD God had caused a deep sleep to fall upon the man...

to avoid the idea that 2.21ff. is an account of the creation of woman distinct from that implied in 1.27.

There can be no doubt that there are duplications between Genesis 1 and 2. In the former, human beings are made at vv. 26-30, while at 2.5 humanity does not yet exist and a man is made in 2.7. Again, 2.19 implies, against ch. 1, that the beasts of the field or birds of the air do not yet exist. On the other hand, the following differences between the two chapters are significant. In ch. 2 there is no explicit account of the creation of light, darkness, day, night, sun, moon, stars or firmament. There is also a detailed account, not found in ch. 1, of the location of the Garden of Eden and of the rivers which flowed from it (vv. 8-14). On the basis of the content of 1.1–2.4a and 2.4b-25 it is safest to say that the former is a creation story and that the latter is an origins story. Genesis 1 relates the formation and ordering of the universe, while Genesis 2 presumes the existence of the earth and describes how it was populated and ordered.

7. *One Tree or Two?*

It is usually held that Gen. 1.1-4a and 2.4b–3.24 come from different sources, because of the contrasting style and language of these chapters and the fact that they use different names for God. In 1.1–2.4a the Hebrew term for God is *ᵉlōhîm* while in 2.4b–3.25 it is *yhwh* *ᵉlōhîm*. These are represented respectively in English translations as 'God' and 'Lord God'. However, some interpreters also find within 2.4b–3.25 itself an earlier story in which there was no mention of the tree of the knowledge of good and evil. According to this view, ch. 2 was an account of the creation of humankind and animals, now contained in 2.4b-8, 15bβ ('to till the ground and keep it') and 18-24. 2.10-14 may have been part of this account or may have been added later. But in order to link ch. 2 and 3 it was necessary for an editor to add to ch. 2 the following verses: 9, 15a, and 15bα (up to 'Garden of Eden'), 16-17 and 25.

In ch. 3, vv. 22-24 create a problem in that Adam and Eve are driven from the garden not because they disobeyed the command to eat from the tree of the knowledge of good and evil (compare 2.16-17 where only the eating of the fruit of the tree of the knowledge of good and evil is forbidden) but in order to prevent them from eating the fruit of the tree of life (3.22). There is the further problem that in 3.3 it is the tree in the midst of the garden that is prohibited, and in 2.9 that tree is the tree of life. What the humans eat is the fruit of the tree of the knowledge of good and evil. This leads to the further suggestion that, in its original form, Genesis 3 was not set in a special garden from which the offenders were then expelled. The expulsion theme, and with it the existence of the tree of life, was a literary device needed to link the original form of ch. 2 to 3.1-21. Thus the following stages of the growth of 2.4b–3.24 have been suggested:

1. There first existed two separate stories:
   (a) 2.4b–8, (10–14), 15bβ, 18–24
   (b) 3.1–21
2. The stories were linked by adding to ch. 2 the verses 15a, 15bα-17 and 25. These provided a context for 3.3 ('you shall not eat of the fruit of the tree which is in the midst of the garden') and for 3.7 ('they knew that they were naked').
3. The theme of the expulsion from Eden was introduced by the addition of 2.9 and 3.22-24, which mention the tree of life.

It is not maintained here that there were necessarily three separate stages, nor is it being denied that these suggestions are simply theories, and that is it possible to account for the paradoxes of the narrative on the hypothesis of a single author narrating a story without using pre-existing traditions. The chief value of the exercise is in alerting readers to elements in the text. For readers who are convinced by the analysis, it has the value of helping them to compare the suggested 'original' stories with other ancient traditions.

8. Genesis 3 and Ezekiel 28.11-19

The closest parallel to Genesis 3 in ancient literature comes from Ezek. 28.11-19. Although this passage is an oracle against the king and city of Tyre, it has the following similarities with Genesis 3:

1. The chief actor is placed in the Garden of Eden (v. 13).
2. He was originally perfect but later found to have iniquity (v. 15).
3. He was driven from the divine mountain by a guardian cherub.

There are also differences, in that Genesis 3 does not mention a holy mountain, nor precious stones. The reason for the downfall of Tyre is pride linked to the desire for riches. There is no mention in Ezek. 28.11-19 of a serpent, disobedience in eating from a tree, or the cursing of the ground.

On closer inspection, the Ezekiel passage is closest in content to Gen. 3.22-24, which describes expulsion from Eden and the activity of the guardian cherub. There are no exact parallels with 3.1-21, and there is no mention of the garden of *Eden* in 3.1-21, but merely of a garden. This is interesting in the light of §7 above, where the view was outlined that 3.22-24 is a literary device to link the original stories of Genesis 2 and 3 and to remove Adam and Eve from the Garden of Eden. It is difficult to escape the conclusion that, in the formation of Gen. 3.1-24, a story similar to that in Ezek. 28.11-19 was used, even if it was only to provide a narrative unity for stories different from that in the Ezekiel passage.

9. Cain and Abel

Genesis 4.1-16 has parallels with 3.1-21, and can be regarded as either from the same source as 3.1-21 (J) or as deliberately composed in order to refer back to 3.1-21. The most striking similarities are:

1. the divine questions to the wrongdoers (3.9 and 4.9)
2. the curses (3.17 and 4.11).

From the thematic viewpoint, the story in 4.1-16 expands the wrongdoing of the human race. In Genesis 3 the man and woman quarrel over their responsibility for their disobedience to God (3.11-12). In 4.1-8, the sons of the man and woman quarrel, and one kills the other.

The narrative contains certain difficulties. We are not told why God preferred Abel's offerings of livestock to Cain's offerings of the produce of the land. Was Cain trying to ignore the curse upon the land of Gen. 3.17? Another difficulty is that, according to 9.6, the penalty for murder is death, but Cain is spared that. It could be argued, from the order of events in the narrative of Genesis 1–11, that Cain is not subject to a law not yet promulgated. However, in v. 14 Cain says that he will be killed by anyone who finds him wandering on the earth. This can hardly be in revenge for the murder of his brother, since that duty would fall within the family of Abel, and not simply anyone whom Cain chanced to meet. This last theme raises, of course, two questions: from where would these people come who might slay Cain, given that only three humans exist (Adam, Eve and Cain if we read the narrative literally); and who will avenge Cain sevenfold if he is slain?

If these problems were recognized by Israelite readers or hearers of this material, they were probably not a cause for anxiety. Cain, like Adam and Eve, is a type, and he represents human beings who violate the closest bonds of kinship. The narrative expresses God's condemnation of such action, while at the same time containing hints of the dangers of living the itinerant life of metal workers, who are descended from Cain (vv. 17-22).

The most important passage in the story is that which describes how the shedding of innocent blood affects the fertility of the land (vv. 10-12). The created order is not a machine that functions regardless of the behaviour of human beings. As pointed out above (§5) there is a link between human morality and obedience to God, and the fertility of the land. Even crimes not noticed or detected by human beings are an affront to God, bringing punishment to the offenders and loss of strength to the earth. The passage expresses the conviction of Old Testament faith that to believe in creation is to believe in an order in which human relationships play their part. The action of Cain is, in effect, an undoing of creation. However, Genesis 4 ends with an important reference to God's graciousness at work in the midst of human evil. The birth of Seth (v. 25) sets up the line from which Noah will come, and people begin to call on the name of Yhwh.

10. *Long-Lived Patriarchs*

Between the Cain and Abel narrative and that of the Flood there is a list of ancestors, whose function is to show how the world became populated. In Gen. 5.1-28, 30-32 we have what is ascribed by source criticism to the P source; and it is interesting that the list of ancestors has similarities with what is regarded as the J passage of 4.17-21. These can be shown as follows:

4.17-21	5.1-28, 30-32
[Adam]	Adam
	Seth
	Enosh
Cain	Kenan
Mehujael	Mahalalel
Irad	Jared
Enoch	Enoch
Methushael	Methuselah
Lamech	Lamech
Noah (5.29)	Noah

The order of the generations in 4.17-21 is different from that in 5.1-28, being Cain–Enoch–Irad–Mehujael–Methushael–Lamech, but the similarities are sufficiently strong to suggest (if one accepts source division) that J and P had access to similar traditions about the descendants of Adam to the time of Noah.

Genesis 5.29 is assigned by source criticism to J because of its reference back to the cursing of the ground and the toil of labour (3.17; 4.12). The English translations are not always helpful for this verse, and the Hebrew verb rendered (in RSV) as 'bring...relief' strictly means 'comfort'.

If source division is correct, then 5.1 in the P source resumes from 2.4a, and P has no 'fall' story until it reaches 6.11. Striking are the great ages attained by the descendants of Adam, with Methuselah reaching the greatest age of all, 969 years. In this, Genesis 5 can be compared with the Sumerian king lists (*ANET*, pp. 265-66) according to which the kings who reigned before the Flood had much longer reigns than those who came after the Flood. Before the Flood, the first two kings reigned for 64,800 years, whereas after it twenty-three kings achieved only just over 24,510 years. The Genesis figures are modest by comparison, but they are sufficiently out of line with normal human expectations to make the point that the people who lived before the Flood lived in an age which is no longer accessible.

The case of Enoch, who did not die but was 'taken' by God because of his close relationship with God (5.24) is an expression in the Old Testament of the view that fellowship with God cannot be broken by death. However, this is very much a minority theme in the Old Testament.

11. *Gods, Women and Giants*

Genesis 6.1-4 is a strange and fascinating passage. In one sense, it adds nothing to the overall narrative since, if there are sources, 6.5 (J) refers back to 4.24 as the reason for the Flood while P gives its reason for the Flood at 6.11. On a 'final form' reading the passage connects with the very long lives of the ancestors, and reduces the life-span of humans to 120 years as a punishment either for the inter-marriage of the 'sons of God' and the daughters of man or for the wickedness described in ch. 4. However, as is clear from 11.10ff., the descendants of Noah lived to be well over 120 years (Shem lived for 600 years according to 11.10-11) although their longevity gradually declined as the generations descended towards the time of Abraham. A good case can be made for seeing 6.1-4 as a tradition that was added quite late to the composition as a whole, not only on account of its awkwardness in its context and its contradiction of other material, but on linguistic grounds (the Hebrew phrase rendered 'for' — *bᵉšaggam* — looks like later Hebrew). Scholars disagree as to whether the 'sons of God' are divine beings who marry human women, or are mighty rulers who arbitrarily take women for their harem (cf. the end of 6.2). On the face of it, the explanation that 'sons of God' means mighty rulers is less obvious than taking 'sons of God' at face value to mean divine beings. But in that case, why should God punish humankind in v. 3 for acts committed by divine beings?

Against the background of ancient literature it can be noted that the increase in human population is the prelude to the Flood in the *Atra-Ḥasis* story (Lambert and Millard, *Atra-Ḥasis*, p. 73). We may also notice that in the context of the idea of creation as order, 6.1-4 implies a confusion of boundaries, with divine beings and possibly giants inter-marrying with human beings.

If Gen. 6.1-4 is puzzling in its present context, it became the basis of much speculation in later interpretation. From it developed the idea of the fall of angels who lusted after the daughters of men, and thus the passage provided a basis for the dualistic understanding of the world that we find in inter-testamental Judaism and in Christianity.

12. *One Flood Story or Two?*

The source division of Genesis 1–11 into J and P is fairly straight-forward in chs. 1–5. But from 6.5 to 9.28, the source theory entails that two independent stories of the Flood have been woven together to form a single narrative. It is also supposed that it is possible to recon-struct these sources. This section will outline the reasons for the divi-sion into two sources, and will point to some difficulties which it involves.

The strongest argument for the existence of two sources is the pres-ence of repetitions ('doublets'), and of distinctive verbs and divine names.

1. 6.5-8 is parallel to 6.11-13 in subject matter. In the case of the former, the divine name is Yhwh (LORD) while in the latter it is *ᵉlōhîm* (God). Also, the verb 'blot out' is used in v. 7 (Heb. *māḥâ*) whereas 'destroy' (Heb. *šḥt*) is used in v. 13.
2. 7.1-5 is parallel to 6.19-22, and the passages have the divine names Yhwh (LORD) and *ᵉlōhîm* (God) respectively. In 7.1-5 Noah is instructed to take into the ark seven pairs of clean and one pair of unclean animals, but in 6.19-22 he is to take pairs of everything.
3. 7.7-10 is parallel to 7.13-15. Both passages relate an entry into the ark.

4. 7.22-23 is parallel to 7.18-21. Genesis 7.21 says that all creatures remaining on earth died, a sentiment immediately repeated by 7.22. Genesis 7.23 reads, 'He blotted out every living thing', but there is no close antecedent for the 'he', which suggests that this passage has been taken from a source in which there was an antecedent.

On the basis of these, and other, considerations, it can be suggested that the following passages belonged to the separate sources:

J	P
6.5-8	
	6.9-21
7.1-5	
	7.6
7.7-10 (part)	
	7.11, 13-15, 18-21
7.22-23	
	7.24–8.5
8.6-12	
	8.13a, 14-19
8.20-22	
	9.1-17

Not all verses have been assigned to sources, as there are some uncertainties.

If we examine the proposed sources, we see that P is a more complete story than J. In J there is no command to build an ark, nor any account of Noah's leaving the ark after the Flood. On the other hand, the J passages link well together, especially 8.20-22 which looks back to 6.5-8. Both passages mention the evil imagination of the human heart, while the reference to not cursing the ground again (8.21) is reminiscent of 5.29, 4.11 and 3.17 (all of which are verses ascribed to J), although 8.21 uses a different Hebrew verb from that in the other passages.

If the narrative was compiled from two sources there are two views as to how this was done. According to one view, the P writer incorporated the J material into his narrative. According to the other view, a later redactor combined P and J, using P as the main narrative.

Against the source division theory, it can be asked why P, or a redactor, should have left the parallel passages, detailed above, side by side, while presumably eliminating the J versions of the manufacture of the ark and Noah's exit from it after the Flood. A partial answer can be given in that 6.5-8 and 8.20-22 provide an artistic beginning and end to the story, and the retention of 6.5-8 then produces a parallel with 6.11-13. On the other hand, it is difficult to explain why P or the redactor should have retained the parallel and contradictory accounts of the entry into the ark. There is a further problem in that one of the J passages (7.7-10) has the 'wrong' divine name and does not discriminate between clean and unclean animals as it is supposed that J does. If 7.7-10 has been edited by a redactor in order to make it conform to the P account, as is often supposed, then why did this editor do such a minimal job of trying to remove the inconsistencies?

It is often urged against the source division that we have no evidence from the ancient world that authors combined separate narratives together. This, however, has recently been contested by Tigay (Tigay, 'Evolution'). The evidence of Tigay does not prove the source division theory in the case of the Flood, but removes the argument that the use of sources is supported by no examples from the ancient world. That the case for sources in Gen. 6.5–9.17 is not absolutely conclusive is indicated by the continuing discussion of the matter (see the literature in the Bibliography).

13. *Noah's Drunkenness and Canaan's Curse*

Genesis 9.20-27 contains an obvious difficulty. Why is it that Noah curses not Ham, whose wrongdoing is described in v. 22, but Ham's son Canaan (v. 25)? The probable answer is that in 9.20-27 two originally separate traditions have been combined together. The first, in vv. 20-23, is similar to the tradition in 4.22. In the latter passage, Tubal-Cain is described as the (original) forger of bronze and iron implements. Here Noah is named as the first tiller of the soil, who planted a vineyard. In other stories set in beginning time, there is mention of the founders of institutions known to the readers. It is interesting that in the case of Noah, his extension of the benefits of civilization is not an unqualified success. It leads to drunkenness, and to his being naked in his tent. The offence of Ham was not so much that he saw his father naked, but that, unlike his brothers, he did nothing to remedy his father's disgrace. The whole passage indicates that the family from which the whole human race is to descend is capable of actions that are not worthy of humanity at its best.

The poem of 9.25-27 is similar to the curses that have preceded it in Genesis, as well as being similar to the blessings and curses given by the patriarch Isaac (27.23-29, 39-40) and Jacob (49.3-27). These pronouncements reflect political circumstances known to the readers, and invest these circumstances with a sanctity derived from the reputation of the speaker of the blessings and curses. That 9.25-27 is an ancient poem is probably indicated by its obscurities. Verse 25 is comparatively straightforward. The cursing of Canaan in terms of condemning him to slavery no doubt reflects the situation in the reigns of David and Solomon when the Canaanites were subordinate to the Israelites. Verse 26 is less easy. On the face of it, it means 'Blessed be the LORD, the God of Shem' (see RSV footnote) but it makes no sense in a blessing of sons, hence the RSV's text 'Blessed by the LORD my God be Shem' which involves a slight revocalization of the Hebrew. Even this is inane, and one wonders whether the text has been lost or hopelessly corrupted.

The blessing of Japheth seems to retain the original text, since there is a pun on the name Japheth and on the verbal form translated 'enlarge' (*yepet* and *yapt*). It is difficult, however, to know what it means when the text says 'let him dwell in the tents of Shem'. On the face of it, this implies a displacement of Shem by Japheth, but this is difficult because Shem is the ancestor of the Hebrews and Japheth is the ancestor of sea-going peoples and islanders. The commonly accepted explanation that the verse refers to the employment of foreigners at the court of David or Solomon is not obvious. We have to say that we do not know what this verse meant either 'originally' or to readers in context. What is clear is that, generally speaking, 9.20-27 taken together functioned to show that the human race after the flood was not perfect, and that the subjugation of the Canaanites by the Israelites was a punishment ordained by the principal human survivor of the flood.

14. *The Genealogies (Genesis 10)*

According to source division, Genesis 10 is composed of two types of narrative. The P narrative is characterized by a formulaic mode of expression (10.1a, 2-7, 20-23, 31-32): 'The sons of n: a, b, c... The sons of a: d, e, f etc.', concluding with 'these are the sons of n with their families, language(s), lands'. The J material (10.1b, 8-19, 21, 24-30) is much more of a narrative with various anecdotes about individuals and nations. Even if readers do not accept the source theory, they must notice that we have two types of material juxtaposed: the formulaic and the narratival/anecdotal.

These two types of material perform two functions. The formulaic material indicates how the descendants of Noah spread all over the earth, in fulfilment of the command of 9.1 to 'be fruitful and multiply, and fill the earth'. The narrative/anecdotal material informs Israelite readers about the origins of peoples familiar to them either from their reading of Genesis as a whole, or from their knowledge of the ancient world. Thus, among the places and peoples mentioned in 10.10-14, the names Babel (Babylon), Nineveh, Egypt and Philistines occur, while in 10.15–19 the significant names include Canaan, Sidon, the Jebusites, Gerar, Gaza, Sodom, Gomorrah, Admah and Zeboim. Well-known names in 10.25–29 are Sheba, Ophir and Havilah.

The narratival/anecdotal material is reminiscent of 4.17-22, where Jabal is the father of those who dwell in tents and have cattle, and Tubal-Cain is the (original) forger of metal instruments (4.20, 22). In 10.8, Nimrod is the first on earth to be a mighty man—a statement that appears to contradict 6.4, which mentions mighty men before the flood.

A possible key verse for the understanding of the chapter is v. 9, where Nimrod is described as a 'mighty hunter before the LORD'. Nimrod is apparently unknown elsewhere in ancient literature, although the present passage generated many traditions about him in later Jewish and Islamic writings. If, as seems most likely, the verse is taken to be a compliment to Nimrod, then we have a non-Israelite described both as a founder of civilization in Babylon and Assyria, and as standing in some sort of relationship to God. From this we could conclude that the chapter is saying that not only did the nations consist of men and women created by the God worshipped by Israel, but that among these nations were individuals who enjoyed the favour of the God worshipped by Israel. We must not overlook the fact that the Old Testament has a strong sense that foreign nations can be used by God (cf. Isa. 10.5; 45.1), and that God's purpose in calling Abraham is to bring blessing to all nations (Gen. 12.3).

The material that makes up Genesis 10 is a necessary narrative device to populate the world following the reduction of the human race to one family by means of the flood. However, in the process of describing the spread of the human race, the chapter makes the world more 'friendly' for Israelite readers by mentioning cities, countries and peoples familiar to them, and by implying that the knowledge of the God worshipped by Israel was not entirely missing among these peoples.

15. *The Tower of Babel*

Read in sequence, Genesis 10 and 11.1-9 appear to be contradictory. 11.1 says that the whole earth had one language, whereas 10.5, 20 and 31 imply that each nation had its own distinct language. Even if we invoke source criticism, and say that 11.1-9 comes from J while 10.5, 20 and 31 are 'P' passages, the difficulties are not entirely removed.

10.10 states that Nimrod ruled over Babylon (Babel) while 11.9 can be read to indicate that the destruction of the tower led to the founding of Babel.

It is quite possible that the writer or editor of Genesis 1–11 saw 11.1-9 as a flashback to a time early in the spread of the nations over the earth, and that the scattering described in 11.9 was then part of the process of the spread of the nations.

Within the overall structure of Genesis 1–12, ch. 11 sets up a contrast between the scattering of the people because of their desire to assert themselves apart from God, and the obedience of Abram in 12.1-3, which will be the basis for a blessing of the nations.

The story has some similarities with Genesis 3, not only in content but in language. In Genesis 3 the man and woman eat a fruit which will help them to become 'like God'. Here, the desire of the human beings seems to be to reach heaven, God's dwelling place (11.4). The theme of the violating of boundaries can be observed here, and as in Genesis 3 God addresses himself in the first person plural, and determines to prevent further action by the human beings.

> Behold, they are one people…and nothing that they propose to do will
>   be impossible for them (11.6).
> Come, let us go down, and there confuse their language (11.7).

In Genesis 3 God expels the human beings from the garden; here he scatters the human race from the plain in the land of Shinar.

A closer reading of the story indicates one or two unevennesses. For example, in v. 7 God determines to confuse the people's languages, but. in v. 8 he scatters them abroad. No doubt the act of scattering peoples will result in the development of different languages, but one wonders whether the biblical writer or his presumed readers knew about how languages develop. There is also the fact that twice God 'comes down' (vv. 5, 7) although on the second occasion this is expressed as a resolve to do so. Because of these unevennesses, it has been suggested that two stories have been woven together here, one dealing with the origin of languages (11.1-2, 6-7), the other concerning an attempt to build a city, which God frustrated (11.3-5, 8). The explanation for the name of Babel would, on this view, have been added after the two stories were joined. Whether or not this is convincing, it draws attention to elements in the text.

An interesting question is whether there is any basis in fact to the story. It has good local colouring, in that building in Babylon was done in bricks baked from clay, whereas in Judah and Israel there was an abundance of stone for building. One candidate for an unfinished building that might have inspired the story is the Etemenanki Temple in Babylon, begun in the reign of Nebuchadnezzar I (1123–1101 BCE) and apparently not completed for many centuries (von Soden, 'Etemenanki', pp. 134-47).

16. The Date of Genesis 1–11

This question has been left until last partly because it is difficult to settle, and partly because it can distract readers from looking at the text closely. The simple answer to the question of date is that Genesis 1–11 is part of the larger work containing Genesis to 2 Kings (minus Ruth, which appears elsewhere in the Hebrew order of books of the Bible). This complete work did not reach its final form until during or after the Babylonian exile in the sixth century BCE. However, the date of the final editing does not determine the date of the individual items to be found in Genesis 1–11.

If one accepts the source theory, there are two possibilities. Most source critics would agree that P^g was composed during the exilic or post-exilic periods; and if the writer of P^g used older materials, it is impossible to determine their age. On the date of J there is a majority view that places it in the period of the Israelite monarchy, possibly as early as the reign of Solomon. A growing minority view, however, is that J was composed during the exilic or post-exilic periods.

The arguments about the dating of J are circumstantial and not conclusive. As far as Genesis 1–11 is concerned, we saw in Chapter 2 that Wittenberg assumes a Solomonic date for J because he believes that he can detect in Genesis 3 and 11 a critique of royal building activities and the attempt of the king to assume wisdom that is appropriate only to God.

However, it is possible to argue in quite a different way. For example, if it is maintained that part of Genesis 3 is dependent upon Ezek. 28.11-19, then Genesis 3 must be dated to the exile at the earliest, since the Ezekiel passage is to be placed in the first half of the sixth century. Again, the story of the Tower of Babel can be said to fit best into the period when the Israelites were in exile in Babylon. In that case, the story would be a condemnation of the greatness of Babylon, and a declaration of its nothingness compared with the might of the God of Israel.

Attempts to date elements of Genesis 1–11 are at best plausible rather than probable, and involve circular arguments. This is not to say that it is wrong to try to date parts of Genesis 1–11, but rather that we should not allow such attempts to make us read the text superficially, as though we knew all that it has to say once we have assigned a date and setting. Even if we could be certain about dates and settings, we should still have to consider the following questions: how do the narratives function within the whole, and what interest do we, the readers, bring with us to the interpretation of Genesis 1–11?

FURTHER READING

Anderson, B.W., 'Creation and Ecology', in *idem* (ed.), *Creation in the Old Testament* (London: SPCK, 1981), pp. 152-78.

—'From Analysis to Synthesis: The Interpretation of Genesis 1–11', *JBL* 97 (1978), pp. 23-39.

Anderson, B.W. (ed.), *Creation in the Old Testament* (London: SPCK, 1984).

Beauchamp, P., 'Création et fondation de la loi en Gn 1,1–2,4', in F. Blanquart (ed.), *La Création dans l'orient ancien* (Paris: Les Éditions du Cerf, 1987), pp. 139-82.

Bentzen, A., *King and Messiah* (Oxford: Basil Blackwell, 1970).

Bird, P.A., ' "Male and Female He Created Them": Gen. 1.27b in the Context of the Priestly Account of Creation', *HTR* 74 (1981), pp. 129-59.

Boesak, A., *Black and Reformed: Apartheid, Liberation and the Calvinist Tradition* (Johannesburg: Skotaville, 1989), pp. 148-57.

Brett, M.G., 'Motives and Intentions in Genesis 1', *JTS* (1990).

Brueggemann, W., *Genesis* (Interpretation; Atlanta: John Knox Press, 1982).

Bryan, D.T., 'A Reevaluation of Gen. 4 and 5 in Light of Recent Studies in Genealogical Fluidity', *ZAW* (1987), pp. 180-88.

Burns, D.E., 'Dream Form in Genesis 2.4b–3.24: Asleep in the Garden', *JSOT* 37 (1987), pp. 3–14.

Calvin, John, *Genesis* (trans. John King; repr., Edinburgh: Banner of Truth, 1965 [1874]).

Carroll, M.P., 'Genesis Restructured', in B. Lang (ed.), *Anthropological Approaches to the Old Testament* (London: SPCK, 1977), pp. 127-35.

Childs, B.S., *Introduction to the Old Testament as Scripture* (London: SCM Press, 1979).

Clines, D.J.A., *The Theme of the Pentateuch* (JSOTSup, 10; Sheffield: JSOT Press, 1978).

Coats, G.W., *Genesis with an Introduction to Narrative Literature* (FOTL, 1; Grand Rapids: Eerdmans, 1983).

Collins, A.Y. (ed.), *Feminist Perspectives on Biblical Scholarship* (SBL Centennial Publications, 10; Chico: Scholars Press, 1985).

Crüsemann, F., 'Autonomie und Sünde. Gen 4,7 und die "jahwistische" Urgeschichte', in W. Schottroff and W. Stegemann (eds.), *Traditionen der Befreiung. I. Methodische Zugänge* (Munich: Chr. Kaiser Verlag, 1980), pp. 60-77.

Cunchillos, J.-L., 'Peut-on parler de mythes de création à Ugarit?', in Blanquart (ed.), *La Création dans l'orient ancien*, pp. 79-96.

Davies, P.R., 'The Sons of Cain', in J.D. Martin and P.R. Davies (eds.), *A Word in Season: Essays in Honour of William McKane* (JSOTSup, 42; Sheffield: JSOT Press), pp. 35-56.

Day, J., 'Creation Narratives', in R.J. Coggins and J.L. Houlden (eds.), *A Dictionary of Biblical Interpretation* (London: SCM Press, 1990), pp. 147-50.

Delano, J.H., 'The Exegesis of "Enuma Elish" and Genesis 1 — 1875 to 1975: A Study in Interpretation' (PhD dissertation, Marquette University; Ann Arbor: University Microfilms, 1969).

Delitzsch, Friedrich, *Babel and Bible* (London: Williams and Norgate, 1903).

Dockx, S., *Le Récit du paradis. Gen. 2–3* (Paris: Duculot, 1981).

Driver, S.R., *The Book of Genesis* (London: Methuen, 1904).

Fiorenza, E.S., 'Remembering the Past in Creating the Future: Historical-Critical Scholarship and Feminist Interpretation', in Collins (ed.), *Feminist Perspectives*, pp. 43-63.

Gibson, J.C.L., *Genesis* (The Daily Study Bible; Edinburgh: St Andrews Press, 1981), I.

Gros Louis, K.R.R., 'The Garden of Eden', in *idem* (ed.), *Literary Interpretation of Biblical Narratives* (Nashville: Abingdon, 1974), I, pp. 41-58.

Hauser, A.J., 'Genesis 2–3: The Theme of Intimacy and Alienation', in D.J.A. Clines *et al.* (eds.), *Art and Meaning: Rhetoric in Biblical Literature* (JSOTSup, 19; Sheffield: JSOT Press, 1982), pp. 20-36.

Jacobsen, T., 'The Eridu Genesis', *JBL* 100 (1981), pp. 513-29.

Jobling, D., 'Myth and its Limits in Gen. 2.4b–3.24', in *idem*, *The Sense of Biblical Narrative*. II. *Structural Analyses in the Hebrew Bible* (JSOTSup, 39; Sheffield: JSOT Press, 1986).

—'The Myth Semantics of Genesis 2.4b–3.24', *Semeia* 18 (1980), pp. 41-49.

Joines, K.R., 'The Serpent in Gen. 3', *ZAW* 87 (1975), pp. 1-11.

Jónsson, G.A., *The Image of God: Genesis 1.26-28 in a Century of Old Testament Research* (ConBOT, 26; Stockholm: Almqvist & Wiksell, 1988).

Laffey, A.L., *An Introduction to the Old Testament: A Feminist Perspective* (Philadelphia: Fortress Press, 1988).

Lambert, W.G., and A.R. Millard, *Atra-Hasis. The Babylonian Story of the Flood* (Oxford: Clarendon Press, 1969).

Larsson, G., 'The Documentary Hypothesis and the Chronological Structure of the Old Testament', ZAW 97 (1985), pp. 316-33.

Link, C., 'Der Mensch als Schöpfer und als Geschöpf', in J. Moltmann (ed.), *Versöhnung mit der Natur?* (Munich: Chr. Kaiser Verlag, 1986), pp. 15-47.

Lohfink, N., *Unsere grossen Wörter. Das Alte Testament zu Themen dieser Jahre* (Freiburg im Breisgau: Herder, 1977; English translation by R. Walls, *Great Themes from the Old Testament* [Edinburgh: T. & T. Clark, 1982]).

—'Die Schichten des Pentateuch und der Krieg', in *idem* (ed.), *Gewalt und Gewaltlosigkeit im Alten Testament* (Quaestiones Disputatae, 96; Freiburg im Breisgau: Herder, 1983).

Meyers, C., *Discovering Eve: Ancient Israelite Women in Context* (New York: Oxford University Press, 1988).

Moberly, R.W.L., 'Did the Serpent Get it Right?', *JTS* NS 39 (1988), pp. 1-27.

Mosala, I.J., *Biblical Hermeneutics and Black Theology in South Africa* (Grand Rapids: Eerdmans, 1989).

Müller, H.-P., 'Das Motif für die Sintflut. Die hermeneutische Funktion des Mythos und seiner Analyse', *ZAW* 97 (1985), pp. 295-316.

—'Mythische Elemente in der jahwistischen Schöpfungserzählung', *ZTK* 69 (1972), pp. 259-89.

—'Mythos–Anpassung–Wahrheit. Vom Recht mythischer Rede und deren Aufhebung', *ZTK* 80 (1983), pp. 1-25.

Oded, B., 'The Table of Nations (Genesis 10) — A Socio-Cultural Approach', *ZAW* 98 (1986), pp. 14-31.

Oden, R.A., Jr, 'Divine Aspirations in Atrahasis and in Genesis 1-11', *ZAW* 93 (1981), pp. 197-216.

Patte, D. (ed.), *Genesis 2 and 3: Kaleidoscopic Structural Readings* (Semeia, 18; Atlanta: Scholars Press, 1980).

Pettinato, G., *Das altorientalische Menschenbild und die sumerischen und akkadischen Schöpfungsmythen* (Abhandlungen der Heidelberger Akademie der Wissenschaften; Phil.-Hist. Klasse 1; Heidelberg: Heidelberger Akademie der Wissenschaften, 1971).

Rad, G. von, 'The Theological Problem of the Old Testament Doctrine of Creation', in Anderson (ed.), *Creation in the Old Testament*, pp. 53-64.

Rogerson, J.W., *Anthropology and the Old Testament* (Oxford: Basil Blackwell, 1978 [repr., Sheffield: JSOT Press, 1984]).

—'Anthropology and the Old Testament', in R.E. Clements (ed.), *The World of Ancient Israel: Sociological, Anthropological and Political Perspectives* (Cambridge: Cambridge University Press, 1989), pp. 17-37.

—'Genesis 1-11', *Currents in Research: Biblical Studies* 5 (1997), pp. 67-90.

—'Herders Bückeburger "Bekehrung"', in *Bückeburger Gespräche über Johann Gottfried Herder 1979* (Rinteln: C. Bösendahl, 1980), pp. 17-30.

—'Myth', in R.J. Coggins and J.L. Houlden (eds.), *A Dictionary of Biblical Interpretation* (London: SCM Press, 1990), pp. 479-82.

—*Myth in Old Testament Interpretation* (BZAW, 134; Berlin: W. de Gruyter, 1974).

—*Old Testament Criticism in the Nineteenth Century: England and Germany* (London: SPCK, 1984).

—'The Old Testament', in J. Rogerson, C. Rowland and B. Lindars, *The Study and Use of the Bible* (Basingstoke: Marshall Pickering, 1988), pp. 1-150.

Rogerson, J.W., and P.R. Davies, *The Old Testament World* (Cambridge: Cambridge University Press; Englewood Cliffs, NJ: Prentice–Hall, 1989).

Scharbert, J., *Genesis 1-11* (Die neue Echter Bibel; Würzburg: Echter, 1983).

Schelkle, K.H., *Der Geist and die Braut. Die Frau in der Bibel* (Düsseldorf: Patmos, 1977). (Chapter 1: 'Schöpfung und Schuld').

Schmid, H.H., 'Creation, Righteousness, and Salvation: "Creation Theology" as the Broad Horizon of Biblical Theology', in Anderson (ed.), *Creation in the Old Testament*, pp. 102-17.

Schmidt, W.H., *Die Schöpfungsgeschichte der Priesterschrift. Zur Überlieferungsgeschichte von Genesis 1,1-2,4a und 2,4b-3,24* (WMANT, 17; Neukirchen-Vluyn: Neukirchener Verlag, 2nd edn, 1967).

Schottroff, L., 'Die Schöpfungsgeschichte Gen 1,1-2,4a', in L. Schottroff and W. Schottroff, *Die Macht der Auferstehung, sozialgeschichtliche Bibelauslegungen* (Munich: Chr. Kaiser Verlag, 1988).

Schottroff, W., 'Arbeit und sozialer Konflikt im nachexilischen Juda', in L. Schottroff and W. Schottroff (eds.), *Mitarbeiter der Schöpfung. Bibel and Arbeitsmelt* (Munich: Chr. Kaiser Verlag, 1983), pp. 104-48.

Seuz, M.-J., 'La Création du monde et de l'homme dans la littérature suméro-akkadienne', in Blanquart (ed.), *La Création dans l'orient ancien*, pp. 41-78.

Shea, W.H., 'A Comparison of Narrative Elements in Ancient Mesopotamian Creation-Flood Stories with Genesis 1-9', *Origins* 11 (1984), pp. 9-29.

Soden, W. von, 'Etemenanki vor Asarhaddon nach der Erzählung vom Turmbau zu Babel und dem Erra-Mythos', in H.-P. Müller (ed.), *Bibel und Alter Orient. Altorientalische Beiträge zum Alten Testament* (BZAW, 162; Berlin: W. de Gruyter, 1985), pp. 134-47.

Steck, O.H., *Die Paradieserzählung. Eine Auslegung von Genesis 2,4b–3,24* (Biblische Studien, 60; Neukirchen–Vluyn: Neukirchener Verlag, 1970).

—*Der Schöpfungsbericht der Priesterschrift* (FRLANT, 115; Göttingen: Vandenhoeck & Ruprecht, 2nd edn, 1981 [1975]).

Tigay, J.H., 'The Evolution of the Pentateuchal Narratives in the Light of the Evolution of the *Gilgamesh Epic*', in *idem* (ed.), *Empirical Models for Biblical Criticism* (Philadelphia: University of Pennsylvania Press, 1985), pp. 21-52.

Tischler, N.M., *Legacy of Eve: Women of the Bible* (Atlanta: John Knox, 1977) (chapter 1: 'Eve—The Complete Woman').

Trible, P., *God and the Rhetoric of Sexuality* (Overtures to Biblical Theology, 2; Philadelphia: Fortress Press, 1978).

Van Dyck, P.J., 'The Function of So-Called Etiological Elements in Narratives', *ZAW* 102 (1990), pp. 19–33.

Van Seters, J., 'The Primeval Histories of Greece and Israel Compared', *ZAW* 100 (1988), pp. 1-22.

Vawter, B., *On Genesis: A New Reading* (London: Geoffrey Chapman; New York: Doubleday, 1977).

Volkmar, F., '"Solange die Erde steht"—Vom Sinn der jahwistischen Fluterzählung in Gen. 6–8', *ZAW* (1982), pp. 599-614.

Wenham, G.J., 'The Coherence of the Flood Narrative', *VT* 28 (1978), pp. 336-48.

Wenham, G.J., 'Genesis: An Authorship Study and Current Pentateuchal Criticism', *JSOT* 42 (1988), pp. 3-18.

—*Genesis 1–15* (WBC, 1; Waco: Word Books, 1987).

West, G., 'Reading "The Text" and Reading "Behind the Text": The "Cain and Abel" Story in a Context of Liberation', in D.J.A. Clines *et al.* (eds.), *The Bible in Three Dimensions: Essays in Celebration of Forty Years of Biblical Studies in the University of Sheffield* (JSOTSup, 87; Sheffield: JSOT Press, 1990), pp. 279-99.

Westermann, C., *Genesis 1–11: A Commentary* (trans. J.J. Scullion; London: SPCK, 1984).

Wittenberg, G.H., *King Solomon and the Theologians* (Pietermaritzburg: University of Natal Press, 1988).

Wolde, E.J. van, *A Semiotic Analysis of Genesis 2–3: A Semiotic Theory and Method of Analysis Applied to the Story of the Garden of Eden* (Studia Semitica Neerlandica, 25; Assen: Van Gorcum, 1989).

Wyatt, N., 'Interpreting the Creation and Fall Story in Genesis 2–3', *ZAW* 93 (1981), pp. 10-21.

Zenger, E., *Gottes Bogen in den Wolken. Untersuchungen zu Komposition und Theologie der priesterschriftlichen Urgeschichte* (Stuttgarter Bibelstudien, 112; Stuttgart: Katholisches Bibelwerk, 1983).

Part II
GENESIS 12–50
R. Walter L. Moberly

Chapter One

HOW SHOULD WE READ THE TEXT?

The stories of the patriarchs are among the most famous and memorable of all the stories in the Bible. Abraham is called by God to leave home and family, waits many years for a son and then is called to sacrifice that son to God; Jacob sees a ladder up to heaven at Bethel and wrestles with a mysterious adversary at the ford of the Jabbok; Joseph dreams prophetic dreams, rises to power in Egypt after being sold as a slave by his brothers, and rescues his family in time of famine. Although these stories are generally less well known now than they used to be, they are not only deeply embedded in the culture of Western civilization, but they also retain their ability powerfully to capture the imagination of the modern reader who encounters them.

Despite, or perhaps even because of, their great imaginative power, the best way to read these stories in the context of modern biblical scholarship has become problematic. Particularly at the present time, the whole question of method and approach in reading the Old Testament has become controversial, and nowhere are the problems more acute than with the stories of the patriarchs.

The General Context of Debate

On the one hand, the predominant approach to Genesis 12–50 in modern times has been that of the ancient historian. The primary concern has been to analyze the text in the way that ancient historians analyze any ancient narrative text. Thus questions of authorship, date and context of composition, possible underlying sources and traditions, genre and historical worth of content, editorial bias, and other similar matters have largely filled works of scholarship. Although recognition of the imaginative power of the stories has not been lacking, it has often been doubtful whether this recognition has made any genuine difference to the way the text has been studied; that is, the significant scholarly agenda has been that of the ancient historian, and the imaginative force of the stories has tended to function as a matter for comment in passing rather than as presenting an important agenda for study in its own right. Nonetheless, the gains from this historical agenda have been considerable, and there has emerged a much clearer understanding of the patriarchal stories as ancient texts in a way which greatly enhances their interest for most readers.

On the other hand, in recent years there has been a growing reaction to the predominance of the historian's agenda, precisely because it leaves important dimensions of the text, in particular its extraordinary imaginative power, largely or wholly untouched. In general terms, the move by some scholars has been to the agenda of literature rather than that of history. Literary approaches have been extremely diverse, but there has generally been a concern to try to analyze how and why it is that these stories make their memorable impact. Thus questions of storytelling technique (stance of narrator, plot, structure, characterization, recurrent and variant motifs, creation and resolution of suspense etc.) have come to the fore. Interest in the biblical writer, if present at all, now tends to be less to do with what may be learned about him as a historical figure (date, context, reason for writing etc.) than in what may be learnt about his skills as a literary artist.

One of the less helpful features of some modern debate is the suggestion, either explicit or implicit, that these two different approaches are somehow incompatible. One can work through the fine historical commentary on Genesis of, say, C. Westermann, and have little greater awareness or understanding of the imaginative power of the stories. Alternatively, in one of the outstanding works of literary study, M. Sternberg's *Poetics of Biblical Narrative*, there is a clear statement of principle that historical and literary approaches are not mutually exclusive. But in his practice Sternberg consistently opts for literary rather than historical explanations of puzzles in the text, even when there is a reasonable *prima facie* case for a historical explanation; the only historical insight that is consistently utilized is a knowledge of Hebrew as an ancient language. There is, however, no instrinsic reason why one should have to choose between historical and literary approaches, or why one should not opt for 'both–and', rather than 'either–or'. Nonetheless, the practical tendency of many scholars to opt for 'either–or' can make it difficult for the student to see how the varying approaches to the text may best be combined with each other.

Although discussions of approaches to the text are often couched in terms of the historical and the literary as the only two alternatives, it is important not to forget what might perhaps best be called 'committed' approaches, which relate the biblical text to the issues of life

today and read the text explicitly in the light of contemporary concerns. Of these, the one that has probably attracted most attention in
recent debate is feminism (which of course overlaps in varying ways
with historical and literary approaches; for a literary-feminist
approach, see, e.g., Phyllis Trible's reading of the story of Hagar in
her *Texts of Terror*). It is important not to forget, however, that the
classic Christian approach to the Old Testament is a 'committed'
approach. Indeed, it is most probably for religious and theological
reasons—because these stories are part of Scripture—that most people
still today want to study the stories in the first place. This is not to
deny that the stories may legitimately be studied from historical or
other perspectives without regard to their continuing religious value;
it is simply that in practice the religious reason for reading tends to be
predominant.

But what difference does a religious approach make? In the first
place, it is clear that a religious approach is a *motive* rather than a
method. It may well be that religious motives can be satisfied through
literary and historical methods. And this assumption seems to characterize most modern Old Testament studies and commentaries.

Secondly, however, it should be noted that for most of the last two
thousand years, until relatively recent times, it has been generally
supposed that a religious approach did bring with it a method of its
own (just as a committed feminist approach self-consciously develops
its own methodology). For example, the assumption that the text may
have a meaning other than solely that of its face value, and that
special methods are in order to dig out these further meanings, has
characterized the vast majority of pre-modern Old Testament studies,
and still survives among sophisticated modern commentators. Perhaps the best known forms of this approach are typology and allegory. It is unfortunate that, because both typology and allegory so
easily lend themselves to far-fetched interpretations of the text, and
have so often been used badly, they have fallen into general dis-
repute; for when used well they may in fact be valuable means of
applying the text to the life of the community of faith (for a sophisticated modern typology, see von Rad's treatment of Gen. 22 at the end
of Chapter 6).

Another way of posing the issue of the difference that a religious
approach may make is to ask whether the Bible should be interpreted
'like any other book'—as the issue was put by the distinguished Vic-
torian classicist, Benjamin Jowett, in his famous essay, 'On the Interpretation of Scripture', in the 1860 volume of *Essays and Reviews*.
Jowett was objecting to the enormous diversity of conflicting inter-

pretations that attach to Scripture in a way he felt to be uncharacter-istic of any other book, and he argued that biblical interpretation could be greatly improved if the Bible was read like any other book and the interpreter concentrated solely on recovering the original sense of Scripture, with its history of later interpretations cut away (i.e. Jowett's statement was programmatic for the historical approach to Scripture that has predominated ever since). The response to Jowett's proposal, at least from the point of view of Christian theo-logy, must be both yes and no. Yes, in the sense that the Bible was written in known ancient languages and according to the known (or generally able to be inferred) conventions of ancient literature. No, in the sense that the material has a certain unique content which has always been integrally related to the continuing life of communities of faith. This latter point affects the material in at least two ways. First, it means that the material itself has acquired something of an internal history through having new insights incorporated into it over a period of time prior to the fixation of the text in its canonical form; this makes the quest for its 'original' meaning peculiarly problematic. Secondly, it means that the material is read in a way unlike that in which any other book is read—it is both constantly read and expounded in public gatherings of Christians and Jews, and it is constantly re-read and pondered in private devotional reading. One assumption underlying this public and private use of the material as Scripture is that it is able to inform and mould the conscience and so shape the beliefs, values and practices of believers. However much other books may be valued, they are not read in this same kind of privileged way. It is important, therefore, that in any account of an Old Testament book, or portion of a book, such as Genesis 12–50, one should be aware of the issues raised by the material's function as Scripture for those who approach it from the perspective of its con-tinuing religious significance.

Part of the difficulty in deciding how best to approach the patri-archal narratives lies in the possible assumption that one should be able to resolve the issue simply by looking at the text and at the dif-ferent methods of interpretation available. For one indispensable ele-ment must in fact be the interests and concerns of the reader. That is to say, different readers quite legitimately have different questions and concerns in mind when they approach the biblical text (for an entertaining account of this from a Jewish perspective, see J. Magonet, *A Rabbi's Bible*). To the person who is interested in historical ques-tions, explanation of the imaginative power of the text may be of limited significance; and vice versa. In short, *how* we read the text will vary according to *why* we read the text. The search for *one* 'correct' reading is largely illusory, and one must accept a plurality of interpretations corresponding to the plurality of legitimate agendas with which the text may be approached. This does not mean that 'anything goes', for there will always be criteria to distinguish better readings from worse readings. The point is simply that the question of better and worse interpretations cannot be decided in isolation from a consideration of the assumptions and priorities held as a consensus view within the context(s) where the interpreter is working.

One of the things that may make biblical study difficult for many students is precisely the uncertainty as to which interpretative context they belong. A student from a Church background may have been taught in that context to read the text in one kind of way (e.g. devotionally and practically); when that student comes to university, he or she may be encouraged to read the text in a different kind of way (e.g. with a critical analysis unrelated to devotional and practical concerns). Particularly if, as is often the case, people in each of those contexts say, or at least imply, that their way is the only proper way to read the text, questions of identity may be acute for the student. Yet they may never be explicitly addressed if discussion is restricted to the biblical text and different interpretative methods, and little or no attention is given to the life situation of all concerned. Nonetheless, such wider concerns should never be an excuse for not paying careful attention to the specific features of the biblical text.

Finding a Starting-Point within the Text

How, then, might one in practice approach the patriarchal narratives? I suggest that one good way is via reflection on the traditional ascription of Genesis 12–50 (along with everything else in the Pentateuch) to Moses. The significance of this ascription lies not simply in the question of whether or not Moses himself wrote the material, and it is a pity that since modern scholarship has judged that Moses is extremely unlikely to have written Genesis 12–50 (and the rest of the Pentateuch) the ascription has received little further thought. For part of the significance of the ascription resides in the basic context it provides for understanding the text.

Although the historical questions about the origins of Israel's religion are both complex and disputed, there is a general consensus that so far as anything can be said about the origins of Israel's religion it is likely that it began with Moses. Essentially, therefore, scholars follow the lead given by the Pentateuch itself, where the foundations of

Israel's faith—God's self-revelation as Yhwh, the Exodus, the pass-over, Sinai and the giving of Torah, Israel's sacrificial worship—are all ascribed to God's dealings with Moses. Of course, scholars vary con-siderably in their assessments of the likely antiquity of all these ele-ments, and so vary correspondingly in the extent of divergence from the biblical narrative in their critical historical reconstruction. But the point that the biblical narrative is followed, at least in outline, is clear (and although some scholars recently have wanted to abandon the biblical outline altogether—see, e.g., N.P. Lemche, *Ancient Israel*—it is not clear that any alternative account poses fewer historical difficulties).

The corollary of recognizing that Israel's religion began with Moses is the recognition that the patriarchal material is intrinsically *non-Israelite*. Of course, it is not seen as alien to Israel's religion, but is seen as Israel's precursor, that is, pre-Israelite, with which Israel in some way stood in continuity. As we shall see, the patriarchal stories are full of divergences from normative Israelite religion, which implicitly witness to their intrinsically non-Israelite status. And here too, modern scholars, following the lead of Alt in his seminal essay, 'The God of the Fathers', have been inclined to follow the lead of the biblical text, at least in outline, and to recognize in the patriarchal material genuinely ancient material which antedates Israel's Mosaic religion.

It is in the light of these points that the significance of the ascription of Genesis 12–50 to Moses can be appreciated. For what it means is that these stories, although intrinsically and originally standing out-side Israel's faith, have been told from a perspective within Israel's faith. This means, first, that these stories have in some way been appropriated by Israel as its own, and, secondly, that by ascription to Moses, they are told as part of the authoritative and normative account of Israel's story. The modern recognition that the material was most probably not written by Moses but by a variety of authors in a variety of periods all subsequent to Moses in no way affects this basic point that the context from which the patriarchal stories are now told is Israel's context, a context different from that which they originally had. The present position of the patriarchal stories in the Pentateuch makes them part of Israel's authorized story of itself.

All this entails that reading the patriarchal stories is not a simple or straightforward matter. For the text presents both what the stories now *are*, part of Israel's story, and what the stories once *were*, part of a non-Israelite story. Although the more important of these two for the writers was clearly what the stories now are, for that is how they were to function as significant and authoritative within Israel, it remains true that many indicators of what the stories once were have been left in the text and not deliberately removed from it, and this not unnaturally encourages the inquisitive reader to enquire further about this historical dimension of the text. Whether the reader today is genuinely in a position to get behind the presentation of the material as it now stands in the biblical text is a moot point, on which opinions widely differ. But the point is that the enquiry is in principle a valid one, and one in some ways invited by the text itself.

This general point does not just arise from the traditional ascription of the material to Moses, but is present within the text itself. The one explicit and unambiguous place in Genesis 12–50 where the writer obtrudes his own Israelite perspective is Gen. 34.7, where the writer comments on the indignation of the sons of Jacob after the rape of Dinah with the words that Shechem 'had wrought folly in Israel by lying with Jacob's daughter'. For here 'Israel' is clearly used in the sense of a national community, a sense which it could not have in the patriarchal period.

If this general perspective on the patriarchal stories is correct, it still needs qualification in certain ways. For, as we shall see, there is much in the patriarchal stories that is not told in Israel's terms but retains its own distinctiveness. Moreover, the degree to which the patriarchal stories are told in Israel's terms varies from story to story. Generally speaking, it is in the stories of Abraham that the language and concerns characteristic of Yahwism are most present. It is likely, therefore, that it was the story of Abraham that received most reflection and incorporated most retelling when Israel made the patriarchal stories its own. A fuller sense of the varying character of the patriarchal stories should emerge in the course of the following chapters.

To summarize, the question of how to read the patriarchal narratives is not straightforward, both because of the legitimate difference of interest that readers may have, and because of the inherent tension within the text caused by the telling of non-Israelite material from the perspective of Israel. However, this complexity may add to the interest of the study—as will, I hope, become clear as this book progresses.

Chapter Two

AN INTRODUCTION TO THE TEXT OF GENESIS 12–50

Within the compass of one short chapter it is hardly possible both to introduce all the content of Genesis 12–50 and also to indicate all the different ways of reading the text that have been proposed. What follows, therefore, is a selective introduction which seeks to highlight some of the major points of which the student should be aware.

The Character and Role of God in Genesis 12–50

As the narrative of Genesis 12–50 now stands, there are five major characters: Abraham, Isaac, Jacob, Joseph—and God. The most important of these is God, and it is he who provides the unity within Genesis 12–50 as a whole; as the human figures die and pass on, it is the consistent hidden presence and purpose of God who is preparing for his people Israel that runs through the material (compare e.g. Gen. 12.1-3 with 50.24).

The character of God is never described, but the fundamental assumption that is made is that this God is Israel's God, Yhwh, and so some facets of his character can be presupposed in the light of what is said about Yhwh elsewhere, especially in the four passages about the name, that is, character, of Yhwh in the book of Exodus (Exod. 3.13-15; 33.19; 34.5-7; 34.14). However, the fact that, according to the explicit statement of Exod. 6.3, God was not known as Yhwh to the patriarchs suggests that at least sometimes in Genesis there may be important differences in his character from his self-revelation in Exodus.

For the most part Yhwh is a presence who speaks and who can be spoken to, but who does not usually appear in a form accessible to sight and touch. However, he does sometimes appear in the form (apparently) of a normal human being, most famously to Abraham at Mamre (Gen. 18.1-33) and to Jacob at the ford of Jabbok (Gen. 32.22-32), and is sometimes represented by an 'angel' (*mal'āk*, literally messenger) who is virtually indistinguishable from Yhwh himself (Gen. 22.11). Apart from his sometimes speaking and being spoken to in

apparently everyday circumstances (Gen. 13.14-17; 16.7-14; 17.1),
there is a marked tendency for God to appear and speak in visions
and dreams (Gen. 15.1, 12; 20.3; 28.10-17; 31.24; 46.2). Sometimes the
dreams are more pictorial and indirect in their message—that is, they
need interpretation, as is consistently the case in the story of Joseph
(e.g. Gen. 37.5-11; 40.8; 41.1-45, esp. vv. 25, 32).

It is Yhwh who provides the major continuity between the stories,
as everything that happens is to be seen as part of his clear purpose,
which is set out at the beginning of the patriarchal stories (12.1-3).
This purpose, which will make of Abraham a 'great nation', not only
links the patriarchal stories to one another but also links them to the
story of Israel which follows in Exodus, so that the Israelite who reads
(or hears) the stories will know that they are all part of Israel's story.

Genesis draws attention to the meaning of the names of all its principal human characters (Abraham, 17.5; Isaac, 17.17, 19; Jacob, 25.26;
the twelve sons of Jacob, 29.31–30.24; 35.16-18; the two sons of Joseph,
41.51-52; the fact that it never does so with the names of any of the
women, most notably the absence of any comment on the naming of
Dinah, 30.21, is one small but significant aspect of the 'patriarchal'
outlook of the text). One might therefore expect Genesis to do the
same with the name of God. This does not happen, probably because
the meaning of Yhwh is given in Exodus to Moses to whom the name
is revealed, and also because the Pentateuch retains the tradition
(Exod. 6.3) that the name Yhwh was not known to the patriarchs
(despite the freedom with which it is used in the stories as they now
stand). It remains interesting, however, to see how often terms other
than Yhwh are used for God—terms which once might have functioned as names, though not any longer as Israel's God has only one
name, Yhwh, and therefore other such terms are now to be understood as titles and epithets.

The most common alternative to Yhwh is simply the generic term
'God' (*'elōhîm*). This is the main way of referring to God in the Jacob
and Joseph stories. One significant feature of this usage is that it lacks
the exclusivity implied by the name Yhwh (who is specifically the
God of Israel), and so is appropriate to those stories where there is a
general openness about people's relationship with God. Thus when
God speaks to Abimelech, king of Gerar (ch. 20) or to Pharaoh, king of
Egypt (ch. 41), in much the same way as he speaks to Abraham or to
Joseph, then it is the general, non-exclusive term *'elōhîm* that is consistently used. As we shall see later, there is a consistent openness
about the depiction of God in Genesis 12–50, which forms a notable
contrast to Exodus 3 onwards.

The title for God to which attention is drawn in Exod. 6.3 as characterizing God's self-revelation to the patriarchs is *El Shaddai*. The precise significance of this name is unclear, but it usually appears in contexts of a promise of future descendants (Gen. 17.1; 35.11; 48.3; 49.25). Traditionally it has been taken as a term expressing God's sovereignty—hence its traditional rendering as 'God Almighty'. Modern etymological study has suggested that its original meaning may have been 'God of the Mountain' (see, e.g., the discussion in Westermann, *Genesis 12–36*, pp. 257-58), but, even if this is correct, it is likely to have been unknown to the writers of Genesis for whom something like the traditional rendering is probably to be understood.

The Abraham Cycle: Genesis 11.27–25.18

The first of the patriarchs is Abraham (for convenience I shall consistently use the familiar longer form of his name, even though in terms of the story he does not acquire the name until Gen. 17.5). As already noted, it is in his stories that the divine name Yhwh is most used, and so it is here that we most naturally look for the figure who was of most importance to the writers as preparing for, and in some ways prefiguring, Israel's faith.

Although Abraham is an individual figure, he is also often a representative or embodiment of Israel as a people. The opening words of Yhwh to Abraham (12.2) draw attention to the fact that he is to be a great nation, and in 18.19 he is to teach his descendants to obey Yhwh 'so that Yhwh may bring Abraham what he has promised him'. As this refers to Abraham in the future, in the context of his descendants, it is clear that here Abraham himself somehow represents the people of Israel. Moreover, as we shall see, Abraham's stories are sometimes embodiments of Israel's story, both the Exodus and Sinai traditions. Thus the Abraham stories often need to be read on different levels, both for what they say about Abraham in his own right, and for what they show about Abraham as a type of Israel.

All the stories featuring Abraham are brief, usually corresponding to the length of a biblical chapter. This is somewhat different from the Jacob stories—some of these also are short, but those concerning Jacob and Laban form a more extended sequence. This is again different from the Joseph story which is predominantly one extended narrative. It is generally thought that these differences relate to the origins and transmission of the material, the Abraham stories having originally been short oral units, while the Joseph story has a more novel-like character. In terms of present function, the Abraham stories can more easily be used for didactic purposes, each one usually having some distinct moral or point.

From the outset, Abraham is a man of faith (though this has been questioned; see Gunn and Fewell, *Narrative*, ch. 4, and Davies, 'Male Bonding', both of which I have discussed in my *The Bible, Theology, and Faith*, ch. 5). When God asks him to relinquish everything that has constituted his identity and security—homeland, people and family (12.1)—Abraham quite simply obeys ('So Abram went, as Yhwh had told him', 12.4a). The first two things he does in the land of Canaan are to build altars to Yhwh, thus indicating his responsive reverence to God's leading (12.7-8); the second time he builds an altar, it is also said that he 'called on the name of Yhwh', that is, he prayed (cf. e.g. Ps. 116.[2], 4, 13, 17).

The most famous individual story of Abraham is Genesis 22, in which he is called to sacrifice his hope for the future in the person of his long-awaited son (see Chapter 3). This is the last story in which there is dialogue between God and Abraham, and Jewish tradition has often fruitfully linked it with the first dialogue in 12.1-3. There is indeed a verbal link between the two passages, in that each of God's addresses (12.1; 22.2) contains the otherwise unparalleled form of an idiomatic phrase, *lek lᵉkā* ('Go', but in fact similar to the archaic English idiom 'get thee' as in Hamlet's words to Ophelia, 'Get thee to a nunnery'). In ch. 12 Abraham is asked to go and relinquish his past, in ch. 22 he is asked to go and relinquish his future. Each time he trusts God and obeys without reservation. It is not surprising that Abraham has been looked to as a father of faith by Jew, Christian and Muslim alike.

Probably the overarching concern of the Abraham cycle is God's promise to Abraham of a land and a son (12.1-3), a promise whose fulfilment is delayed, so that Abraham has to live in hopeful faith. The promise of the land is to be fulfilled only in Abraham's descendants (12.7), so the crucial promise for Abraham himself is that of a son, since without a son there will be no descendants. For years Abraham has to wait. He jeopardizes the promise when he is willing to pass off Sarah into Pharaoh's harem (12.10-20); the promise is, however, renewed more than once (13.16; 15.5); yet although he trusts God in his promise (15.6), the actual fulfilment comes apparently no closer. Sarah's action of giving Hagar to Abraham may reasonably be read as showing impatience with the lack of fulfilment of the promise (16.1-6). When the news finally comes that a son is soon to be born to Sarah, this seems incredible (laughable) to both Abraham and Sarah (17.15-21; 18.9-15). The promise is jeopardized again when Sarah, presumably already pregnant, is passed off into Abimelech's harem (20.1-18). At last, Isaac is born (21.1-7). Yet even now nothing can be taken for granted, for it is now that God tells Abraham to sacrifice his son, and it is only when Abraham has passed the supreme test of faith (22.1-19) that Isaac's future is secure.

Other specific examples of Abraham's piety are not hard to find. In ch. 13 he is prepared to allow Lot the first choice of land (and it is ironic that when Lot chooses what looks to be the most fertile part of the land, the southern Jordan Valley ['towards Zoar', 13.10; 19.15-22], the reader knows that this is about to become the most notoriously barren part of the whole land). In ch. 14 Abraham rescues Lot, is blessed by Melchizedek, and declines any profit from his booty. In chs. 15 and 17 he receives a covenant from God. In ch. 18 he not only shows hospitality to strangers but is singled out as chosen by God for moral purposes (18.19) and has the stature to engage with God on the question of righteousness, probing the justice and mercy of God (18.22-33). In ch. 20 he is seen as a man of intercessory prayer (20.7). In ch. 21 he is recognized as someone of whom it can be said, 'God is with you in all that you do' (21.22). And finally the fact that Abraham dies 'in a good old age' (25.8) is a sign of the divine blessing which he enjoyed in his life.

Particularly important is the fact that Abraham is the recipient of a covenant with God in chs. 15 and 17. The word 'covenant' (Heb. $b^e rît$) is a term of central theological significance in the Old Testament generally, as this is how Israel's relationship with God at Sinai is understood (Exod. 19.5 etc.). Three points about this covenant may be noted here. First, unlike the covenant at Sinai, where great emphasis is laid upon Israel's responsibilities within the covenant and there are severe warnings of judgment for disobedience (see esp. Deut. 28), the covenant with Abraham lays its emphasis upon what God promises to do for Abraham, to give him both descendants and land. In this it is similar to the other three covenants in the Old Testament that are made with individuals, Noah (Gen. 9.8-17), David (2 Sam. 7; 23.5; Ps. 89) and Phinehas (Num. 25.10-13), all of which are essentially promises of God; indeed it is notable in Ps. 89.3 [Heb. 4] that 'I have made a covenant' is in poetic parallelism with 'I have sworn'. It is not that there is no note at all about what Abraham is to do (Gen. 17.1b); nonetheless the nature of the covenant is clearly different from that at Sinai. The similarities between the covenants with Abraham and David have sometimes been considered evidence for the dating of the patriarchal material in the period of the united monarchy.

Secondly, it is a notable emphasis elsewhere, particularly in

Deuteronomy, that God's election and deliverance of Israel are in ful-filment of the oath sworn to the fathers (esp. Deut. 7.6-8). Although this could refer to all the promises to the patriarchs, it is presumably particularly to the formal promissory covenant with Abraham that the reference should be understood. It is deeply characteristic of Israel that, although it sees its own faith as beginning with Moses, it roots its understanding of God's dealings in the pre-Mosaic patriarchal period and sees a strong continuity between the two.

Thirdly, it is initially perhaps a little surprising that the making of the covenant with Abraham is contained in two separate chapters. This is generally explained by the supposition that these were ori-ginally two separate accounts belonging to different sources (ch. 15, J and/or E; ch. 17, P—see Chapter 4 below), and this may well be so; certainly their styles are different, as ch. 15 has a vivid mixture of nar-rative and speech in a scene that is imaginatively memorable, while ch. 17 is almost entirely speech in a scene that has little development. Nonetheless, as the text stands there is a complementarity between the two. Gen. 15.7-21, with its mysterious ritual, focuses on the promise of land (15.7-8, 18), while ch. 17 focuses on the promise of descendants (vv. 2, 4) and on the need for circumcision as a sign of this. Presumably a major point of circumcision is that in the very act of sexual intercourse there should be an intimate reminder to both male and female within Israel that the child which is begotten is not simply the result of human processes but is also a gift from God in fulfilment of his promise.

Although piety is a major feature of Abraham's life, his piety is not incompatible with elements which are not generally, considered pious. Abraham's first recorded words to God are words of question-ing (15.2), and his response to the first promise of a son specifically through Sarah is incredulous laughter (17.16-17). Indeed, it is remark-able that in the very chapter in which Abraham's faith is singled out for mention (15.6) and in the one in which he first receives the cove-nant, he responds to the two divine promises—which one would sup-pose should simply be accepted with gratitude—with questions about how he is to trust the promises (15.2, 8). This is in fact a phenomenon akin to the laments in the Psalter, in which the life of faith is envis-aged as containing space for questioning God without undermining the integrity of faith.

More questionable are two occasions when Abraham acts in fear, jeopardizes the divine promise and brings misfortune upon his host (12.10-20; 20.1-18), and also when he weakly allows Sarah to deal harshly with Hagar (16.6; cf. 21.10-11). The point is that even with someone as exemplary as Abraham, the biblical writer is concerned to show the reality of life with 'warts and all' lest an artifical kind of piety should convey an atmosphere of unreality. As T.W. Mann has put it,

> Because the biblical authors persistently refuse to moralize, their charac-
> ters are adamantly earthy creatures. Far from being cardboard stereo-
> types of moral virtue — or vice — they are 'credible' men and women of
> great and ultimately impenetrable complexity (*Book of the Torah*, p. 8).

Yet if there is a sense of moral ambiguity about Abraham, it must readily be admitted that it is as nothing compared to that which surrounds the figure of Jacob.

Isaac

The figure of Isaac is the least developed of all the major patriarchs. Indeed, it seems a little surprising that the traditional patriarchal trio is Abraham, Isaac and Jacob, when the patriarchal stories actually concentrate on Abraham, Jacob and Joseph. Nonetheless, the text treats Joseph differently, for it is only to Abraham, Isaac and Jacob that God appears and delivers his promise (12.1-3 etc.; 26.2-5; 28.13-15) — God is never shown as speaking directly to Joseph. Thus Isaac does in some basic way stand on a level with Abraham and Jacob, as distinct from the twelve sons of Jacob.

One common attempt to explain the brevity of the Isaac material has involved appealing to its probable history of transmission at an early, oral stage. It is said to be a well-attested principle in oral and legendary material that a character who is originally of great promi-nence should recede into the background and have his position of prominence taken over by another character who becomes important at a later stage. In the light of this, it has been suggested that ori-ginally Isaac was a more prominent figure than Abraham. As Noth puts it,

> It is striking, even on first glance, that in the final form of the tradition
> which has been preserved for us, Isaac seems to be completely over-
> shadowed by Abraham... Now the fact that Isaac recedes into the back-
> ground in contrast to Abraham, the figure that manifestly evolved later,
> speaks for Isaac's priority... In comparison to Isaac, therefore, Abraham
> is to be regarded as the more 'modern' figure who, at the expense of
> Isaac, obtained more and more space in the tradition (*History of Penta-
> teuchal Traditions*, p. 103).

While this is not impossible, one wonders how one should dif-ferentiate a figure who originally was prominent and later became relatively insignificant from a figure who was relatively insignificant in the first place—and given our lack of evidence or clear controls, such an issue can never be resolved.

In any case, Isaac is the least active and significant of the patriarchs. Alter interestingly refers to him as

> manifestly the most passive of the patriarchs. We have already seen him as a bound victim for whose life a ram is substituted; later, as a father, he will prefer the son who can go out to the field and bring him back provender, and his one extended scene will be lying in bed, weak and blind, while others act on him (*Art of Biblical Narrative*, p. 53).

Most of the stories about Isaac are primarily stories about either Abraham or Jacob (chs. 22, 24 [Abraham]; 25.19-34; 27.1–28.9 [Jacob]). Only in ch. 26 is there a sequence of stories in which Isaac is the sole patriarch to feature. Yet even here almost everything has a parallel with what is said of Abraham:

26.1	A famine, as in the time of Abraham (12.10).
26.2-5	Divine promises, as to Abraham (12.1-3; 22.15-18).
26.6-11	Isaac passes off his wife as his sister, as did Abraham (12.10-20; 20.1-18).
26.12-14	Isaac attains great wealth, as did Abraham (13.2, 6).
26.15-22	Disputes with Philistines over wells (cf. 21.25).
26.23-25	Yhwh appears to Isaac, who builds an altar and calls on the name of Yhwh (cf. 12.7-8).
26.26-31	Isaac enters into a covenant with Abimelech and the Philistines (cf. 21.25-32).
26.32-33	The naming of Beersheba (cf. 21.31).

The effect of these similarities is to give a deep sense of pattern and continuity between Abraham and Isaac—'like father, like son'. Although there are differences within the similarities, and these are important (see Chapter 4 below for the wife as sister episode), it is the sense of continuity that is predominant. The writer wishes to show a pattern of piety and blessing continued between the generations, though the advent of Jacob in particular means that Isaac's final scene (ch. 27) shows him as a less august figure than Abraham in his old age.

The Jacob Cycle: Genesis 25.19–36.43

Jacob is the most complex and enigmatic of the patriarchs—a cunning and unscrupulous deceiver, who yet becomes a man of God. He is the one who becomes Israel and so is the eponymous ancestor of the nation. One might have expected that someone of the character of Abraham would have this honour of being the eponymous ancestor of a nation called to be holy to Yhwh (Exod. 19.5-6; Deut. 7.6). Yet the fact that it is self-seeking Jacob and not faithful Abraham who gives his name to his descendants speaks volumes for Israel's under-standing of the nature of human life under God, and in particular the ambiguous and paradoxical relationship between the call of God and the moral response of the people called.

Jacob not only becomes the eponymous ancestor of the people Israel. In some way he actually typifies and embodies Israel. This is made clear at two crucial moments early in his story. First, when Rebekah is suffering in her pregnancy with Esau and Jacob she receives a message from Yhwh that not just two babies but 'Two nations are in your womb' (25.23). Secondly, at the climax of Isaac's blessing of Jacob, Isaac says, 'Let peoples serve you, and nations bow down to you' (27.29) — something which happens to Israel the nation in the time of David and subsequently, but not to Jacob the indi-vidual. However much, therefore, the story of Jacob and Esau can and should be read and understood as a struggle between two individual people, it needs also to be understood as in some way typifying the larger issue of the struggling relationship between nations, especially between Israel and Edom, who were generally at odds with each other in Israel's history.

This point, however, should not be applied automatically, as though everything in the story of Jacob and Esau were a cipher for the history of Israel and Edom. For, most obviously, the magnificent for-giveness with which Esau receives Jacob on his return from Paddan-Aram (Gen. 33.4 — which Jesus may have used as the model for the father of the prodigal son, Lk. 15.20) is in no way expected in the light of the known history of Edomite dealings with Israel. This shows that the portrayal of Jacob and Esau as individuals has a value in its own right.

As the story of Jacob stands, it revolves around two remarkable encounters with God. The first is when Jacob is fleeing from home after cheating Esau out of his father's blessing in the memorable story of the deception of Isaac (ch. 27). While asleep in the open, he has a dream in which he sees a ladder set between earth and heaven, with angels ascending and descending and with God at the top speaking to him. The content of the divine address, God's first words to Jacob, is striking; not a word of rebuke for the deception of Isaac and Esau; instead, a self-introduction and four promises — land, descendants, blessing by the families of the earth, divine company and protection. (This emphasis on promise with no corresponding moral demands is, as we shall see, one of the many ways in which patriarchal religion differs from Mosaic religion.) When he wakes, Jacob is awed by the place, sets up the stone he used as a pillow as a sacred pillar, renames the place Bethel, and makes a vow (although he does not address God directly).

One attempt to do justice to the theological dimensions of the text has been to focus upon Jacob's statement 'how awesome is this place!', which has been taken as a classic expression of holiness, the sense of a *mysterium tremendum et fascinans* (see Otto, *Idea of the Holy* — although in fact, significantly [see Chapter 5], the Hebrew word for 'holy' [*qādôš*] is not used). A different facet of the text's significance is Jacob's association with Bethel. In Israelite history, Bethel became an important sanctuary (Judg. 20.18, 26; 1 Sam. 10.3), and so was chosen by Jeroboam as one of the two major shrines of the northern kingdom (1 Kgs 12.29). The present narrative explains how Bethel became such a holy place. What is perhaps surprising is the implicitly positive view of Bethel that the text contains, which has often led to the bulk of the text being ascribed to the Elohist (see Chapter 4) writing in the ninth century BCE in the context of the northern kingdom where Bethel was venerated. For elsewhere in the Old Testament, Bethel is usually viewed negatively, both by the writer of 1 Kgs 12.25–13.34 and 2 Kgs 23.15, and by Amos (3.14; 4.4; 5.5) and Hosea (10.15). Moreover, given the implicitly positive view of Jerusalem in Genesis 22 (see Chapter 3), one might expect a less positive view of Bethel in Genesis 28. Perhaps the explanation is quite simply that the writer was anxious to preserve the distinctive character of the patriarchal period as impervious to the later religious conflicts of Yahwism.

In any case, Jacob's dream at Bethel makes clear that God is involved in the life of Jacob, and this is important as a context for understanding the following narrative of Jacob's stay with Laban where there is little obvious divine engagement with the situation and where Jacob and Laban take it in turns to deceive each other. While Jacob is with Laban he acquires his two wives, Leah and Rachel, and also eleven of his twelve sons.

The birth of the sons is interesting for the remarkably matter-of-fact way in which it is told. One might have expected that the birth of the eponymous ancestors of the tribes of Israel would be surrounded by uplifting themes, but the opposite is the case. For example, there is a famous little vignette (30.14-24) of Leah gaining the right to sleep with Jacob through Rachel's bartering acquisition of mandrakes (a traditional aphrodisiac) gathered by Leah's son, Reuben. This leads to the birth of more offspring, not only for Leah but also, at last, for Rachel too. Although the writer is at pains to show how in all this petty feuding God was present and working his purposes out (30.17, 22), the mundane nature of the proceedings is not disguised. All this is consistent with the emphasis elsewhere in the Pentateuch that God's choice of the people of Israel was not because of special qualities inherent in Israel (esp. Deut. 7.7-8).

A decisive turning point for Jacob comes when he has to return home with his wives and children, for now he is afraid of what Esau is likely to do to him. When he is told that Esau is coming to meet him with four hundred men, this seems to confirm his worst fears. This leads to Jacob offering his first prayer to God (32.9-12), in which there is a note of genuine humility and supplication (although, characteristically, Jacob has already started making his own practical arrangements to deal with the problem). But after further arrangements we read, 'And Jacob was left alone; and a man wrestled with him until the breaking of the day' (32.24). Of all Old Testament stories, this is perhaps the hardest to comment on, largely because the deliberately allusive and mysterious nature of the text makes the story appeal powerfully to the imagination but leaves it not very amenable to rational, discursive explanation. Is Jacob's adversary a spirit of the night, a river spirit, Esau, a projection of his subconscious, or God? As the text stands, it is clearly none other than Yhwh in human form (32.30). But the fact that the story is suggestive of these other interpretations—perhaps because in earlier versions they were an actual part of the story—makes it likely that in a sense they are all true, as they all belong to the immediate or wider context of the story. God confronts Jacob not only in human form, but as Esau, whom he fears, as a night spirit, belonging to the time when his fears are at their sharpest, as a river spirit because he is crossing a perilous boundary into the territory of Israel, and as the embodiment of the deepest hopes and fears of his own mind. The writer boldly incorporates these folkloristic motifs in order to try to convey something of the mysterious depth of the occasion.

In the struggle Jacob is both victor and vanquished; he comes out with a new name, Israel, representing a new character as one who embodies what was best in the old character—he has striven with God and men, and prevailed (32.28)—and as one who limps, and will never stand upright in his own strength again.

Hereafter, although Jacob/Israel is still recognizably the same person, a change has occurred. After his reconciliation with Esau, Jacob builds an altar for the first time and calls it 'God is the God of Israel' (33.20). Abraham from the outset built altars as a mark of his faith in God; now Jacob does so too. Some time later Jacob makes his family purge themselves of 'foreign gods' (the sole example in the patriarchal narratives of a concern for religious purity in a characteristically Yahwistic sense) and he builds another altar at Bethel (35.7). In later years Jacob still appears as a poor parent who shows favouritism among his children (37.3-4) and does not react well to adversity (37.34-35; 42.35–43.15), nonetheless he is a venerable figure who blesses Pharaoh (47.7, 10) and all his sons (Gen. 48–49). The character of Jacob presents a fascinating study in the difference that God does, and does not, make in a wilful and recalcitrant personality.

One final point that may be noted about the Jacob cycle is that it has certain similarities to the early story of Moses. These may be noted as follows (for a fuller list, including some looser parallels, see Hendel, *Epic of the Patriarch*, pp. 137-65, esp. 140):

1. Both Jacob and Moses do something that is morally ambiguous (deception of father [Gen. 27], killing of Egyptian [Exod. 2.11-15]) and consequently have to flee.
2. Both have a meeting with God at a holy place, which prepares them for what lies ahead (Bethel, Gen. 28.10-22; Horeb, Exod. 3.1–4.17).
3. Both meet their wife-to-be at a well (Gen. 29.1-14; Exod. 2.15b-21).
4. Both are told by God to return to the place from which they originally fled (Gen. 31.13; Exod. 4.18-20).
5. Both have mysterious and threatening night encounters with God (Gen. 32.22-32; Exod. 4.24-26).

How should these similarities be explained? Hendel suggests that they show a common underlying oral narrative tradition, and this may well be so. A shared tradition of storytelling about significant figures in Israel's beginnings could well portray different characters in similar ways. However, this may suggest that the process could be largely unintentional. As we shall see later, the pentateuchal writers have a predilection for patterning and typology. It may equally be the case that Moses, as the founder of Israel's faith, was deliberately patterned on Jacob, the eponymous ancestor of the nation (or vice versa) to create a study in the similarities and the differences in the way God deals with the great figures of Israel.

The Joseph Cycle: Genesis 37–50

The main narrative about Joseph is the lengthy, novel-like story in Genesis 37, 39–45. Thereafter the material becomes more episodic, and Westermann (*Genesis 37–50*, pp. 22-24) argued that some of the material in chs. 46–50 originally belonged to the Jacob cycle. As the text stands, however, Joseph is the predominant figure. Chapter 37 starts with Joseph as a young man, and ch. 50 ends with his death.

Another distinctive characteristic of the Joseph material is the fact that unlike Abraham or Jacob there is never any hint in the text that Joseph typifies or embodies Israel as a people. Joseph is always and only an individual person, whose exemplary character is presumably intended to be taken as a model for other individuals also.

Although we first encounter Joseph as a somewhat priggish teenager (ch. 37), his experience of suffering seems rapidly to mature him into a serene man of faith who patiently endures unjust imprisonment, ultimately being rewarded by promotion to viceroy of Egypt. Although the precise extent to which he should be seen as an exemplary character is a matter of debate, there can be no question but that some exemplary elements are present in the text.

One of the most influential modern interpretations of the Joseph story was von Rad's essay 'The Joseph Narrative and Ancient Wisdom'. This has given rise to considerable debate (for a brief survey and bibliography, see Emerton, 'Wisdom', pp. 221-27, and the critique by Weeks, *Early Israelite Wisdom*, pp. 92-109). Insofar as much of Proverbs (a) deals with behaviour at court (e.g. Prov. 22.29), which is where Joseph flourishes (Gen. 41.37-45), (b) commends the fear of (i.e. obedience to) Yhwh (Prov. 1.7) which Joseph displays (Gen. 39.9; 42.18), (c) commends self-discipline (Prov. 14.29) such as Joseph shows in adversity, and (d) also generally portrays the prosperity of the righteous (e.g. Prov. 10.6), just as Joseph finally prospers, there are certain obvious general affinities between the Joseph story and that strand of wisdom literature represented by Proverbs. Within the story, Pharaoh explicitly refers to Joseph as wise (41.39; cf. 41.33). The key theological statements of the whole Joseph story are Joseph's words to his brothers, 'So it was not you who sent me here but God' (Gen. 45.8) and 'You meant evil against me, but God meant it for good' (50.20). Such an understanding of God's providential sovereignty is also spelled out in Prov. 19.21, 'Many are the plans in the mind of a man, but it is Yhwh's purpose that will be established' (cf. Prov. 16.9; 20.24). Even though there are facets of Joseph that do not so readily relate to the emphases of Proverbs—for example his skill in the interpretation of dreams and his mysterious dealings with his family—there are still enough similarities between Joseph and the concerns of Proverbs for the parallel to be illuminating in reading the text.

The explicit references to God's providential sovereignty (45.8; 50.20) are all-important since they provide the context for understanding all else that happens, in particular the dreams that are crucial in the early chapters. Elsewhere in Genesis, dreams are the context for a divine epiphany or oracle (e.g. 15.12-21; 28.12-17), but here they are always in the form of a sequence in their own right; they do not feature God as such (in this the dreams are akin to parables) but are given by God as adumbrations of the future. Joseph's recounting of his dreams to his brothers may have been foolish (an example of when he did not hold his tongue [cf. e.g. Prov. 18.7]), but the dreams are clearly to be seen as God-given anticipations of the story to come. The same is true of the dreams of the butler and baker when Joseph is with them in prison: he has the God-given ability (40.8) to interpret them, and they come to pass as he has said. Most obviously is this the case with the dreams of Pharaoh which only Joseph is able to intepret (ch. 41). These dreams have received less attention than they might in theological discussions of the Joseph story, yet they are striking in that they go beyond the point that God can bring good out of evil intentions (45.5; 50.20) and show God knowing the future before it happens. Particularly striking is the statement of 41.32: 'And the doubling of Pharaoh's dream means that the thing is fixed by God, and God will shortly bring it to pass.' This implies that although sometimes there may be indeterminacy about the course of the future, this is not always the case. It is characteristic also of the practical nature of Hebrew faith that God's determination of a famine is seen not as an occasion for speculative questioning of the purposes of God, but for practical action on the part of the person (in this case, Joseph) who fears God.

Although Joseph is the central figure of these chapters, we are not given the insight into his character that might be expected. This has particularly puzzled readers of chs. 42–44 when Joseph does not reveal himself to his brothers but puts them through a series of hardships. What is his motive? Anger? Revenge? Testing? The text does not explicitly say. However, there are perhaps two clues. One is Joseph's tears when confronted by his brothers, which are the same for his brothers generally as they are for Benjamin in particular (42.23-24; 43.30; 45.1-3); this suggests that his heart is not set against them. The other is the explicit linkage between his harsh behaviour and his initial dreams (42.9); although the nature of the linkage is not spelt out, the fact that the reader knows that the dream is a God-given anti-cipation of the future suggests that Joseph's behaviour is somehow to be linked to the fulfilment of God's purposes. It is probable, therefore, that Joseph's behaviour towards his brothers, despite its puzzling nature, should be seen as some kind of well-intentioned test.

One final point about the Joseph story relates to its possible functions within Israel. One striking feature is its presentation of a

Hebrew operating successfully in a foreign environment, and in this it appears to have been a model for the later books of Esther and Daniel (cf. Humphreys, 'A Life-Style for Diaspora'). Certainly, when Jews found themselves in exile the story could have taken on an added significance as embodying some of the possibilities open to those who were willing to believe that Yhwh could still be with them in exile. It may even be that the story received some editing in the exilic period. The otherwise slightly puzzling reference to Joseph's family being 'preserved as a remnant' (45.7) may perhaps make best sense if seen as a rewording of the story in the exilic period when this was precisely how the Jews in exile felt and when the story of Joseph was seen as offering some model for interpreting their situation.

Genesis 12–50 as Israelite Scripture

One final question to ask in this context is why Israel should have preserved the stories of the patriarchs. After all, Israel's own story begins with Moses and the Exodus, and it is only in this context that Israel's distinctive knowledge of God as Yhwh is given. Although a partial answer may be that the writers of the Pentateuch wished to show a historical continuity between Israel and its antecedents, that of itself would not suffice to explain the position that Genesis 12–50 has at the outset of Israel's sacred writings, particularly when the religious ethos and practice of the patriarchs (see Chapter 5) is so at odds with that of Mosaic Yahwism.

I have suggested in *The Old Testament of the Old Testament* that Genesis 12–50 stands in relation to the rest of the Old Testament rather in the same way that the Old Testament stands in relation to the New Testament. Or, to put the same point the other way round, the familiar problem that the Christian has with the Old Testament is similar to the problem that Mosaic Yahwism and the writers of the Pentateuch had with the patriarchal traditions — in each case there is a conviction that it is the same God, but this recognition has to be combined with the recognition that somehow things then were different, a difference classically expressed in terms of old and new dispensations.

Although part of the reason why Christians have preserved the Old Testament as Christian Scripture is to show the historical continuity between Christian faith and its Hebrew and Jewish antecedents, this has not been the primary use to which the Old Testament has been put. Rather the Old Testament has been used as a resource for the life of faith, on the assumption that one can sit light to many of its specific religious *practices* (circumcision, sacrifice, food laws etc.), and yet retain most of its religious *principles*. As long as there is a shared assumption that human life has value and dignity, that life is to be lived responsibly in trust and obedience under God, and that prayer is an essential medium of communication between God and humanity, then the religious principles that give rise to one set of religious practices in one context may still inform a distinct yet related set of religious practices in another context. It is likely that this kind of understanding accounts not only for Christian retention and use of the Old Testament as Christian Scripture, but also for Yahwistic retention and use of the patriarchal traditions in Genesis 12–50 as Hebrew Scripture. The primary interest of Israel in the patriarchs was therefore in them as people who could in one way or other exemplify the dynamics of life under God and so would inform and instruct successive generations of Israelites. This was in no sense a moralistic kind of exemplification, as we have seen that the portrayal of Jacob most obviously (though the same applies to a lesser extent to Abraham) is anything but moralistic—but is still usable to exemplify how life under God should (and should not) be lived.

If this understanding of Genesis 12–50 is at all valid, it should also be related to the well-known debate about the origins of Scripture as a significant concept within Israelite faith. It is customarily maintained that early Israel had little sense of texts as normative for faith, and that only with the advent of Deuteronomy in the late seventh century did there begin a movement in this direction. Certainly there is much in this notion, and one can easily see in Deuteronomy a concern for normativity that is lacking in other law codes (e.g. Deut. 1.5; 4.1-8; 12.32 [Heb. 13.1]; 31.9-13), and no doubt this did give considerable impetus towards Judaism's becoming increasingly centred upon a book rather than upon sacrifice in the temple. Nonetheless, if my proposed understanding of Genesis 12–50 is at all on the right lines, it suggests a concern for a narrative text such as Genesis 12–50 as also authoritative for Israel's faith. To be sure, it functions as authoritative in a way quite different from Deuteronomy, for Genesis 12–50 is a nondirective text, which much more obviously needs interpretation if it is to function as religiously authoritative than is the case with the legal precepts of Torah. Moreover, we do not know the date when Genesis 12–50 was recognized as authoritative for Israel, and whether this was earlier or later than Deuteronomy. Nonetheless, the point remains that any discussion about the origins and development of scriptural authority in Israel's faith needs to do justice not only to the laws of Deuteronomy but also to the narratives of Genesis 12–50.

Chapter Three

A SPECIMEN TEXT: GENESIS 22

I propose in this chapter further to introduce the patriarchal stories in general by focusing on one story in particular, Genesis 22 (the interpretation offered here is developed more fully in my *The Bible, Theology, and Faith*, ch. 3). The hope is that the kinds of issues that are seen to be relevant to understanding this chapter will then be able to be applied elsewhere without too much difficulty. There is of course the danger that Genesis 22 may not be wholly typical of the patriarchal narratives. Indeed, it is in many ways distinctive in the range and depth of its content and in its mode of telling, and it is probable that the story has received more attention than others already in the time of the biblical writers, as well as subsequently. Nonetheless it is in my judgment sufficiently typical that it may serve to illustrate more clearly than most the kind of material that is found in a number of the patriarchal stories; it also shows the kinds of processes that we should suppose, to greater or lesser extent, to have been involved in the patriarchal narratives in general.

An Interpretation of Genesis 22

1. The first task is to read and interpret the story as it now stands. The best way to do this is to follow the lead of the story-teller. This, however, may be easier said than done, because, according to a famous analysis of the story by E. Auerbach in his *Mimesis*, Genesis 22 is a model of restraint on the part of the storyteller. The story is told in a taut, suspense-filled way, in which much is left unspecified by the narrator: 'time and place are undefined…thoughts and feelings remain unexpressed, are only suggested by the silence and the frag-mentary speeches; the whole…remains mysterious and "fraught with background"' (*Mimesis*, pp. 11-12). There is much of value in Auer-bach's analysis; however, he has somewhat overstated his case, for the writer does in fact provide strong clues about the way in which the story should be understood.

Generally speaking, Old Testament storytellers do not stand outside a story and comment upon it, but rather so tell it that it conveys
its own meaning (there are important similarities between the conventions of Old Testament narrative and those of contemporary
novels and films). The points at which the storyteller usually places
what he considers most important are usually the speeches made by
the main characters at the dramatically crucial moments, though
sometimes repetitions and wordplays also serve this function. In this,
Genesis 22 is no exception.

Genesis 22 is, however, exceptional in that the narrator does comment on the story and provides an explicit interpretative key right at
the outset, presumably because the story is not only of prime importance but also because it may be liable to misinterpretation. Thus the
story begins, 'After these things God tested (*nissâ*) Abraham.' The
precise sense of 'test' will be crucial to understanding the story, but it
should not be taken on its own, for there is one other word that
should be taken in conjunction with it. The speech of the angel of
Yhwh at the critical moment of sacrifice refers to the result of the test,
a result which presumably constituted its purpose in the first place,
and so is essential to understanding it. Verse 12 reads, 'Do not lay
your hand on the boy, and do not do anything to him, for now I know
that you fear God (lit. you are a fearer of God, *yᵉrē' ᵉlōhîm 'attâ*), since
you have not withheld your son, your only son from me.' Here the
crucial thing is that Abraham fears God. Thus the two words which
together provide the primary key to understanding the story are 'test'
(*nissâ*) and 'fear' (*yārē'*).

The meaning of these words is best discovered by examining their
usage elsewhere. First, it should be noted that 'fear' in Gen. 22.12 has
its predominant Old Testament usage in a religious context; that is, it
does not indicate fright, or even religious awe, but rather moral obedience. 'Fear' of God concerns doing rather than feeling (see e.g. Deut.
5.29, where fearing God is connected with keeping his commandments, or Job 28.28, where the fear of the Lord is parallel to departing
from evil).

Secondly, the words *nissâ* and *yārē'* occur together in one other passage in the Old Testament, that is Exod. 20.20, a key passage because
in it Moses explains the purpose of God giving the Ten Commandments, the heart of Torah (the Hebrew word traditionally, but often
misleadingly, rendered as 'Law'), to Israel. Here Moses says to Israel,
'Do not fear (i.e. be frightened), for God has come to test (*nassôt*, the
infinitive of *nissâ*) you, and so that the fear of him (i.e. obedience;
yir'ātô, the noun from *yārē'*) may be before you to keep you from sin.'

The purpose of Torah is thus in some way to challenge and draw out Israel into a fuller obedience to God. It should be noted, moreover, that although the specific words 'test' and 'fear' are not found in conjunction elsewhere, the concept that they represent is. For it is a recurrent notion, especially in the major theological treatment of Israel's position as the people of God—Deuteronomy, and literature related to Deuteronomy—that Yhwh tests Israel so as to enhance their obedience to him; thus Exod. 16.4 interprets the giving of the manna in the wilderness as a matter of testing (*nissâ*) Israel, whether they will be obedient to Torah or not; Deut. 8.2 interprets the whole forty years in the wilderness as a time of God's testing (*nissâ*) whether Israel would be obedient to God's commandments; Deut. 13.3 [Heb. 4] interprets a wonder-working prophet who preaches apostasy as Yhwh's testing (*nissâ*) Israel to prove whether they love him wholly and solely (cf. Deut. 33.8-9; Judg. 2.22; 3.4).

How then is the connection between Genesis 22 and these other passages to be understood? The linkage between the passages is routinely noted by most Genesis commentators, but most make little of it. Even Westermann (*Genesis 12–36*, p. 356), who has an excursus on *nissâ*, merely makes some observations about the history of the concept and points out that the usage of 'test' with regard to Israel as a people appears to be older than with regard to an individual person (such as Abraham). Yet the interpretation of Genesis 22 can be taken further than this.

Initially, it should be noted that the notion of God testing is primarily a part of a theology of Israel and Torah, for this is where the language overwhelmingly occurs, particularly in the key passage Exod. 20.20. It follows from this that the use of this language with regard to Abraham is an extension or reapplication. Why should this be? This is another instance where a basic perspective on the patriarchal stories as non-Israelite material told from Israel's context is illuminating. This may perhaps best be appreciated if we stand back initially and consider a well-known Christian analogy.

The Old Testament, as Christian Scripture, poses a well-known hermeneutical problem. If Jesus Christ is the supreme revelation of God, how is the Christian to understand and appropriate material from a pre-Christ context? One characteristic Christian assumption is that the Old Testament contains patterns and analogies to the revelation of God in Christ, a hermeneutical approach known as typology. Thus the basic Christian stance with regard to the Old Testament is Christological, that is, it starts with Christ and reads the Old Testament looking for patterns and analogies to him.

Less well known is the fact that the Old Testament itself contains a closely similar hermeneutical problem. For Israel, the supreme revelation of God is Torah, given by God through Moses to Israel at Sinai. Yet Israel used as part of its Scripture these stories of Israel's ancestors, the patriarchs, who lived in a pre-Torah context. How, then, was Israel to understand and appropriate these stories (Green, *Devotion and Commandment*, helpfully characterizes traditional Jewish awareness of, and responses to, this problem)? The natural assumption is that they would want to show patterns and analogies to Torah, and to do so particularly with Abraham as the supreme exemplar of the life of faith under God. It is therefore not surprising when there is one explicit statement to this effect within the text (Gen. 26.5), and another of similar import (18.19), and when post-biblical Jewish tradition, from the Book of Jubilees in the second century BCE onwards, extensively develops the notion that the patriarchs obeyed Torah even before it had been given at Sinai. Yet in fact it is not Gen. 26.5 that provides the best textual foundation for this notion, but rather Gen. 22.1, 12, where Israel's language of testing with a view to Torah obedience is applied to Abraham. For this makes Abraham an exemplary type of Israel, one who demonstrates as a representative individual the kind of Torah obedience to God that should characterize Israel as a whole.

2. The second main interpretative issue to consider, which is the one with which people tend to begin, is the fact that God is asking Abraham to take the life of a child. In any modern context this would be considered morally repugnant, and anyone who claimed to have been told by God to kill a child would find no credence for such claims from any responsible person, believer or non-believer. There is a modern tendency, encouraged (in different ways) by people of the stature of Kant and Kierkegaard to suppose that this modern moral judgment must also apply to the story in its ancient context. Yet such an approach is a classic example of anachronism and demonstrates the importance of having an informed historical perspective when reading the Old Testament. Our first point, about the nature of testing, indicates that the story is to be seen as a positive moral example, and this is confirmed by further considerations.

The general attitude to children in the ancient world was almost the exact opposite of that generally found in the modern West. Where the modern world has a high estimate of the value of children, which easily lapses into sentimentality, the ancient world had a low estimate, which easily lapsed into cruelty (most obviously in the widespread practice of the exposure, i.e., abandonment in the open to death, of unwanted children). The adult, in particular the father, was considered the norm of life, and children, until they themselves reached adulthood, were considered as significant to the extent that they enhanced the worth of the father. Although the Old Testament generally encourages a humane attitude towards children (and towards orphans and widows, being those most vulnerable in society because left without domestic male protection), it does not generally question their subordinate importance in relation to the father, and this is particularly evident in some of the older strata. For example, on two occasions in Genesis (other than ch. 22), the story takes for granted that a father can make life and death decisions about his child (38.24, Judah with regard to his daughter-in-law, Tamar; 42.37, Reuben with regard to his two sons). The law of Deut. 21.18-21 envisages a father's making a life and death decision with regard to a rebellious son, and Exod. 21.7 envisages a man's selling his daughter as a slave. Jephthah sacrificed his daughter in fulfilment of a vow (Judg. 11.34-40). The assumption common to all these passages is that the role and worth of the child is relative to, and dependent upon, the father. The material is, in one important sense of the term, patriarchal in outlook.

In the light of these passages, it is clear that Genesis 22 is making a similar assumption—Abraham naturally has the right of life and death over Isaac. Indeed, throughout the story of Abraham, Isaac is always seen as significant in terms of Abraham, for the birth of Isaac means that Abraham will no longer be without an heir by Sarah, and that the promise to Abraham made by God will be fulfilled. At the beginning of Genesis 22 something is said about Isaac, not about Isaac in himself but about his significance for Abraham ('your son, your only son Isaac, whom you love', v. 2), and at the end of the story it is Abraham who is commended and promised further blessing because he has not withheld his only son from God (22.16-18). The significance of Isaac in Genesis 22, therefore, is not that of a unique human being whom it would be immoral to kill. Rather, as Abraham's son, he is Abraham's hope for the future. Isaac is Abraham's most precious possession, a possession all the more significant because promised by God and waited for over so many years. What Abraham's test of obedience consists in, therefore, is a willingness to surrender to God that which is most precious to him, that in which he could most legitimately have confidence and hope, precisely because it was promised and given by God in the first place.

One other possibly relevant factor in this context is the widespread belief in the ancient Near East, shared also by Israel, that the first of all new life belonged to God (an illuminating discussion is Levenson, *Death and Resurrection*). The underlying assumption was that as God was the giver of life, so he had the right to receive back the first and best of what he had given. In this, Yhwh expected no less than any other deity, for in the context of the passover (itself a story about Yhwh's life-and-death authority over the firstborn) we read, 'Consecrate to me all the firstborn; whatever is the first to open the womb among the people of Israel, both of man and of beast, is mine' (Exod. 13.2). Moreover, in Exod. 22.29-30 (Heb. 28–29) there are some old laws about such offerings: first, agricultural produce ('You shall not delay to offer from the fulness of your harvest and from the outflow of your presses'); secondly, children ('The firstborn of your sons you shall give to me' [the normal verb 'to give', *nātan*, is used]); thirdly, livestock ('You shall do likewise with your oxen and with your sheep'); fourthly, there is a note that seems to apply to both sons and livestock ('Seven days he/it shall be with his/its mother; on the eighth day you shall give him/it to me'). It is often suggested that ancient Israel at one stage countenanced the sacrifice of children to God, and that Genesis 22 is a protest against such practice. But whatever the underlying historical developments may have been, the natural way of reading the Genesis text as it now stands is rather different.

First, the premise on which the story rests is certainly that God has the right to ask for Abraham's son (his firstborn by Sarah), but less on the ground that this is God's right to the firstborn than on the more general ground that God has a right to ask for whatever he has given to Abraham. It is worth noting that there are many similarities between Genesis 22 and Job 1–2, both stories where God tests a godly person, and where the test consists of relinquishment of that which is most precious. The attitude towards God contained in the famous words of Job is not without relevance for Genesis 22: 'Yhwh gave, and Yhwh has taken away; blessed be the name of Yhwh' (Job 1.21). The point in Genesis 22, however, is that God is prepared not to exact his right to take away, but will accept obedience and the symbolic sacrifice of a ram instead.

Secondly, despite some resonance with the issue of God's right to the firstborn, it may be correct to see that particular issue as already dealt with, as the text now stands. The ancient law of Exod. 22.29-30, cited above, does not specify the form that 'giving' the firstborn to God should take, and only requires that it be done after eight days. There is one obvious resonance with this requirement that a child be given to God after eight days, and that is the practice of circumcision on the eighth day (Gen. 17.12). Although Genesis 17 applies the requirement to every male child and not just the firstborn, it remains natural to see the law of male circumcision as a generalization of the principle of Exod. 22.29-30. This means that the practice of circumcision is, among other things, to be understood as the giving of a child to God. In the case of Isaac, this has already been carried out prior to Genesis 22 (Gen. 21.4).

In short, therefore, whatever moral scruples the story of Genesis 22 may initially arouse in a modern context, in its own context any notion of immorality is out of place. It is a story about God's demand of Abraham to relinquish to God that which is most precious to him, as the essence of what true faith ('fearing God') involves. God is able to demand this not only because of his intrinsic right to that which is best, but also because Isaac's life was God's gift in the first place. It is only as Abraham is willing to obey this hard command that he discovers that he will not in fact lose by it, but instead will gain great blessing (22.16-18).

3. A third major issue concerns the location of the story, something to which the story itself draws attention, both by naming the territory as Moriah (v. 2), and by recounting a special name given by Abraham in token of what had happened there (v. 14), a name given special significance by a wordplay (vv. 8, 14; see below). Where is this place?

The name Moriah occurs elsewhere in the Old Testament only in 2 Chron. 3.1: 'Then Solomon began to build the house of Yhwh in Jerusalem on Mount Moriah, where Yhwh had appeared to David his father, at the place that David had appointed, on the threshing floor of Ornan the Jebusite.' Although, surprisingly, reference is made only to the story of David (2 Sam. 24 // 1 Chron. 21) and not to the story of Abraham, there can be little doubt that the Chronicler's Moriah is the same as that of Genesis 22, and that a comparison of the passages means that the Temple is built on the site of Abraham's offering of Isaac. It is generally thought, however, that the identification of Jerusalem as the site of Genesis 22 is a later interpretation of the text which is not intended in the story's own Genesis context. Von Rad, for example, comments that 2 Chron. 3.1

> refers without doubt to the mountain on which the Temple stood. But our narrator means a land of Moriah about which we know nothing at all... He [the narrator] gives no place name at all [in Gen. 22.14], but only a pun which at one time undoubtedly explained a place name. But the name of the place has disappeared from the narrative... Perhaps the ancient name was lost because of the later combination of the narrative with the 'land of Moriah' (*Genesis*, pp. 240, 242, 243).

There are, however, good reasons for supposing that a reference to Jerusalem is indeed intended as an integral part of the Genesis story as it now stands, and is the point of the pun in v. 14.

There is an emphasis in the story upon 'seeing' (*rā'â*, 22.8, 13, 14; usually rendered 'provide' for reasons of sense in context), which is related as a general principle to one place where God supremely sees (22.14a) and is seen (22.14b). This is probably to be connected with the name of the territory where the story happens, Moriah (22.2), understood as a noun from the verb *rā'â* with the sense 'Place of Seeing'. Within the Old Testament generally, there are two places in particular where God is seen: first, Sinai (esp. Exod. 24.9-11; cf. 1 Kgs 19.9-18), and secondly Jerusalem (e.g. 2 Sam. 24.15-17; Isa. 6.1; Ps. 84, esp. vv. 5, 8 [Heb. 6, 9]). Since the story envisages a location within the central territory of Israel, three days' journey from Beersheba, it is naturally Jerusalem rather than Sinai that is indicated.

Furthermore, the site of the story is linked with 'the mountain of Yhwh' (*har Yhwh*, 22.14b). Elsewhere in the Old Testament the phrase 'the mountain of Yhwh' is only ever used of Jerusalem (Ps. 24.3; Isa. 2.3; Zech. 8.3), with the sole exception of Num. 10.33 where it is used of Sinai.

Finally, with regard to location, one may note that the story has to do with sacrifice, which for Israel, according to the prescriptions of the Old Testament, should supremely take place within the Temple in Jerusalem. Abraham offers his sacrifice to God at a place which God selects for him (22.2, 3), which is similar to God's requirement for Israel's worship 'at the place which Yhwh will choose to put his name there' (Deut. 12.5 etc.), a place which is to be understood as Jerusalem (1 Kgs 14.21).

4. A fourth major element in the story, which has not yet been considered, is the extended address by the angel of Yhwh when he calls a second time from heaven (22.15-18). This is notable for at least two reasons. First, it renews God's promise of blessing and does so in uniquely emphatic terms, stronger than anywhere else in the Abraham story. Secondly, it links this promise of blessing to Abraham's obedience ('because you have done this…because you obeyed my voice', vv. 16, 18).

It is this second point that is theologically most interesting, because elsewhere God's promises to Abraham are unconditional statements given with no grounding, thus implicitly being grounded in the character and purposes of Yhwh himself. I have studied this in detail elsewhere and have come to the following conclusion:

Abraham by his obedience has not qualified to be the recipient of blessing, because the promise of blessing had been given to him already.
Rather, the existing promise is reaffirmed but its terms of reference are
altered. A promise which previously was grounded solely in the will
and purpose of Yahweh is transformed so that it is now grounded *both*
in the will of Yahweh *and* in the obedience of Abraham. It is not that the
divine promise has become contingent upon Abraham's obedience, but
that Abraham's obedience has been incorporated into the divine
promise. Henceforth Israel owes its existence not just to Yahweh but
also to Abraham.

Theologically this constitutes a profound understanding of the value
of human obedience—it can be taken up by God and become a moti-
vating factor in his purposes towards man. Within the wider context of
Hebrew theology I suggest that this is analogous to the assumptions
underlying intercessory prayer... ('Earliest Commentary', pp. 320-21).

5. Although the main interest of Genesis 22 is in vv. 1-19, it would be
wrong to overlook vv. 20-24. At first sight the verses are unpromising,
just another of those Genesis genealogies which seem to offer little to
the modern reader. Yet it is not accidental that the genealogy of the
twelve sons of Nahor, Abraham's brother, has been placed directly
after the preceding narrative, for in addition to the twelve sons, there
is the intrusive mention of one woman, the granddaughter Rebekah
(v. 23). The full significance of this woman within the Genesis story
will not become clear until Abraham's servant goes in search of a wife
for Isaac (Gen. 24), although the reader who, like the writer, stands
within the context of Israel may already smile knowingly. What the
narrator is doing is preparing the way for the fulfilment of the
renewed promise of descendants to Abraham through Isaac (vv. 16-
18) by quietly introducing, in a normal way, the human character
whose life will soon be taken up into the fulfilment of the divine
promise.

6. One final point may be made about the way in which the story is
told. The restraint of the storyteller, which Auerbach interpreted in
terms of suspense, may also be part of an imaginative desire to be
faithful to the context of the patriarchs themselves which he is portraying. That is, although the writer is showing the linkage of
Abraham with Torah and Jerusalem, he does not explicitly mention
either, but rather leaves them implicit, to be inferred by the thought-
ful reader from the clues provided in the text. Perhaps part of the
reason for this is the recognition that in Abraham's own context
neither Torah nor Jerusalem had the significance which they had for
Israel. The writer's subtle, inferential reference to both makes it

possible on the one hand to show Abraham's connections with what was central for Israel and on the other hand to respect his difference from Israel.

To sum up, what we have in Genesis 22 is a remarkable story of Abraham as a model of Israel's Torah-shaped obedience to God. He is willing to offer to God that which is dearest to him and he also offers sacrifice on the site of Israel's worship on the mountain of the Temple in Jerusalem, thereby showing that the symbolic meaning of sacrifice is unreserved self-offering to God. This obedience is understood to be of such value that it is incorporated by God into the heart of his purposes towards Israel.

From the point of view of a reader within the context of Israel, it is also a story about how Israel's very existence hung, apparently, by a thread, for, had the sacrifice been carried out, there would have been no Israel. Yet the very fact that the story can be told presupposes that there is an Israel, and so from the outset the outcome is presupposed. Thus, together with the sense that God may himself imperil Israel's very existence, there is a sense that Israel will not fail, primarily because of the ultimate good purposes of the God who imperils, but also, and notably, because of the quality of human obedience that Israel's paradigmatic ancestor displayed. If the story is rightly understood, it is not only in God but also in an obedient human being that Israel's confidence for its existence is based.

A Critical Analysis

I have offered an interpretation of Genesis 22, and something of its riches and depths has been seen. Perhaps the best way to proceed further is by asking 'Is it true?' This question is the more important because of another feature of the way the story is told, as noted by Auerbach, and developed by M. Sternberg. As Auerbach puts it,

> Without believing in Abraham's sacrifice, it is impossible to put the narrative of it to the use for which it was written… The Bible's claim to truth…is tyrannical—it excludes all other claims… The Biblical narrative…seeks to overcome our reality: we are to fit our own life into its world… (*Mimesis*, pp. 14, 15).

Similarly, Sternberg refers to the

> Bible's determination to sanctify and compel literal belief in the past. It claims not just the status of history but, as Erich Auerbach rightly maintains, of *the* history—the one and only truth that, like God himself,

brooks no rival... The Bible shows a supreme confidence in its facts. Any rival version, it implies, would be absurd, if at all conceivable (*Poetics of Biblical Narrative*, pp. 32, 126).

It is not important here to analyze the basis for such claims, for in one way or other some such understanding would be widely granted. The present concern is to explore precisely how credence might be given to some such claim about the truth of the text. This is not a question that can be answered without some careful exploration of precisely what is meant by truth in this context.

There is a recurrent tendency in much modern biblical study to approach the question of truth in a narrative via the question of its historical accuracy. For the great narratives of the Old Testament are certainly in some way historical narratives, telling the story of Israel from beginnings to exile. Moreover, from a theological point of view it has often been felt important to maintain at least a basic historicity of content in Israel's stories, lest the denial of such content would evacuate their value for the Jewish or Christian believer who is committed to a belief in God's genuine engagement with life in this world. If, then, we approach Genesis 22 with the question of its historical accuracy in mind, what do we find? The short answer is — a problem.

The basic reason for this is the point I have emphasized as essential for understanding the patriarchal narratives, that they are pre-Israelite material told from an Israelite perspective. That is to say, by the very nature of the situation, the stories are told from a perspective that was not their own originally, and so far as this Israelite perspective has been incorporated into the text, so far has the original historical nature of the material faded into the background. If, for example, I am correct in the contention (see Chapter 4) that the Old Testament is consistent that the name Yhwh was first revealed to Moses, and that all the uses in Genesis represent a Yahwistic retelling of the stories based on the conviction that Yhwh the God of Israel is none other than the God of the patriarchs, then however much one may justify the procedure as theologically legitimate and in keeping with storytelling practice, the point remains that from a strictly historical perspective anachronism is involved — the patriarchs themselves in their historical context did not know God as Yhwh.

To say all this does not mean that there may not be anything genuinely pre-Israelite still present in the patriarchal stories. As we will see in Chapter 5, there is considerable evidence that the Yahwistic tellers of the patriarchal stories were not only aware of the distinctively pre-Yahwistic, pre-Israelite nature of the stories, but also preserved this distinctiveness in many ways when one might have expected them to obliterate it. Nonetheless, the point remains that the writers did feel free to retell the patriarchal stories in their own terms and categories, and this makes the modern historical quest for the original form of the stories, not to mention their possible historicity, particularly elusive.

With regard to Genesis 22, this basic problem is obviously acute. The story as it now stands presupposes that Jerusalem is a holy site for Israel, and Jerusalem only first became Israelite under David in the early tenth century BCE (2 Sam. 5.6-10; cf. Judg. 19.10-12). More specifically, it presupposes that the reader knows that the Temple stands in Jerusalem, which means that the story must be not earlier than the time of Solomon who built the Temple (1 Kgs 5–8). We do not know the date at which Israel developed its theology of testing and Torah, but it is most prominent in Deuteronomy and in Judges 2–3 which is written in the light of Deuteronomy, and these texts are conventionally dated to the seventh and sixth centuries; although Gen. 22.1, 12 and Exod. 20.20 may be earlier than these, it is obviously difficult to establish the point with much confidence. Finally, I have myself argued that the second address by the angel in Gen. 22.15-18 is an addition to a story that was already otherwise complete, an addition possibly made in the time of the exile in the mid-sixth century when the Abraham stories were probably being reappropriated as a foundation for Israel's future life after the exile (cf. Isa. 51.1-3).

For the content and composition of Genesis 22 as it now stands, we thus have to look to one or more periods within the general range of the tenth to sixth centuries BCE. Yet on the timescale of the story itself, it is set sometime in the early second millennium BCE—perhaps some 800 years before Solomon, and some 1200 years before the exile. If this timescale is to be taken at even approximately face value, then, for the historian, whose access to past events depends in the first instance on establishing the nature of the sources and establishing their likely degree of proximity to the events they relate, this means that strictly limited weight can be put on Genesis 22 as a historical source. For Genesis 22 simply stands at too great a remove from its narrated events.

The virtual impossibility of using Genesis 22 in its present form as a historical source may be illustrated by a consideration of one attempt to utilize it as such. For example, W. Harold Mare discusses the archaeology of Jerusalem in the Middle Bronze period (early second millennium). He notes Kathleen Kenyon's dating of a wall (above the

Gihon spring on Mt Ophel) to c. 1800 BCE, with its implications for population in the area at the time, and then comments: 'That Abraham did not encounter any opposition when he came to Mount Moriah to offer Isaac (Genesis 22) suggests that the inhabitants of the area were not strong enough or belligerent enough to organize resistance against him' (*Archaeology of the Jerusalem Area,* p. 24). The difficulty with such an inference from the text of Genesis 22 is that it seems to assume that had the local inhabitants been a significant problem, then they would have been mentioned (presumably as in Gen. 21.25-34; 26.17-22). Yet as Genesis 22 stands, such an issue is surely an irrelevance—the story is simply impervious to the question of what the inhabitants of the district might have been doing or thinking when Abraham was there. As far as the story goes, the only significant figures are Abraham, Isaac and God, and other people, outsiders, might as well not exist for all the difference they make. The assumption that Genesis 22 is just a simplified, selective account of historical events can, it is true, hardly be definitively refuted. But it is thoroughly implausible, partly because it does not take seriously the question of dating the source, partly because it does not take seriously the Yahwistic context from which originally non-Yahwistic material is now told, and partly because it does not sufficiently consider what type of material the story might be.

There are two main ways of trying to make progress in this apparent impasse. The first concerns the historian's desire to penetrate behind the present form of the narrative to try to recover something of its original pre-Yahwistic form. The classic modern work in this regard was Gunkel's analysis of the story in his *Genesis* commentary, which has been widely adopted in subsequent works. Gunkel assumed that the story told of the founding of a sanctuary (it being common practice in ancient and mediaeval times for holy places to have official stories of how they came to be), but that this must originally have been somewhere other than Jerusalem. By assuming that the uses of Yhwh in v. 14 replace an original 'God' in the form *'ēl* or *'elōhîm,* and that the wordplay on 'see' (*yir'eh,* from *rā'â*) is original to the story, he suggests that the original place name given by Abraham in v. 14 was Jeruel, a place near Tekoa mentioned in 2 Chron. 20.16, 20. Further, he assumes that the sacrificial element was original to the story, and that originally it told of actual child sacrifice to God at Jeruel, though in time a ram came to be substituted for the child.

Such proposals are ingenious, but the obvious difficulty with them is their speculative and untestable nature. Although one may affirm the legitimacy in principle of seeking an earlier form of the story, it seems arbitrary to retain the wordplay and yet discount the links with the name Moriah and with Jerusalem as the place of seeing, and also to retain the element of sacrifice and yet discount the testing element altogether. The main strength of Gunkel's suggestions lies in comparative religio-historical study where stories about the founding of holy places are not only common but are also liable to retelling in the light of the concerns of those who happen to be dominant at the holy place at any given time. But even this really only reinforces the original insight, that the story has been retold from a perspective different from that which it originally had, and does not give any clue as to what the likely original form may have been.

The alternative to penetrating behind the story is to focus on the story as it stands, and in particular to ask what kind of material the story is. The obvious category that comes to mind is that of legend. This is a term that is often used so loosely and diversely that it needs definition if its use is in any way to clarify matters (see Auerbach, *Mimesis*, pp. 19-21; Hals, 'Legend'; von Rad, *Genesis*, pp. 31-43).

Broadly speaking, the main sense of legend is that of a story, usually attached to and originating from some outstanding and remarkable person or event, which is constantly told and retold and which in the retelling takes on a life of its own. This is a phenomenon attested in all cultures, and almost invariably the earliest history of a culture is cast in the form of legends (for example, the Homeric stories for the Greeks, the Arthurian stories for the British). Insofar as people have a sense of identity that is related to these stories, their retelling tends to embody the values and beliefs that are important to those who do the retelling. When the legend is of a religious nature, it often has a strongly moral element, aimed at encouraging imitation. This means that in due course the legend will usually come to say more about the beliefs and values of those who tell it and cherish it than it does about the person or event which originally gave rise to it — though obviously the relationship varies greatly from legend to legend.

It is in some such sense of the term 'legend' that Genesis 22 is probably to be understood. For it is clear first that it is a story important to Israel's self-understanding and identity; secondly, that it is a story embodying a high degree of moral content of an exemplary nature; thirdly, that it was told and retold over a long period of time; fourthly, that in its present form it dates from a time when its content tells us primarily about the beliefs and values of those who told it.

There are at least two consequences that follow from this. First, we can only be agnostic about the bearing the story may have on 'the historical Abraham', for we simply do not have the necessary evidence either to affirm or to deny suggestions about the likely original date and content of the story.

Secondly, and more importantly, it should be clear that the question of the truth of the story is not primarily a question about the historicity of what it relates, but rather a question about the beliefs and values incorporated in the story by those who have related it. Presumably these beliefs and values arise out of Israel's life as a people under Yhwh and have been incorporated in the story precisely because they have been found through practical experience of life under God to be true. Because the great figure of Abraham was the outstanding exemplar of the potential of the life of faith under God, it was felt to be appropriate to express Israel's understanding of basic truths about such life in the context of retelling Abraham's story where such truths were already at least implicitly present. In the legendary story of Abraham there is a merging of past and present (von Rad's account of this in the final section of the introduction to his Genesis commentary is particularly interesting).

This means that the question about the truth, or otherwise, of the story cannot be answered except by engaging with the beliefs and values that the story portrays. Is it true to the character of God, and is it true to the nature of human life? These are not questions that can be answered without reference to one's basic stance as a person. In general terms, those who stand in some kind of continuity with the ancient community of faith which cherished and wrote the story and who themselves cherish it as part of scripture will be inclined to affirm that the story is true. Those without that commitment may answer differently.

Chapter Four

WHEN, WHERE, BY WHOM AND HOW
WAS GENESIS 12–50 WRITTEN?

The short, and disappointing, answer to the questions of when, where, and by whom was the text of Genesis 12–50 written is that we do not know. The answer is the more disappointing because of the enormous expenditure of energy over the last 200 years or so into trying to determine the answer, and because, for most of the last century until the last 30 years or so, it was confidently thought by the consensus of biblical scholars that the answer was known, and was known in some detail.

The consensus may briefly be stated as follows. Some time during the reign of Solomon (c. 960–920 BCE) an authoritative account of Israel's history, showing how God had led Israel to the highpoint of the United Monarchy was composed in Jerusalem by a writer known as the Yahwist ('J'—see below), who collated existing earlier traditions and transformed them into one consecutive account. This comprises the greater part of the narrative of the Pentateuch.

After the division of the kingdom following the death of Solomon, the northern kingdom of Israel produced a history of its own covering much the same ground as the Yahwist's history (which remained the official history of the southern kingdom centred on Jerusalem). The writer is known as the Elohist ('E'—see below), and the content and style of his history was influenced by the growing contemporary phenomenon of prophecy (especially Elijah and Elisha) in the northern kingdom. After the fall of the northern kingdom in 721 to the Assyrians, this Elohistic history was preserved and taken to Jerusalem, where it was combined with and merged into the earlier work of the Yahwist to produce one new work ('JE').

In the seventh century, at about the time of Judah's breaking free from Assyrian suzerainty and of the initiation of Josiah's reform (2 Kgs 22–23) the book of Deuteronomy was written. Although Deuteronomy is a collection of laws and exhortations distinct from the narratives of the Pentateuch, the importance which it attaches to covenant as central to understanding Yhwh's relationship with Israel may have led to some rewriting of the JE account of the Sinai covenant in Exodus 19–24 and 32–34.

In the sixth century, at the end of the exile and during the early years of the return from exile, there was another reform movement, concerned that Israel should not repeat the sins that had led to the exile. This movement was characterized by the compilation of a large number of laws in such a way as to regulate Israel's life as a holy nation. Because of the central importance given to the priesthood and the correct performance of worship, this material is known as the Priestly document ('P'). Although most of the material is presented in the form of laws at Sinai, there is also a brief prefatory narrative covering the major points of Israel's traditional story, to show how Israel's life as a worshipping nation was intended by God from the outset.

In due course this most recent Priestly account of Israel's history was combined with and merged into the earlier JE account to produce one comprehensive account of Israel's history. Although most of the narrative content of the history was JE, the P material was used to provide the framework for the whole.

This, in rough outline, is an account of the consensus view of the Pentateuch. It was classically formulated by J. Wellhausen in his *Die Komposition des Hexateuchs*, and his *Prolegomena to the History of Ancient Israel*. It was mediated and reinforced in the English-speaking world by scholars such as S.R. Driver, in his *Introduction to the Literature of the Old Testament*, and in his *Genesis* commentary, each of which went through many editions. It was modified by a variety of scholars, especially von Rad, who, in his 'The Form-Critical Problem of the Hexateuch' and his 'The Beginnings of Historical Writing in Ancient Israel', won a consensus for dating the Yahwist to the time of Solomon, at least a century earlier than the date proposed by Wellhausen. In general terms, there can be no doubt that it is a reconstruction of the composition of the Pentateuch that makes perfectly good sense.

So why is the situation so difficult today? The short answer is that scholars have increasingly pressed the question 'But how do you *know*?' For the fact is that the biblical writers made themselves anonymous and invisible. They aimed to let the text speak for itself, and nowhere in any of the texts of the Pentateuch does the writer draw attention to himself or to his context and his purposes in writing. Although by careful analysis of the text it is indeed possible to discern differences of vocabulary, style and emphasis and to make some suggestions as to possible authorship in the light of these, the task is inevitably a tentative and hypothetical undertaking. Although the documentary hypothesis has commanded a scholarly consensus for many years, there has always been a minority of scholars who have dissented from the consensus (often ultimately for religious motives, on the ground that the consensus view impugned the integrity of the text, but still advancing many cogent considerations). More recently, a growing number of scholars, with no particular religious position to defend, have questioned whether the scholarly consensus is really as well founded as was supposed. The most cogent such questioning is R.N. Whybray, *The Making of the Pentateuch*.

Admittedly the situation is far from being simply a return to square one. Many scholars still maintain the documentary hypothesis as the best available explanation of the text, and even those who have abandoned it as a total explanation usually retain elements of it (particularly relating to the Priestly document). Nonetheless, the mood of the debate has changed. It is academically respectable, in a way that it was not previously, not to accept the documentary hypothesis (although whether the respectability will endure will depend on the strength of the proposals offered to replace it), and those who do maintain the documentary hypothesis are conscious of the need to justify and defend it afresh (see esp. Nicholson, *The Pentateuch*). Until recently it would have been unthinkable for a reputable scholar to write, as does D.M. Gunn, 'It is no exaggeration to say that the truly assured results of historical critical scholarship concerning authorship, date and provenance would fill but a pamphlet' ('New Directions', p. 66).

Even though the documentary hypothesis no longer holds sway in the way it once did, it will never be possible to understand modern scholarly debate about Genesis 12–50 without some knowledge of it, and so it will be appropriate to give further attention to certain aspects of the hypothesis, with special reference to the basic arguments adduced in its favour.

The story of the development of the documentary hypothesis has often been told and is easily available; for short accounts, see almost any Introduction to the Old Testament, and for a fuller account, see R.J. Thompson, *Moses and the Law in a Century of Criticism since Graf*. For present purposes it will probably be most helpful to give a brief and highly selective survey of the issues before moving on to examine one or two specific examples to give a more detailed and first-hand awareness of the problems.

The first clear setting of an agenda for a modern historically oriented approach to the Bible was probably that of Spinoza in the seventeenth century, for it was he who formulated the principle that, in study of the Old Testament, 'We must consider who was the speaker, what was the occasion, and to whom were the words addressed.' Instead of simply considering what the text meant, and issues arising from that, there was a new interest in when and where the text was written, and in then interpreting the text in the light of that knowledge. This was clearly a fundamental move in the direction of 'reading the Bible like any other book' (as Jowett later put it; cf. Chapter 1), specifically any other ancient historical text. As one recent Introduction puts it, 'The valid religious truth or "message" of the Hebrew Bible could only be brought to light when seen as the religion of a particular people at a particular time and place as expressed in these particular writings' (Gottwald, *The Hebrew Bible*, p. 11).

Originally the assumption was made, following the tradition of both Jews and Christians, that Moses had written the pentateuchal text. Even on the assumption of Mosaic authorship, however, which would have meant that Exodus–Deuteronomy were contemporary with Moses, the book of Genesis posed particular problems; for what sources would Moses have had available to him, given that he lived some four hundred years (Gen. 15.13) after the patriarchs? Thus the composition of Genesis was the real issue in early pentateuchal criticism (and still today Genesis 12–50 poses problems different from those of the rest of the Pentateuch). Consequently, one of the earliest works of modern pentateuchal criticism was published in 1753 by Jean Astruc (physician to Louis XV) with the title *Conjectures sur les mémoires originaux dont il paroit que Moyse s'est servi pour composer le livre de la Genèse* ('Conjectures about the original documents which it would appear that Moses used to compose the book of Genesis').

One aspect of the text to which Astruc paid particular attention was the use of varying terms for God, in particular the regular alternation between 'Jehovah' (as he vocalized Yhwh) and 'God' (*ʾelōhîm*). In Jewish tradition this was an aspect of the text well known since antiquity, and was usually interpreted solely in terms of difference of meaning, Yhwh indicating God in his mercy, and *ʾelōhîm* indicating God in his justice. As a total explanation of the alternations, however, this rapidly becomes forced and implausible (as do various more recent attempts always to explain the difference in terms of deliberate variation of meaning; for a sophisticated recent reformulation see Brichto, *Names of God*). Astruc's contribution was to reformulate the categories within which the phenomenon was interpreted, for he suggested that it was to be explained by two different source documents used by Moses, each of which had consistently used one particular term for God. Although Astruc's own analysis is not particularly cogent (for example, he simply divided Gen. 22 between his two sources—A, 22.1-10; B, 22.11-19—entirely on the basis of the use of *'elōhîm* in vv. 1-10 and Yhwh in vv. 11-19 without regard for other considerations), the important thing was that he established categories which seemed plausible to the increasing historical awareness of scholars and which could be duly refined by others in the course of time.

Once the notion of sources distinguished by different terms for God became increasingly accepted, it was also not long before the assumption of Mosaic use of different sources was abandoned, mainly because of a growing awareness of different historical levels within the pentateuchal text. There was an awareness of the apparent anachronism of Gen. 12.6 and 13.7, which would seem to have been written at a time when the Canaanites were not (obviously or prominently, rather than at all) in the land, that is, subsequent to Israel's entry into the land after the death of Moses. There was also a recognition of the great diversity of laws in Exodus–Deuteronomy, and of the fact that law is usually created and developed to meet everyday situations as they arise, and, consequently, that these laws seem to presuppose Israel's settled life within Canaan.

The factor that appeared to clinch the correctness of using different terms for God as an indication of sources was that of the passages which speak of the revelation of the name Yhwh to Moses (Exod. 3 and 6). For the clear implication of Exod. 3.13-15 is that the name Yhwh was only for the first time revealed to Moses, and the explicit statement of Exod. 6.2-3 is that this is indeed the case, and that God was known to the patriarchs not as Yhwh but as El Shaddai. But how then is one to explain the fact that the name Yhwh is used, and used extensively, in Genesis, where, according to Exodus 3 and 6, it ought to be unknown?

The scholarly consensus in modern times has been that the explanation is quite simple: there were two divergent accounts of the origin of the divine name. Where the name Yhwh is used in Genesis, it is the work of a writer who thought that the name was then known; and so the writer is called 'The Yahwist'/'Jahwist' ('J'). It is supposed that Gen. 4.26b, 'At that time people began to call on the name of Yhwh', is the Yahwist's account of how the name Yhwh was known from primaeval times. Thus the Yahwist's history freely used the name Yhwh throughout, and its existence as a distinct narrative strand is indicated precisely by the discrepancy with Exodus 3 and 6.

With regard to the use of *ᵉlōhîm* the situation is a little more complicated, as *two* sources characterized by this term were postulated. The first is that represented by Exodus 3, whose author believed that the divine name was first revealed to Moses. He is called the 'Elohist' ('E') because in Genesis, prior to the revelation in Exodus 3, he generally refers to God by the generic Hebrew word for God, *ᵉlōhîm*. The second is that of the writer of Exodus 6 — considered to be a parallel account to Exodus 3 of an initial revelation of the divine name to Moses and not a sequel to it — who is known as the 'Priestly Writer' (P'). In Genesis, P generally refers to God as *ᵉlōhîm*, but his most distinctive appellation is El Shaddai (traditionally rendered 'God Almighty'), as specified in Exod. 6.3 and used at the beginning of Genesis 17 (the priestly account of God's covenant with Abraham), Gen. 28.3 (the priestly account of Jacob's departure to Aram) and Gen. 35.11; 48.3 (the priestly account of God's appearance to Jacob at Bethel). (The other two uses of El Shaddai in Genesis, 43.14 and 49.25, are less significant, and opinion has been divided as to whether or not they belong to P.)

The documentary hypothesis has been developed with reference to a large number of other factors. But insofar as it relates to pentateuchal narratives, the above factor of the terms used for God has been central. Thus one can find M. Noth and A. Weiser, two distinguished proponents of the documentary hypothesis, saying, 'Regardless of scholarly ingenuity, no one has offered a more plausible explanation of the usage of the divine names than the view that these were two originally independent narrative works, the 'Yahwist' and the 'Elohist', which were later combined' (Noth, *History of Pentateuchal Traditions*, p. 23), and 'Exod. 3 and 6 enables us to see that the use of different names for God is based on quite definite theories which point to different trends in the separate sources' (Weiser, *Introduction to the Old Testament*, p. 74).

Despite the consensus it has commanded, this approach to the text does create a number of difficulties of its own (see my *The Old Testament of the Old Testament*, ch. 2, for fuller discussion), of which perhaps the most serious is the question whether the writers of the Pentateuch, if they had supposed themselves to possess two fundamentally divergent accounts of a matter so important as the origin of the name of Israel's God, would have juxtaposed the discrepant sources in the way the hypothesis requires without making some resolution of the problem.

As already noted, the scholarly consensus around the documentary hypothesis has never been unanimous. A traditional and modern conservative alternative, persistently held by a minority of scholars, has been to argue that the name Yhwh was indeed known to the patriarchs prior to Moses, and that the point of Exodus 3 and 6 is not the giving of a new name but simply the giving of a new meaning and significance to an already familiar name. Thus there is no discrepancy of traditions. This argument, however, faces two major obstacles. One is the explicit statement of Exod. 6.3, 'I appeared to Abraham, to Isaac, and to Jacob as El Shaddai, and by my name Yhwh I was not known to them', which has to be forced to have a meaning other than the plain sense of the Hebrew. The other is the simple fact that the meaning which the divine name has in Genesis in no way differs from that which it has elsewhere.

This leaves us with one other possible resolution of the problem. This is to suppose that the Old Testament is indeed consistent in its contention that the name Yhwh was first revealed by God to Moses, and that all the uses of the name in Genesis simply indicate the retelling of the patriarchal stories from the context and perspective of Mosaic Yahwism. That is, the Genesis narrators stand within Israel whose God is Yhwh, but they take for granted that Israel's God is one and the same as the God of Israel's ancestors, the patriarchs, and so feel free to use the familiar name for Israel's God when telling the patriarchal stories. Although from a strictly historical perspective such usage involves anachronism, this kind of merging of perspectives is common practice among storytellers both in the ancient world and subsequently. The issue at stake, therefore, is not that of differing views as to the origin of the divine name, maintained by different sources. Rather it is essentially a theological issue, a combination of the particularist conviction that Yhwh has only revealed his name and commandments within Israel, with the universal conviction that Yhwh is the one true God and that he is therefore the God with whom Israel's ancestors had to do.

Why then the alternation between different terms for God? On my proposed view, the basic and original term for God in the patriarchal stories was *'elōhîm*. As a generic title for God, without the particularity implied by Yhwh, it is consistent with what we shall see to be the open and inclusive religious outlook of the patriarchal narratives generally (see Chapter 5). The name El Shaddai is a particular name, used on occasion in certain circumstances, whose precise significance is unclear, but which is generally connected with promises of blessing and descendants. El Shaddai is in fact one of a number of divine appellations compounded with El (e.g. El Elyon, Gen. 14.18, 19, 20, 22; El Elohe Israel, 33.20). As we know that the high God of the indigenous religion of Syria and Canaan in the second millennium BCE was called El (see the Ugaritic texts from Ras Shamra in N. Syria, conveniently available either in *ANET* or Winton Thomas, *Documents from Old Testament Times*), it again fits well with the inherently non-Yahwistic character of patriarchal religion. The name Yhwh is used in general because of the telling from a Yahwistic perspective, and so sometimes could be a term loosely interchangeable with *ʾelōhîm* for no particular reason. It is, however, notable that the name Yhwh is most used in the stories of Abraham, and it is precisely here that one finds the greatest other evidence for Yahwistic perspectives also. That is, it is apparent that it was the figure of Abraham that received most theological reflection and moulding from the Israelite narrators (as seen most clearly in Gen. 22), and that therefore the extensive use of Yhwh in the stories of Abraham is part of a much wider theological appropriation of the material.

If this is at all on the right lines, it suggests that the basic model of different sources may not be as such incorrect but may still not be the best way of conceptualizing the issue. Rather, the model of retelling from anew perspective may be much more helpful. Take, for example, the Joseph story (Gen. 37–50). Although this is a narrative conventionally divided between J, E and P, it is notable that the divine name Yhwh only occurs in three contexts. It appears in Gen. 49.18 in what looks to be a comment that has been added to the text. It appears in Gen. 38.7, 10 in two comments which draw an explicit moral lesson, in a story whose relationship to the surrounding Joseph story is in any case somewhat unclear. And it appears eight times in the narrator's interpretative comments at the beginning and end of the story of Joseph and Potiphar's wife in Genesis 39 (vv. 2, 3, 5, 21, 23), where it may naturally be seen as an explicit telling of this part of Joseph's story in terms of the purposes of Yhwh, thereby setting the context for all else that happens to Joseph in Egypt. Surely the best explanation of this phenomenon is not that of a distinct source using Yhwh, but rather of a narrator and/or editor retelling existing material and adding explicit reference to Yhwh in the process. It would also be in keeping with what we saw to be the case in Genesis 22, where the story of Abraham and Isaac has been much retold and has incorporated perspectives from its retellings.

Nor is this kind of proposal unprecedented in recent debate, for the main alternative to the documentary hypothesis has been R. Rendtorff's proposals in his *The Problem of the Process of Transmission in the Pentateuch*, which have been further developed by his pupil E. Blum in his *Die Komposition der Vätergeschichte*. Rendtorff argues that instead of thinking of sources which run as continuous threads through the Pentateuch (the originally independent and parallel histories of J, E and P), we should think of distinct traditions which originally existed in their own right and then were subsequently brought together and edited to establish links between them. Rendtorff's own specific proposals for seeing the divine promises as such a link are in my judgment somewhat tenuous, but his basic model has much to commend it (a persuasively modified version of Rendtorff's proposal is his 'The Paradigm is Changing'). If it is right to see the patriarchal narratives as a whole as a body of tradition appropriated and retold in a Yahwistic context, then similar processes may also have been at work within the individual patriarchal narratives, the stories of Abraham, Jacob and Joseph as originally told separately having been subsequently combined and retold.

A Test Case: The Patriarch in Danger through his Wife

Apart from the criterion of different terms for God as a clue to how the text of Genesis was written, the other criterion most appealed to in this context is that of 'doublets' in the text. M. Noth even puts this as the first of his criteria:

> Fundamentally only one of the usual criteria for the disunity of the old Pentateuchal tradition is really useful, though this one is quite adequate and allows a thoroughgoing literary analysis. I refer to the unquestionable fact, attested time and again throughout the tradition, of the *repeated occurrence* of the same narrative materials or narrative elements in *different versions*... The only possible explanation of the matter is that in the old Pentateuchal tradition several originally independent parallel strands of narrative were later connected with one another (*History of Pentateuchal Traditions*, pp. 21, 22).

One of the examples of this phenomenon most cited in this connection is the story of the endangering of the patriarch through his wife in Gen. 12.10–20 // 20.1–18 // 26.6–11, so it will be worth considering this in some detail.

A quick review of the three stories will show that they have a certain basic plot in common. Each time the patriarch travels south to alien territory and sojourns there; each time the patriarch fears death because of his wife; each time the patriarch resolves the problem by passing off his wife as his sister; each time the patriarch is found out by the foreign ruler, who upbraids him with the words 'What have you done to me/us?' How should this be understood? As the text stands, these are clearly consecutive episodes which show a strong sense of pattern and repetition within the patriarchal story. However, just as the understanding of the phenomenon of different terms for God was seen by Astruc as evidence for different underlying sources, so too with the phenomenon of doublets. The usual assumption that has been made is that one writer would not have repeated himself in the manner of the present text, and so the different forms of the story must derive from different sources. Moreover, the similarities between the different accounts show that in fact there is really only one story with which we are dealing. There was one original story which was told in a variety of ways in a variety of contexts, the differences of detail between the present versions being essentially an accident of the retelling process. The different pentateuchal sources each knew of the same story in a different form, and when the sources were combined by a redactor they were then made into successive, rather than parallel, episodes—either because the differences of detail led the redactor to suppose that the stories were in fact distinct, or because to make them sequential was the only way in which the redactor could preserve all the versions of the story without having to lose any.

The question which story should be ascribed to which source is then reasonably straightforward, at least for Genesis 12 and 20. Gen. 12.10-20 is considered to be the work of the Yahwist, partly because the story uses the name Yhwh (v. 17), and partly because the brevity with which the story is told, lacking elaboration or justification, is suggestive of its great antiquity. J. Skinner, for example, commented that the content of the story is 'treated with a frank realism which seems to take us down to the bed-rock of Hebrew folklore' (*Genesis*, pp. 247-48). Genesis 20, by contrast, is the work of the Elohist. The term *ʾelōhîm* is used throughout (apart from v. 18, which looks like a later explanatory gloss); Abraham is said to be a prophet, thus revealing the links of the Elohist with the prophetic movement in the northern kingdom; and the story throughout shows a much more developed moral and religious awareness than is the case in Genesis 12 and so is not only later but also most probably linked to the moral concerns of the prophetic tradition (note such words as 'righteous' [v. 4], 'integrity' [vv. 5, 6], 'sin' [vv. 6, 9], 'fearing' [vv. 8, 11]). Gen. 26.6-11 is the most difficult story to place, since there is no term for God, nor do any distinctive vocabulary or concepts occur in it. However, the use of Yhwh in the surrounding context (vv. 2, 12), together with the general narrative style, has inclined commentators to ascribe the story to J, although some have indicated their unease (it would require repetition within J, when one of the basic premises is that J would not have repeated things) by proposing that it may be a later version of, or addition to, J.

As to the original form that the story took, this can only be a matter of surmise. Although Genesis 12 is considered the oldest form of the stories as they now stand, it does not follow that it is necessarily the original. K. Koch compares the stories under eight headings and arrives at the following reconstruction:

> The original version will thus have run: Because of famine Isaac travelled from the desert in southern Palestine to the nearby Canaanite city of Gerar, to live there as 'sojourner', i.e. to keep within the pasturage rights on the ground belonging to the city. He told everyone that his wife was his sister so that his life would not be endangered by those who desired her. However, Rebekah's beauty could not pass unnoticed. The king of the city, Abimelech, took Rebekah into his harem, amply compensating Isaac. As a material sin was about to be committed, God struck the people of the palace with a mysterious illness. Through the medium of his gods, or a soothsayer, Abimelech recognised what had happened. Abimelech called Isaac to account: 'What is this that you have done to me?' He then restored him his wife and sent him away, loaded with gifts (*Growth of the Biblical Tradition*, p. 126).

What should one make of this? First, in general historical terms, there is clearly no difficulty in imagining the kind of process here proposed, which is both coherent and plausible as an account of how a story can develop and change. Secondly, one may always legitimately quibble at details of the proposed original version, which must necessarily be hypothetical. One major decision is that the story originally belonged to Isaac rather than Abraham, on the principle, noted above, that often in oral tradition figures change their importance, a principle whose application is necessarily controversial.

Thirdly, one should note some difficulty with the initial assumption that similar stories are really variants of one story from different sources on the grounds that one writer would not repeat himself in this way. For, of course, this is precisely what the hypothesis requires the redactor who put the sources together to have done. One might try to ease the problem by saying that in the original creative period of writing (J and E) such repetition would not have been permitted, but that by the time of the redactor there was less creativity and more sense of the need for reverential preservation of received tradition. Yet even this is of limited validity, partly because it seems an unfounded and romanticist notion to extol J and E as free and creative and to stigmatize the redactor as a pious collator, not least because there is little or no evidence that by the probable time of the redactor literary conventions had changed in any significant way, and partly because of the inconsistency that elsewhere the redactor is at times held to have exercised great freedom in his handling of the traditions before him.

Despite the fact that the proposed process is still not implausible, one should nonetheless ask whether it is a relevant consideration. It is important not to beg the question by assuming that one knows what kind of problem the text presents us with, when a decision here is in fact controversial. Is the interpretation of apparently puzzling factors in the text really best explained on the assumption of different sources? I have argued that this is probably not the case with differing terms for God, which should be understood rather in terms of story-telling technique, retelling old material in new categories. May this phenomenon of similar stories not also be explained similarly? On any reckoning, the fundamental question posed by the Old Testament text relates to the storytelling conventions of the ancient narrator. What conventions were taken for granted by the narrator? Obviously this can never be definitively answered, because all we have to go on is the text itself which offers no explanations. The goal of the scholar is a careful and sympathetic reading of the text that allows one to infer at least some of what the conventions embodied in the text may have been.

Why then should similar stories be told in proximity to each other in the course of the Genesis narrative? Instead of seeing this as a ques-tion of origins, it may be a question of creative storytelling. One way of putting this is to observe that whereas traditional source analysis emphasizes the similarities between the stories, seeing the differences as accidents of oral tradition, it may be the case that it is the differences that are really significant. Robert Alter has argued for the importance in ancient storytelling of 'type-scenes' in which a scenario familiar to both storyteller and audience is presented. Given the fami-liarity of the scenario, the interest lies each time in the particular way each story is told, or, in other words, in those elements of the story that are peculiar to it and which distinguish it from other versions. If this assumption is at all correct—and it too has obvious plausibility— then it is not a problem that a narrator should include similar stories in proximity to each other; rather it is to be expected. Indeed, we have already noted (Chapter 2) that Genesis 26 contains every story that is told of Isaac in his own right, and that each one is parallel to some-thing that is told of Abraham. It is misleading to single out 26.5-11 as though it presented particular problems, when almost everything in the chapter presents the same issue. Thus the clear propensity of the text for repeating material in slightly different form surely directs us in the first instance to a phenomenon of ancient Hebrew storytelling, and is only secondarily, if at all, indicative of the possibly diverse sources and origins of the material.

If then we consider the three stories as type scenes, a number of factors emerge. First, apart from the similarities noted above, there are certain further similarities. On the one hand, on the first two appearances of the type-scene the incident represents a threat to God's promise. The scene first appears just after the promise has initially been given (Gen. 12.1-3). Its second occurrence is when the promise has been finally affirmed for Sarah herself (Gen. 18.14) and when in fact Sarah must already be pregnant with Isaac. Thus on both occurrences there is a sense of human fear and weakness endangering yet not thwarting the divine purpose. On the other hand, each story portrays the patriarch, the recipient of God's promise and the agent of God's future blessing, in a morally ambiguous light. When each time the deceived king asks 'What is this you have done to me/us?' it is difficult not to feel that his moral indignation is justified. The mysterious nature of God's call is thus explored, particularly in Genesis 20, where Abimelech's initial question to God, 'Lord, will you slay an innocent (literally, righteous, *ṣaddîq*) people?', is closely similar to Abraham's own famous interaction with God (Gen. 18.23) — those whom God does not call may still have moral insights similar to those of the ones who are called.

As for the differences between the stories, 12.10-20 should probably be understood typologically, in a way analogous to Genesis 22, where Abraham is a type of obedience to Torah. For here an Exodus typology can easily be discerned. In time of famine in Canaan, Abraham goes down to Egypt, as do the sons of Jacob (cf. Gen. 42–46); there he prospers, as does Israel (cf. Exod. 1.7); Yhwh afflicts Pharaoh and his house with great plagues, as he does at the time of the Exodus (cf. Exod. 7–12); Abraham is subsequently sent out from Egypt, and departs for Canaan as Israel does (cf. Exod. 12.31; 13.4-5); and Abraham leaves with great wealth and possessions, as does Israel (cf. Exod. 12.35, 38).

Genesis 20, by contrast, seems to explore the ambivalent relationship between Abraham, representing Israel, and Abimelech, representing upright (*ṣaddîq*) gentiles. As already noted, Abimelech has a moral insight similar to that of Abraham himself. Nonetheless, the election and responsibility of Abraham is maintained, particularly in v. 7, which may well be a picture of the relationship between Israel and the nations: Israel has the privilege and responsibility of a special relationship with God, and however much this is compromised by doubtful behaviour, the importance of praying for the life and wellbeing of others remains.

Gen. 26.6-11 is again different. First, although the episode appears after a renewed divine promise of multiplying Isaac's descendants, this time the promise is not imperilled, because Jacob and Esau have already been born. This time the reader may relax and smile — the stakes are lowered. Secondly, Rebekah is never taken into a harem. All that happens is told in a wordplay when Abimelech sees Isaac fondling (*yiṣḥāq mᵉṣaḥēq*) Rebekah. Neither of the other stories say anything about what happens to the wife, and now when something does happen it is a bit of conjugal love-play.

Thus the first type-scene depicts Israel's triumph over Egypt, the second depicts a more ambiguous and yet still defined relationship between Israel and gentile neighbours, and the third is a relaxed and humorous variation on the theme.

In conclusion, it may be said that the major problem facing discussions about the composition of Genesis 12–50 is a conceptual one. Within what categories should the data of the text be interpreted? Although the move, epitomized by Astruc, of interpreting data in terms of underlying sources has been profoundly influential, it is not in fact a good starting-point, because it begs the question. The first question that must be asked is about the storytelling conventions and techniques of the Genesis writers, and only when that has been established with as much confidence as is possible can one move on to ask about the evidence the text provides for the history of its composition. And although it may well be the case that different sources are combined in Genesis, I have suggested that the primary model for understanding the compositional processes should be that of the retelling and remoulding of old stories in the light of new perspectives. It is only as one focuses first on the 'how' of biblical storytelling that one may be able to answer questions about the 'when', 'where' and 'by whom'.

Chapter Five

A HISTORICAL PROBE

In the discussion thus far the assumption has been made that the patriarchal narratives in general represent genuinely ancient, pre-Israelite, material which has been retold from the perspective of Mosaic Yahwism. This assumption is itself controversial, however, and it will therefore be appropriate to explore and justify it in this chapter.

One well-known problem which can easily be accommodated on the model of later retelling is that of anachronisms. For example, it has often been argued that in the early second millennium the camel was not yet domesticated (it is an argument from silence, since the camel is not mentioned or depicted where it might be expected, but reasonably cogent nonetheless), and yet the patriarchs are depicted with camels (e.g. Gen. 12.16; 24.10-67). Again, the Philistines are reckoned not to have arrived in Palestine until the end of the second millennium, yet they are depicted as contemporary with Abraham and Isaac (Gen. 20.32; 26.14-18). Assuming, for the sake of argument, that it is correct that these biblical references are anachronistic, what do they show? They need show no more than that the tellers of the patriarchal stories used categories for depicting the patriarchs that were familiar and contemporary to themselves, the storytellers (rather as, say, Rembrandt depicts the patriarchs in the costume and surroundings of the seventeenth century). This is the same phenomenon as that for which I have argued with regard to the use of the divine name Yhwh in Genesis 12–50. Although this can be problematic for the modern historical concern that wants to distinguish different historical periods, the merging of historical horizons in traditional storytelling is a readily comprehensible process and is none the worse for representing a practice supposedly uncharacteristic of the modern West.

The whole question of the historical age of the patriarchal world, however, needs to be pressed more closely. For we saw that a story such as ch. 22 stands at such a remove from a second millennium context that one can only be historically agnostic with regard to it. And many scholars are not just agnostic but are thoroughly dismissive about the likelihood of there being any material of genuine antiquity (i.e. the first half of the second millennium) represented in the patriarchal stories. This, therefore, is the issue that must be addressed.

Probably the most obvious argument for the ancient and pre-Yahwistic character of the patriarchal traditions is the number of religious practices to which they refer which are at variance with normative Mosaic Yahwism, especially as this is set out in Deuteronomy. For example, Abraham plants a tree in Beersheba at a place where he worships God (Gen. 21.33), and also builds altars in two places where some special tree already exists (Gen. 12.6-7; 13.18). Yet the law of Deut. 16.21 states, 'You shall not plant any tree as an Asherah beside the altar of Yhwh your God which you shall make'. Now of course none of the Genesis passages states that the tree which Abraham planted or beside which he built an altar was an 'Asherah' (a sacred tree or pole, consistently associated in the Old Testament with Canaanite religious practice which is prohibited for Israel, e.g., Judg. 6.25-30; 1 Kgs 14.23; 2 Kgs 18.3-4); nonetheless, it is difficult not to feel that even so there is an obvious affinity between Abraham's practice and that prohibited by Deuteronomy. How then is it that Abraham, the model for Israel's faith, can carry out religious practices forbidden to Israel, yet with no adverse comment from the narrator? The obvious answer would appear to be that the writer takes seriously Abraham's context prior to the giving of Torah to Israel, in which the prohibitions of Deuteronomy simply do not apply because they were not yet given. Similar considerations would apply (a) to the pillar which Jacob sets up at Bethel (Gen. 28.18-22; 35.14-15), against which one could set the prohibition of Deut. 16.22, 'And you shall not set up a pillar, which Yhwh your God hates'; or (b) to the fact that Jacob has two wives, Leah and Rachel, and gives preference to the children of his favourite Rachel over the firstborn children of Leah despite the fact that Deut. 21.15-17 explicitly forbids precisely such conduct.

This type of argument was given a completely different slant by Wellhausen in his famous *Prolegomena to the History of Ancient Israel*. Wellhausen's argument is subtle and wide-ranging, but the essential points for our concerns can be stated briefly. Although Wellhausen agreed that much of the religious practice of the patriarchs is at odds with what is prescribed in pentateuchal laws (especially Deuteronomy), he argued that such divergence was not restricted to the patriarchal narratives, but was also characteristic of the narratives in Joshua–2 Kings. For example, Exodus, Leviticus and Numbers envisage the ark as set in the holy of holies where only the high priest may enter once a year (Lev. 16). Yet Samuel, as a young acolyte in the temple at Shiloh, actually sleeps in the place where the ark is (1 Sam. 3.3). Thus the 'abnormalities' of patriarchal religion must be seen as characteristic of early Israelite religion generally.

A major change in Israelite religion came about with Josiah's reform in 621 BCE (2 Kgs 22–23) with its attempt to centralize the worship of Yhwh in Jerusalem. This was also the period to which Wellhausen ascribed the writing of Deuteronomy; only thereafter were the various practices of earlier religion restricted and proscribed. The result of all this is that patriarchal religious practice is indeed as it is because Torah had not yet been given to prohibit it—but this is simply characteristic of all Israelite religion prior to Josiah's reform. Thus it is not Moses and the origins of Israel that mark the real difference between patriarchal and Mosaic religion, but rather Josiah's reform is the real watershed in Israelite history. Prior to Josiah's reform all Israelite religion was inherently pluralistic and akin to Canaanite religion; after Josiah's reform there began to develop a host of norms to regulate and distinguish Israel's religion (culminating in the Priestly legislation—all the laws of Leviticus and Numbers, and most of the laws of Exodus—of the exilic and postexilic period in the late sixth century). Thus the 'abnormal' features of patriarchal religion are not evidence for anything other than an origin prior to Josiah's reform. Since, moreover, Wellhausen considered that all the content of the patriarchal narratives portrayed conditions which existed in their time of writing, which were anachronistically retrojected to a much earlier pre-Israelite period, and that this time of writing was predominantly the period of prophecy in the eighth and seventh centuries (the exception being the later Priestly material), so he considered that there was nothing in the patriarchal narratives that was genuinely of the antiquity which the Pentateuch as it now stands appears to claim for it.

Wellhausen's views about the patriarchal narratives have been influential but have not as such given rise to a scholarly consensus, mainly because of a cogent alternative view that was put forward by A. Alt in his essay, 'The God of the Fathers'. The basic point on which Alt differed from Wellhausen was the latter's contention that the content of the patriarchal stories simply reflected the period of its written composition, for Alt believed that a long period of oral transmission underlay the written text and had preserved material that genuinely was of great, and pre-Israelite, antiquity. The question, of course, is how one can still discern an underlying oral process, and Alt appealed primarily to two factors; first, a careful analysis of differences and anomalies within the written text, which should disclose different levels within it, and secondly a comparison with an independently attested religious phenomenon—Nabatean religion in the early centuries CE—which Alt believed to be comparable to patriarchal religion. What, according to Alt, was attested in Nabatean inscriptions, and could also be seen in the patriarchal narratives, was a pattern of religion in which an individual had a personal deity who was the patron of his clan. The essence of the individual's relation with his deity would centre on the two things that a person needed most in a nomadic context outside settled civilization—first, children to continue the clan, and, secondly, land for the clan to settle in. Since the promise of son and land are both central to the story of Abraham, and since, in particular, they are present in the story of the covenant in Genesis 15, a story with elements 'which give the impression of great antiquity' (p. 65), Alt concluded that here we have genuinely ancient, pre-Israelite, material which was later adopted by Israel into its Yahwistic faith. Although Alt's wide-ranging proposals have been modified in various details by subsequent scholarship, his basic thesis has commanded widespread agreement and has formed the basis of most subsequent accounts of patriarchal religion until very recently.

One important recent development of Alt's work has been made by C. Westermann in his great *Genesis* commentary. Westermann has focused on those elements of patriarchal religion that relate particularly to the familial lifestyle of the patriarchs and the ways in which these differ from the corporate cultic life and worship of Israel. So, for example, he comments that

> The decisive difference between the large-scale cult [viz. of Israel] and that of the patriarchs is that the latter does not construct a domain separated from and independent of ordinary life, but is integrated fully into the life-styles of the small wandering group... Cultic action takes place as part of the life of the group, and arises therefrom; it takes place as required, not because of some cultic prescription (*Genesis 12–36*, pp. 110-11).

Westermann shows how, for example, the places and ways in which the patriarchs worship and offer sacrifice easily fit this basic description.

Once Alt had established the likelihood of the antiquity of at least the core of the patriarchal traditions in terms of their religious practices, further evidence was adduced by W.F. Albright and various other American scholars influenced by him. Here the main concern was to compare the names and customs presented or presupposed in the patriarchal stories with those in texts from elsewhere in the ancient Near East in the second millennium BCE, and to argue that the basic similarity of the patriarchal with the extrabiblical material showed that the world portrayed in the patriarchal narratives is genuinely the world of the second millennium. In particular, Mesopotamian texts from Nuzi (fifteenth century BCE) have legal material on marriage, adoption and inheritance which offers parallels to patriarchal material. For example, a Nuzi text specifies that a wife, if childless, should provide her husband with a substitute for herself— just as Sarah gave Hagar to Abraham (Gen. 16.1-4). A classic presentation of this approach to the patriarchal stories is that of John Bright in his *History of Israel*. In the third edition of this work (1980), even after taking into account the criticisms of this whole approach (see below), Bright concludes his discussion, 'One's conviction that the patriarchal narratives authentically reflect social customs at home in the second millennium is strengthened' (p. 80).

Although the above position, in stronger or weaker formulations, could be said to have represented a scholarly consensus until quite recently, it does so no longer. The current scholarly mood is not in favour of the antiquity of the patriarchal traditions. Several works in particular have been influential in this regard. First, J. Van Seters, in his *Abraham in History and Tradition* (and, more recently, his *Prologue to History*), has attempted to revive what is essentially the position of Wellhausen. He has criticized the view that one can penetrate behind the Genesis text to older, oral traditions, and has argued that the text reflects the period in which it was written, which, in the case of Abraham, he believes to be the exile in the sixth century. He argues, for example, that 'Ur of the Chaldeans', from which Abraham came (Gen. 11.31; 15.7) would not have been so called before the rise to power of the Chaldeans, that is, Babylonians, in the late seventh century. This seems a valid point, since elsewhere in the Old Testament the Chaldeans are first mentioned in late seventh-century texts, for example, Hab. 1.6; Jer. 21.4, 9 (although Van Seters does not consider whether this might not be the updating or contemporizing in the sixth century of an older tradition which originally referred just to Ur or qualified it by some other designation of its inhabitants). And he further argues that the tradition of Abraham leaving Ur of the Chaldees, that is, Babylonia, for Canaan is a coded way of referring to Israel's return from exile in Babylonia to Canaan—a point which depends on the validity of the assumption that the content of the story simply reflects and encodes the concerns of its tellers; although of course an older tradition to this effect would certainly have gained new significance in the exilic period. With regard to the religious practices of the patriarchs, Van Seters argued in a separate article that these simply show the pluralism of Israelite religion prior to Josiah's reform. Although few have been persuaded by Van Seters' own positive proposals, the acuteness with which he has criticized the consensus position has ensured a wide discussion of his views.

A second major contribution is T.L. Thompson's *The Historicity of the Patriarchal Narratives*, which is a critique of the whole approach pioneered and popularized by Albright (Albright is also contextualized and criticized in Whitelam, *Invention of Ancient Israel* and Long, *Planting and Reaping Albright*). Thompson advances two main arguments. First, many of the features of the patriarchal stories which are argued to have second millennium parallels can be found quite as easily to have parallels in the first millennium, and are therefore no proof of antiquity. Secondly, the parallels are much too random, in that they lack chronological precision. If one parallel is from the eighteenth century, another from the fifteenth, and another from the thirteenth, then unless one is willing to discard some of the parallels it is impossible to pin the patriarchal content to a particular period of history, and without some kind of recognizable chronology the material cannot be considered as history.

There are indeed many telling points in Thompson's critique, though it is only decisive against rather simplistic historical claims (which the Albright school on the whole avoided). For if one accepts that the patriarchal traditions have been constantly told and retold, and have incorporated many elements from their retelling, then one would expect the historical sharpness of the traditions to have become more or less blurred. Yet such blurring in no way entails that the origins of the content may not be genuinely ancient. The problem is partly that the nature of the tradition is inherently problematic for the modern historian, and partly that in any case we know so little about the second millennium BC that any historical reconstruction relative to that period must be hypothetical and tentative.

A third major work is the recent German monograph of M. Köckert, *Vätergott und Väterverheissungen*. This is a learned and acute critique of Alt's 'God of the Fathers' and of the whole scholarly consensus (with its various modifications) built upon it. There are perhaps two main elements to Köckert's argument. First, he argues that the patriarchal texts are relatively late (he inclines towards dates in the seventh and sixth centuries) and stand at too great a remove from any supposed patriarchal period. He is sceptical about supposed underlying oral tradition, and emphasizes the primacy of studying the literary processes embodied in the texts as we have them (and it should be noted also that the recent study of P. Kirkpatrick, *The Old Testament and Folklore Study*, denies that oral tradition, if such there was in the patriarchal stories, could have preserved material in recognizable form for even two centuries). Secondly, he argues that many of the supposedly distinctive patriarchal practices are not distinctive at all, but can easily be paralleled from texts of the seventh and sixth centuries. Insofar as there is a distinctive pattern of family-centred religion, this simply shows patterns of family piety that existed within Israel outside the sphere of the official, public cult (i.e. patterns of religion either prior to, or untouched by, Josiah's reform). Thus, with some important modifications, we have a reinstatement of the kind of view of patriarchal religion advocated by Wellhausen.

Although there is much of value in the details of Köckert's analysis, it still leaves important questions unanswered. First, the crucial texts of Exodus 3 and 6, which show Israel's own remarkable awareness of a pre-Yahwistic stage of religion, and which constituted Alt's starting point, receive no discussion by Köckert (or Van Seters or Thompson). Secondly, Köckert gives insufficient attention to basic methodological questions about establishing the dates of texts and their contents. If there are apparent similarities between texts X and Y, this can be explained in a number of ways: X may have influenced Y, Y may have influenced X, both X and Y may have been influenced by Z, the similarities may be accidental, or the similarities may be not be genuine similarities at all. When Köckert finds apparent similarities between the content of patriarchal stories and that of various seventh- and sixth-century texts, he rather consistently assumes that the former must be influenced by the latter, or at best be contemporary with it. Yet until all other ways of understanding the relationship have been explored, the kind of conclusion that Köckert draws cannot be considered well founded.

Perhaps what Van Seters, Thompson and Köckert most clearly show is the difficulty of historical probes into the patriarchal traditions. It becomes extremely difficult, probably impossible, to prove the antiquity of the content of the traditions because of the paucity of evidence and the difficulty of establishing controls. If the patriarchal traditions generally are genuinely ancient but have been subject to retelling and the incorporation of later perspectives—that is, the stories have become more or less legendary (as defined in Chapter 3 above)—then one would expect them to show similarities to texts which had only originated in later periods. In the last resort, it all seems to depend upon one's educated judgment as to the kind of material that the patriarchal stories should be understood to be (a point well illustrated by W. McKane's *Studies in the Patriarchal Narratives*). As noted above, however, the general scholarly mood at present has moved against the view of the patriarchal stories as legends of genuinely ancient origin, and prefers to see them as largely anachronistic retrojections of writers in the monarchical period, or even later. If one examines one recent textbook history of Israel, J.M. Miller and J.H. Hayes, *A History of Ancient Israel and Judah*, one finds no account of the patriarchal period at all, but only a methodological discussion of the problems of using the patriarchal material as a historical source, with a final reluctance to use it at all.

It can hardly be said that the kind of reconstruction offered by Bright has been refuted in detail, and one's basic approach to the question does seem to be largely a matter of mood. All scholars are aware of the historical difficulties posed by the patriarchal texts; it is just that the Albright–Bright tradition of scholars was confident that at least some of the difficulties could be overcome, while more recent scholars, looking at the same evidence, feel the difficulties to be overwhelming.

A Fresh Approach to the Evidence of Patriarchal Religion

There may be a way forward if, rather than addressing the historical questions about patriarchal religion in their familiar form, one focuses on the question whether or not Israel had a consistent tradition about the nature of patriarchal religion consonant with the belief that the patriarchal period was a time when the name Yhwh was not known, a tradition which was maintained by the writers of the patriarchal stories at whatever various historical periods they wrote (see my *The Old Testament of the Old Testament*, ch. 3). Instead of trying to single out possibly ancient elements (especially name of deity, divine promises), as has been customary since Alt, the aim would be rather to depict a consistent religious ethos which was other than that of Yahwism. A detailed study of the material in this way shows at least seven important and interrelated aspects of patriarchal religion (on which see most recently, Pagolu, *Religion of the Patriarchs*).

First, patriarchal monotheism is open and inclusive. Everyone, including Abimelech of Gerar and Pharaoh in Egypt (Gen. 20, 41), relates to one and the same God, and the notion of a plurality of gods, and the need to choose between them, such as is implied by 'You shall have no other gods before me' (Exod. 20.3), is almost entirely lacking.

Secondly, there is no general antagonism between the patriarchs and the religious practices of the natives of Canaan in the kind of way that frequently recurs in the life of Israel. When Abraham imagines that the inhabitants of Gerar would have no fear of God (20.11), the story explicitly rebuts his assumption (20.4-6). Moreover, although Isaac and Jacob seek wives from Aram rather than Canaan, the reason for this (24.1-9; 27.46–28.9) is never that Canaanite wives would cause them to be religiously unfaithful, as Israel is warned elsewhere (e.g. Exod. 34.11-16).

Thirdly, patriarchal cultic practice is different from that prescribed for Mosaic Yahwism. We have noted earlier the issue of trees and pillars, and one may note also the lack of any sense of prescribed places of worship. There is no hint of the patriarchs observing the sabbath or food laws (which came to the fore at the exile), and even though Abraham is commanded to circumcise his family (Gen. 17), the fact that it is Ishmael whose circumcision is primarily narrated means that circumcision does not carry the significance of exclusive identity that it came to have later.

Fourthly, patriarchal religion is unmediated in that it lacks both prophet and priest. The patriarchs never speak or act on God's behalf in the way that Moses does, nor are they thus spoken to by others; and the patriarchs offer their own sacrifices, without a priest to do it for them. Admittedly, on one occasion Abraham is called a prophet (*nābî'*, 20.7), but this is because he is a man who prays for others, as prophets should (e.g. 1 Sam. 12.19, 23), not because he speaks on God's behalf in characteristic prophetic style; and prayer for others is not intrinsically linked to prophecy.

Fifthly, the patriarchs live in Canaan as sojourners, that is, temporary residents dependent on others (*gērîm*; e.g. 17.8; 26.3), with no sense that the land really belongs to them or that they ought to fight for it, as is characteristic of Israel. The patriarchs generally maintain a peaceful existence, and when they want land of their own they buy it from its legitimate owners, the Canaanites (23; 33.19).

Sixthly, there is a general lack of moral emphasis in patriarchal religion, which is consistent with its context prior to Sinai and Torah. Promises of blessing are given, without either stipulations of moral obedience or warnings of judgment for disobedience attached to them. The main exception to this is in the stories of Abraham, where the greater moral emphasis (e.g. 17.1; 18.19; 22.12; 26.5) is probably part of the larger appropriation of these stories by Yahwism, with consequent embodiment of Yahwistic emphases (as argued above).

Seventhly, and finally, the generally open, inclusive and unaggressive nature of patriarchal religion is well summed up by its lack of holiness. The language of holiness in the Old Testament is closely connected to the revelation of God as Yhwh to Moses and Israel. There is no significant use of the language of holiness anywhere in Genesis 12–50; but as soon as God reveals himself to Moses as Yhwh, then for the first time holiness becomes an issue (Exod. 3.5). Although Israel is to be a holy nation set apart for the service of a holy God (Exod. 19)—and with this come all the things that divide Israel from other nations—there is no sense of this in the patriarchal narratives, and that is why their fundamental ethos is distinctive.

What should the historian make of this? A number of points may be made. First, it should be clear that all the above seven points are inter-related and give a recognizable picture of a distinctive religious ethos. Secondly, the ethos of patriarchal religion is clearly other than that of Mosaic Yahwism, certainly as it is presented in the Pentateuch from Exodus to Deuteronomy. Thirdly, it is highly unlikely that such a reli-gious ethos should have been simply invented, least of all by someone who stood within the context of Mosaic Yahwism. If, fourthly, patri-archal religion corresponds to some kind of historical reality, then presumably this is either some form of a genuinely ancient, pre-Yah-wistic religion or something that was an 'unorthodox' strand within Yahwistic religion (e.g. prior to Josiah's reform). The difficulty with the latter suggestion is precisely the complete lack of that holiness and exclusiveness which is one of the most fundamental characteristics of Yahwism. It is difficult to imagine any form of Yahwism that did not in some way share these characteristics. The classic move made by Wellhausen and more recent scholars like Van Seters and Köckert to assimilate 'unorthodox' patriarchal religion to 'unorthodox' Yahwism prior to, or outside the context of, Josiah's reform, and simply to see different manifestations of one and the same phenomenon overlooks this one fundamental point. However much religious practice in Joshua–2 Kings is at variance with the prescriptions of pentateuchal law, the basic sense of the religion as committed to Yhwh as a holy God is consistent.

In conclusion, therefore, it is probably impossible to prove anything about the historicity of the patriarchal period and patriarchal religion because of the paucity of evidence and controls. This does not mean, however, that a good case cannot be made for supposing that the material is, in its origins, genuinely ancient; it is just that a good case will also be able to be made for the opposite point of view, and no doubt for the next few years it is this that will particularly feature in the literature.

Chapter Six

AN INVITATION TO THE IMAGINATION

It was noted in the first chapter that one of the striking features of recent Old Testament study has been a widespread move from reading the text as history to reading it as literature. One of the characteristics of literary approaches is that they put different questions to the text from those put by the historian. For example, there is much greater attention to the patterns and structures of words, and a concern with what the text as text may mean which is not necessarily identical with the meaning that its writer intended. One of the pioneering works in this regard was J.P. Fokkelman, *Narrative Art in Genesis* (1975), the recent reissue of which (1991) presumably attests its continuing significance. A work which studies the disposition of key words in the text is A. Abela, *The Themes of the Abraham Narrative*. And L.A. Turner (*Announcements of Plot in Genesis*) offers some novel readings of the text by approaching it as a 'first-time reader', that is, by excluding from the interpretation all knowledge of developments subsequent to the point in the story under consideration (although this seems a doubtful method in the light of my fundamental point that the patriarchal stories are told from, and presuppose, the context of Israel that is subsequent to them).

There is also in many such literary works a greater openness to a use of the imagination (in other than historical ways) in interpreting the text. Some of the most imaginatively powerful stories, such as Jacob's wrestling at the ford of Jabbok, have attracted particular attention. For example, a famous structuralist reading of this story is R. Barthes, 'The Struggle with the Angel'.

Another characteristic of recent study, less widespread but significant nonetheless, has been a renewed interest in the history of interpretation—which generally means a study of pre-modern commentators, who read the text without the historically minded understanding that has generally characterized biblical study for the last two hundred years. For an example of a detailed study of particular texts, W.T. Miller, *Mysterious Encounters at Mamre and Jabbok*, on the early Jewish and Christian interpretations of Genesis 18 and 32, is full of interesting material.

There has always been some interest in these pre-modern commentators, simply because they constitute part of the history of the discipline. Moreover, for understanding the meaning of difficult Hebrew words and expressions there is a wealth of useful material in mediaeval Jewish commentators, many of whose proposals have been arrived at independently by modern scholars, often unaware of their predecessors. Beyond purely linguistic matters there is much else of interest in pre-modern commentators, although sometimes they have been considered significant primarily insofar as they anticipated something of modern historical insights rather than as being interesting in their own right.

The resurgence of interest in these commentators has not generally been connected explicitly with literary approaches to the text, although sometimes the link is made, as in C. Allen's recent feminist reading of Jacob's deception of Isaac in Genesis 27, 'On Me be the Curse, My Son!' Nonetheless, whether or not the links are made explicit, there is much that is common to the two approaches. For as soon as one ceases to ask the historical questions, and becomes interested in the patterns of the words and their imaginative implications, one may not be doing anything very different from what was done by many pre-modern commentators. It will be appropriate, therefore, in this final chapter to take a few examples from the history of interpretation and to seek to understand how they read the text. This is a study that has both historical and hermeneutical interest.

We shall take examples relating to Genesis 22, since we have already seen how the text may be read from a historically informed perspective, and it will be useful to compare this approach with other readings of the text. Moreover, within the history of Jewish thought and practice the influence of Genesis 22 (which is known as the Akedah, i.e., the Binding [of Isaac]) has been enormous — it has been one of Judaism's key texts, and its significance can hardly be overrated. S. Spiegel (*The Last Trial*) provides a stimulating introduction to the use of Genesis 22 within Judaism, and the recent article of G. Abramson, 'The Reinterpretation of the Akedah in Modern Hebrew Poetry', attests the continuing engagement (albeit often negative and hostile) with Genesis 22 in modern Israel. We shall therefore look first at some examples of Jewish interpretation and only secondarily turn to consider some examples of Christian interpretation.

Jewish Interpretations

1. *The Book of Jubilees*
The *Book of Jubilees* is the oldest extant interpretation of the whole
book of Genesis. It is difficult to date precisely, but is probably to be
dated about 150 BCE. The book is a retelling of the story of Genesis
and, much more briefly, of the first half of Exodus until Israel arrives
at Mt Sinai to receive the gift of Torah. The story is retold with considerable freedom—when compared with the biblical text—so as to
incorporate the perspectives of its teller. Overall, the most striking
characteristic is the desire to show that Torah is of eternal validity and
so was observed by the patriarchs even before Israel came to Sinai.
Thus the distinctiveness of the patriarchal period and religion largely
disappears as the material is conformed to the patterns of Torah. For a
recent study of this whole topic, see J.C. Endres, *Biblical Interpretation
in the Book of Jubilees*.

In the retelling of Genesis 22 there are a number of small differences
from the biblical text, and two major differences, one at the beginning
and one at the end. It was noted above that there are certain similarities between Genesis 22 and the testing of Job in Job 1–2. These
were already appreciated by the writer of *Jubilees*, who expands the
brief reference to testing in 22.1 with the more fully developed scenario of Job 1. That is, he introduces the figure of Satan, as the cynic
who doubts the genuineness of Abraham's faith, with the result that
the test is seen as a demonstration of that genuineness:

> And Prince Mastema [i.e. Satan] came and he said before God, 'Behold,
> Abraham loves Isaac, his son. And he is more pleased with him than
> everything. Tell him to offer him (as) a burnt offering upon the altar.
> And you will see whether he will do this thing. And you will know
> whether he is faithful in everything in which you test him' (*Jub.* 17.16;
> *OTP*, p. 90).

At the climactic moment when God stops Abraham from carrying out
the sacrifice and pronounces his assurance about Abraham's fear of
God, the text correspondingly inserts the words, 'And Prince Mastema
was shamed' (*Jub.* 18.12). This reading of Genesis 22 in the light of Job
1 is a not unnatural imaginative way of trying to understand the text.

The second major addition to the biblical text is at the end, where
reference to one of Israel's festivals is introduced. After Abraham
returns to Beersheba, we read:

> And he observed this festival every year (for) seven days with rejoicing.
> And he named it 'the feast of the LORD' according to the seven days
> during which he went and returned in peace. And thus it is ordained

and written in the heavenly tablets concerning Israel and his seed to
observe this festival seven days with festal joy (*Jub.* 18.18-19).

The identity of this festival is indicated by a temporal reference at
the outset of the story—'in the first month...on the twelfth of that
month' (*Jub.* 17.15), which, allowing for the fact that Abraham arrived
at the place of sacrifice on the third day, means that the story took
place on the fourteenth day of the first month, that is, the day of Passover, which precedes the seven days of unleavened bread (Exod. 12.1-
20, esp. vv. 6, 18). This exemplifies the general point made above,
about the ascription of what is characteristic of Israel already to the
patriarchs. As we have seen that the biblical text itself does this in
subtle fashion, by making Abraham a model for Torah obedience, the
writer of *Jubilees*, although less subtle than the biblical writer, is doing
something perfectly natural for someone operating within a Jewish
context that highly esteems obedience to Torah. In hermeneutical
terms, this is analogous to the common Christian practice of imaginatively assimilating the stories of the Old Testament to the perspectives and assumptions of Christian theology.

2. *The Commentary of Rashi*

By general consent, the greatest of the mediaeval Jewish commentators was Rashi (an acronym for Rabbi Solomon ben Isaac [in
Hebrew, Rabbi Shlomo Yitzhaki]), who lived and worked in France in
the eleventh century. He wrote commentaries not only on the Bible
but also on the Talmud. Rashi's great strength was that he knew and
made use of the great wealth of traditional rabbinic biblical interpretation and at the same time had a sharp eye for the literal and
grammatical meaning of the text. (A useful recent introduction to his
life and work is Pearl, *Rashi*).

Some of Rashi's comments on Genesis 22 are straightforwardly
matter-of-fact. He comments on the reference to 'the land of Moriah'
in v. 2 by noting that this is Jerusalem and making a cross-reference to
the one other mention of Moriah in Scripture, 2 Chron. 3.1, where the
identification of Moriah with Jerusalem is explicitly made. Again,
when Abraham cuts the wood for the burnt offering (v. 3), Rashi notes
that the word for 'cut' in the accompanying targum is also used in
2 Sam. 19.18. For the most part, however, Rashi reads the text imaginatively in the light of general moral and religious concerns.

Rashi's comment on the opening words of Genesis 22 is concerned
to illuminate the concept of testing and will be readily understandable
in the light of the treatment in *Jubilees*—although he is in fact referring
to other texts—and he also gives an additional reason why people

took the text in the way they did. For the Hebrew word *dābār*, usually here rendered 'thing' (e.g. 'After these things...') can also mean 'word' (e.g. 'After these words...'). This then raises the question, Which words? So Rashi comments:

> Some of our Rabbis say [that it means] after the words of Satan who denounced Abraham saying, 'Of all the banquets which Abraham prepared not a single bullock nor a single ram did he bring as a sacrifice to You'. God replied to him, 'Does he do anything at all except for his son's sake? Yet if I were to bid him, 'Sacrifice him to Me', he would not refuse'. Others say [that it means] 'after the words of Ishmael' who boasted to Isaac that he had been circumcised when he was thirteen years old without resisting. Isaac replied to him, 'You think to intimidate me by [mentioning the loss of] one part of the body! If the Holy One, blessed be He, were to tell me, 'Sacrifice yourself to Me' I would not refuse' (translation from Silbermann [ed.], *Pentateuch with Rashi's Commentary: Genesis*, p. 93. Words in square brackets are not in the text but are added to explicate Rashi's concise style of writing).

In v. 2 Rashi notes that Isaac is referred to at some length—'Take your son, your only son, whom you love, Isaac'. Why should the terms be piled up in this way, especially when one assumes that no word in the Torah is ever wasted? So Rashi imagines a conversation between God and Abraham and comments as follows:

> Abraham said [to God], 'I have two sons'. He answered him, 'Thine only son'. Abraham said, 'This one is the only son of his mother and the other is the only son of his mother'. God then said, 'the one whom thou lovest'. Abraham replied, 'I love both of them'. Whereupon God said 'even Isaac'. Why did He not disclose this to him at the very first? So as not to confuse him suddenly lest his mind become distracted and bewildered [and in his confused state he would involuntarily consent, when there would have been no merit in his sacrifice], and so that he might more highly value God's command and that God might reward him for [the increasing sacrifice demanded by obedience to] each and every expression [used here].

One can see that Rashi enters into the world of the text with full imaginative seriousness, and is also seeking to understand developments in such a way that they have paradigmatic moral value.

Other examples of Rashi's close attention to the precise wording are frequent. Given that God intended only to test Abraham and did not want the actual death of Isaac, Rashi notes that the word in v. 2 *wᵉhaᵃlēhû*, traditionally rendered 'offer [as burnt offering]' may be understood differently, since its literal meaning is 'bring him up/ cause him to ascend', and the regular word for 'slaughter/slay [a sacrificial victim]' (*šāḥaṭ*) is not used. So Rashi comments:

He did not say, 'Slay him', because the Holy One, blessed be He, did not
desire that he should slay him, but he told him to bring him up to the
mountain to prepare him as a burnt offering. So when he had taken him
up, God said to him, 'Bring him down'.

Although one may reasonably observe that this is implausible in
terms of normal Hebrew idiom—after all, the same phrase used of
Isaac in v. 2 is used to describe what actually happened to the ram in
v. 13—Rashi's concern is to ask what the text can mean if one is
rereading it and looking for possible hints of the eventual denoue-
ment. Just the same is Rashi's comment on Abraham's words to his
young men in v. 5, 'We will return to you', where he sees significance
in the plural verb and comments: 'He prophesied that they would
both return'; which, incidentally, appears to be the same reading of
the text as in the New Testament, where the plural verb would be the
only textual basis for the comment of the writer to the Hebrews that
Abraham 'considered that God was able to raise even from the dead'
(Heb. 11.19).

Generally speaking, the issue raised by this kind of 'forced' reading
of the text concerns the limits to which one may make the meaning of
the text as text different from the meaning intended by its author (on
the difference between author hermeneutics and text hermeneutics
see Alonso Schökel, *Manual of Hermeneutics*). In general terms, the
issue is similar to that raised by much traditional Christian reading of
Hebrew Scripture as the Old Testament, where the concern is not
necessarily to ask 'What did this originally mean?', but rather 'What
does it now mean when it is read in the light of Christ?' The decision
whether or not to read a text in the light of its original historical
meaning is always a major hermeneutical decision. When the text has
to function as Scripture for either Jew or Christian, it can be a particularly difficult decision to make.

Christian Interpretations

1. *The Genesis Homilies of Origen*

One of the greatest biblical scholars in the patristic period was Origen.
Writing in the first half of the third century CE, Origen commented
extensively upon both Old and New Testaments, and was much
followed by subsequent commentators. Although he is known particularly for his propensity for allegory as a way of handling difficulties
within the text, Origen was well aware of the significance of the literal
meaning also. Generally speaking, Origen's work shows a practical
and pastoral concern to read the Old Testament in the light of Christ

and to relate the biblical text to the life of the Christian community. (A good introduction to his biblical interpretation is provided by M. Wiles in his article 'Origen as Biblical Scholar'.)

Some of Origen's comments on Genesis 22 are those which almost any reader of the story would make. So, for example, Origen comments on God's initial command:

> What do you say to these things, Abraham? What kind of thoughts are stirring in your heart? A word has been uttered by God which is such as to shatter and try your faith. What do you say to these things? What are you thinking? What are you reconsidering? (translation from R. Heine, *Origen's Homilies on Genesis and Exodus*, homily 8, p. 137).

Origen typically answers this rhetorical question not by offering his own speculation but by referring to the New Testament:

> But since 'the spirit of prophets is subject to the prophets' [1 Cor. 14.32], the apostle Paul, who, I believe, was teaching by the Spirit what feeling, what plan Abraham considered, has revealed it when he says: 'By faith Abraham did not hesitate, when he offered his only son, in whom he had received the promises, thinking that God is able to raise him up even from the dead' [Heb. 11.17, 19] (p. 137).

From this Origen deduces that 'the faith in the resurrection began to be held already at that time in Isaac'. This interpretation in the letter to the Hebrews is particularly important for Origen, for he makes use of it again in commenting on Abraham's words to his servants that 'we will return' (v. 5):

> Tell me, Abraham, are you saying to the servants in truth that you will worship and return with the child, or are you deceiving them? If you are telling the truth, then you will not make him a holocaust. If you are deceiving, it is not fitting for so great a patriarch to deceive. What disposition, therefore, does this statment indicate in you? I am speaking the truth, he says, and I offer the child as a holocaust. For for this reason I both carry wood with me, and I return to you with him. For I believe, and this is my faith, that 'God is able to raise him up even from the dead' (p. 140).

Although in these ways Origen engages closely with the question of the literal meaning of the text (when read in the light of the New Testament), he also handles the text more freely and introduces typology where appropriate:

> That Isaac himself carries on himself 'the wood for the holocaust' is a figure, because Christ also 'himself carried his own cross' [cf. Jn 19.17], and yet to carry 'the wood for the holocaust' is the duty of a priest. He himself, therefore, becomes both victim and priest (pp. 140–41).

Since Origen considers that the ram which Abraham offers in sacrifice also represents Christ, this raises a problem of double typology, the problem of how 'both are appropriate to Christ, both Isaac who is not slain and the ram which is slain'. This leads Origen into a discussion, which to most modern readers seems far-fetched, of how the ram represents Christ in the flesh (in which Christ suffered and died, and also was a victim) while Isaac represents Christ in the spirit (in which also he is a priest).

It will be appropriate to conclude our extracts from Origen with two of his comments on Gen. 22.12. First, Origen picks up a problem that has puzzled many a reader:

> In this statement it is usually thrown out against us that God says that now he had learned that Abraham fears God as though he were such as not to have known previously. God knew and it was not hidden from him, since it is he 'who has known all things before they come to pass' [Dan. 13.42, the story of Susanna]. But these things are written on account of you, because you too indeed have believed in God, but unless you shall fulfil 'the works of faith' [cf. 2 Thess. 1.11], unless you shall be obedient to all the commands, even the more difficult ones, unless you shall offer sacrifice and show that you place neither father nor mother nor sons before God [cf. Matt. 10.37], you will not know that you fear God nor will it be said of you: 'Now I know that you fear God' (p. 143).

Secondly, Origen uses Paul's apparent reference to Genesis 22 to draw a classic Christian moral from the story, where the typology is at its loosest:

> But grant that these words are spoken to Abraham and he is said to fear God. Why? Because he did not spare his son. But let us compare these words with those of the Apostle, where he says of God: 'Who spared not his own son, but delivered him up for us all' [Rom. 8.32]. Behold God contending with men in magnificent liberality: Abraham offered God a mortal son who was not put to death; God delivered to death an immortal son for men (p. 144).

2. *The Commentary of Gerhard von Rad*

The German scholar G. von Rad is widely recognized as the outstanding Christian commentator on the Old Testament in the twentieth century. Von Rad's work has proved both seminal and controversial for Old Testament study over the last 50 years. Even his critics generally concede that his reading of the biblical text is marked by unusual freshness and perspicacity. A useful introduction to his life and work is J.L. Crenshaw, *Gerhard von Rad* (Crenshaw also offers a summary account in McKim's *Major Biblical Interpreters*).

One of the reasons why von Rad's work is controversial is that basic methodological questions of precisely what it is that he is doing are not always satisfactorily resolved. That is, much of the time von Rad is working essentially as a religious historian, producing descriptive historical accounts of the religious thought of ancient Israel. Yet fundamentally he works as a Christian theologian, writing from the explicit perspective of Christian faith and seeking to produce constructive theology, relevant to the life of the Church. Although these two tasks need not be incompatible, the relationship between them sometimes seems unclear in von Rad's work.

In his *Genesis* commentary von Rad makes clear that his primary task is to interpret the text as a Christian theologian. For he concludes his introduction by saying:

> We receive the Old Testament from the hands of Jesus Christ, and therefore all exegesis of the Old Testament depends on whom one thinks Jesus Christ to be…in the patriarchal narratives, which know so well how God can conceal himself, we see a revelation of God which precedes his manifestation in Jesus Christ. What we are told here of the trials of a God who hides himself and whose promise is delayed, and yet of his comfort and support, can readily be read into God's revelation of himself in Jesus Christ (*Genesis*, p. 43).

This means that von Rad is identifying himself with the historic Christian appropriation of the Old Testament as Christian Scripture, in which the interpreter's starting-point is a Christological understanding of God and faith. This must necessarily mean that in reading the Old Testament the concern cannot be solely the historian's question of 'What did this text originally mean?', but rather 'What does this text now mean when it is read in the light of Christ?' Given the predominance of the historian's agenda in modern Old Testament interpretation, it is hardly surprising that this theological agenda of von Rad has proved controversial.

When we come to Genesis 22, both the strengths and the weaknesses of von Rad's approach can be seen. The key passages of von Rad's interpretation of the story are as follows:

> One must indeed speak of a temptation (*Anfechtung*) which came upon Abraham but only in the definite sense that it came from God only, the God of Israel… For Abraham, God's command is completely incomprehensible… Isaac is the child of promise. In him every saving thing that God has promised to do is invested and guaranteed. The point here is not a natural gift, not even the highest, but rather the disappearance from Abraham's life of the whole promise. Therefore, unfortunately, one can only answer all plaintive scruples about this narrative by saying

that it concerns something much more frightful than child sacrifice. It has to do with a road out into Godforsakenness (*Gottverlassenheit*), a road on which Abraham does not know that God is only testing him… In this test God confronts Abraham with the question whether he could give up God's gift of promise. He had to be able (and he was able), for it is not a good that may be retained by virtue of any legal title or with the help of a human demand. God therefore poses before Abraham the question whether he really understands the gift of promise as a pure gift (*Genesis*, pp. 239, 244).

A few comments may help elucidate the significance of what von Rad is saying. First, von Rad was a Lutheran, and at the heart of Lutheran theology stands a theology of the cross, an understanding of God and life in the light of Jesus' cry of dereliction in Matthew and Mark's account of the crucifixion—My God, my God, why have you forsaken (*verlassen*) me?' So when Abraham is on a road out into God-forsakenness, his story is being understood by analogy with the crucifixion of Christ.

Secondly, Luther's theology of the cross revolves around two key concepts. On the one hand, the hiddenness of God. For the true revelation of God comes in the cross where God is hidden and so can only be perceived by the eye of faith. This is why for Abraham God's command is incomprehensible and has to be received by faith. On the other hand, *Anfechtung*. This is an impossible word to render in English, but it may perhaps be represented by terms such as affliction, anguish, temptation. What it means is that God works in people by breaking them down, stripping away all customary supports and comforts, and bringing them through suffering to a true recognition of God as he really is. So when von Rad interprets God's testing of Abraham as *Anfechtung*, it is this kind of spiritual process that he is depicting, understood again by analogy with the cross.

In conclusion, three comments may be made. First, von Rad's interpretation is a sophisticated Christian typology. He reads the story of Abraham in the light of Christ and Christian theology, and so presents the story of Abraham as a type of Christ's suffering on the cross. As such von Rad stands in a real continuity with classical Christian commentators, from the Fathers onwards, and well illustrates the way in which the Old Testament, as Christian Scripture, is not read 'like any other book'.

Secondly, although von Rad's interpretation gives a quite different meaning to the story from that which I suggested it had in its Old Testament context, nonetheless there is a real sense in which von Rad is doing the same kind of thing that the ancient Hebrew writer of

Genesis 22 was doing. For we saw that the Hebrew writer interpreted what was originally non-Yahwistic material from the perspective of Yahwism. In doing so the writer assimilated the story to the central theological concerns of Yahwism, particularly obedience to Torah. Von Rad has read what was originally a non-Christian story from the perspective of Christianity, and in so doing has assimilated the story to the central theological concerns of Lutheranism. The hermeneutical assumptions at stake are similar, and the difference in result is the difference in the theological content of the interpreter's standpoint.

Finally, by what yardstick should von Rad's interpretation be assessed? If it is assessed in terms of its conformity to the originally intended meaning of the Hebrew text, then it fares only moderately. A story of Abraham suffering from *Anfechtung* and Godforsakenness is some way from a story of Abraham being shown to be a model for Israel of Torah obedience and true sacrifice at Jerusalem. The strength of von Rad's reading is twofold. On the one hand, it is imaginatively powerful, and has the same validity as any literary creation that manages to capture the imagination. On the other hand, it is in conformity with the norms of the Christian community from which, and for which, von Rad writes. Ultimately, it is likely to be one's stance towards that community which determines one's assessment of the interpretation. As noted at the beginning of the book, the question of what counts as a good reading of the biblical text cannot be divorced from questions about the context and interpretative community within which the reader stands.

FURTHER READING

Commentaries

Brueggemann, W., *Genesis* (IBC; Atlanta: John Knox Press, 1982). Aimed at preachers. Brueggemann discusses the text from the perspective of Christian theology.

Coats, G.W., *Genesis, with an Introduction to Narrative Literature* (FOTL, 1; Grand Rapids: Eerdmans, 1983). Some useful analyses of the text.

Delitzsch, F., *A New Commentary on Genesis* (2 vols.; Edinburgh: T. & T. Clark, 1888–89). Dated, but still an instructive engagement with the text, with much discussion of Hebrew.

Driver, S.R., *The Book of Genesis* (London: Methuen, 4th edn, 1905). The standard commentary in English for many years in the earlier part of this century, it went through many editions. Although dated, still a first-rate exposition of an older critical consensus.

Fretheim, T.E., 'The Book of Genesis', in L. Keck *et al.* (eds.), *The New Interpreters Bible* (Nashville: Abingdon, 1994), I, pp. 319-674. Valuable discussion of most dimensions of the text.

Gunkel, H., *Genesis* (Macon, GA: Mercer University Press, 1997 [ET of 3rd German edn of 1910]). Probably the most influential Genesis commentary of the twentieth century.

Keil, C.F., and F. Delitzsch, 'The First Book of Moses (Genesis)', in *idem, Commentary on the Old Testament* (repr., Grand Rapids: Eerdmans, 1980), I, pp. 33-414. A classic of nineteenth-century conservative commentary.

Kidner, F.D., *Genesis* (TOTC; London: Tyndale Press, 1967). Brief, but with many sharp insights. Kidner eschews most modern perspectives on historical and compositional issues.

Plaut, W.G. (ed.), *The Torah: A Modern Commentary* (New York: Union of American Hebrew Congregations, 1981), pp. 87-360. With Hebrew text and translation. A useful combination of traditional Jewish and modern perspectives.

Rad, G. von, *Genesis* (OTL; London: SCM Press, 1972 [ET of 9th German edn; Göttingen: Vandenhoeck & Ruprecht, 1972]). The outstanding modern theological commentary.

Sailhamer, J.H., 'Genesis', in F.E. Gaebelein (ed.), *The Expositor's Bible Commentary* (Grand Rapids: Zondervan, 1990), II, pp. 1-284. American evangelical interpretation.

Sarna, N.M., *Bereishith/Genesis* (JPS Torah Commentary; Philadelphia: Jewish Publication Society, 1989). With Hebrew text and translation. An attractive combination of traditional Jewish perspectives with sober use of modern critical insight.

Scherman, N., and M. Zlotowitz (eds.), *Bereishis/Genesis: A New Translation with a Commentary Anthologized from Talmudic, Midrashic and Rabbinic Sources* (Artscroll Tanach Series; 2 vols.; Brooklyn, NY: Mesorah Publications, 1986 [originally in 6 separate vols., 1977–82]). A valuable extensive compilation of traditional Jewish insights, but with no concessions at all to any modern insights.

Skinner, J., *Genesis* (ICC; Edinburgh: T. & T. Clark, 1912). Dated, but, like all ICC volumes, packed with useful information especially on historical and linguistic matters.

Speiser, E., *Genesis* (AB; Garden City, NY: Doubleday, 1964). Useful for wider historical background, but otherwise thin.

Vawter, B., *On Genesis: A New Reading* (London: Geoffrey Chapman, 1977). The reading is less new than the title suggests and represents an older consensus approach.

Wenham, G.J., *Genesis 1–15* (WBC, 1; Waco, TX: Word Books, 1987). Probably the most useful commentary for the beginner in Hebrew, since all possibly difficult Hebrew words are parsed and there is discussion of Hebrew usage.

—*Genesis 16–50* (WBC, 2; Waco, TX: Word Books, 1994).

Westermann, C., *Genesis 12–36* (London: SPCK, 1986 [ET from the German edn, Neukirchen–Vluyn: Neukirchener Verlag, 1981]). The most exhaustive modern commentary, indispensable for serious study, although somewhat thin on theology.

—*Genesis 37–50* (London: SPCK, 1987 [ET from the German edn, Neukirchen–Vluyn: Neukirchener Verlag, 1982]).

—*Genesis: A Practical Commentary* (Grand Rapids: Eerdmans, 1987). A popularly oriented condensation of his major commentary.

Works Referred to in the Text

Abela, A., *The Themes of the Abraham Narrative* (Malta: Studia Editions, 1989). A literary discussion of key words and motifs.

Abramson, G., 'The Reinterpretation of the Akedah in Modern Hebrew Poetry', *JJS* 41 (1990), pp. 101-14. Abramson discusses the impact of Genesis 22 in modern Israeli literature.

Allen, C.G., 'On Me be the Curse, My Son!', in R.M. Gross (ed.), *Beyond Androcentrism: New Essays on Women and Religion* (Missoula, MT: Scholars Press, 1977), pp. 183-216; revised in M.J. Buss (ed.), *Encounter with the Text: Form and History in the Hebrew Bible* (Missoula, MT: Scholars Press, 1979), pp. 159-72. A feminist reading of Genesis 27 that draws on pre-modern interpretations.

Alonso Schökel, L., *A Manual of Hermeneutics* (BibSem, 54; Sheffield: Sheffield Academic Press, 1998). A suggestive argument in favour of shifting from author-hermeneutics to text-hermeneutics.

Alt, A., 'The God of the Fathers', in *idem, Essays on Old Testament History and Religion* (The Biblical Seminar; Sheffield: JSOT Press, 1989 [ET from the German edn of 1929]), pp. 1-77. Alt set the agenda for subsequent study of patriarchal religion.

Alter, R., *The Art of Biblical Narrative* (London: George Allen & Unwin, 1981). A stimulating and creative literary approach.

Auerbach, E., *Mimesis* (Princeton, NJ: Princeton University Press, 1968 [1953]), ch. 1. A classic literary analysis of Genesis 22, in which the storytelling style of Genesis is compared with that of Homer.

Barthes, R., 'The Struggle with the Angel: Textual Analysis of Genesis 32.22-32', in *idem, Image–Music–Text* (London: Flamingo, 1984), pp. 125-41 (translated from *Analyse structurale et exégèse biblique* [Neuchâtel: Delachaux et Niestle, 1972]). A famous structuralist reading.

Blum, E., *Die Komposition der Vätergeschichte* (WMANT, 57; Neukirchen–Vluyn: Neukirchener Verlag, 1984). Blum develops the new look on Pentateuchal criticism advocated by Rendtorff.

Brichto, H.C., *The Names of God: Poetic Readings in Biblical Beginnings* (Oxford: Oxford University Press, 1998). Elaborate study, sometimes suggestive, sometimes implausible.

Bright, J., *A History of Israel* (OTL; London: SCM Press, 3rd edn, 1981). A standard textbook for a number of years.

Charlesworth, J.H., *The Old Testament Pseudepigrapha* (London: Darton, Longman & Todd, 1985), II. This volume contains, among other things, an annotated translation of the *Book of Jubilees* by O.S. Wintermute.

Crenshaw, J.L., *Gerhard von Rad* (Makers of the Modern Theological Mind; Waco, TX: Word Books, 1978). An introduction to von Rad's life and work.

—'Von Rad, Gerhard', in D. McKim (ed.), *Historical Handbook of Major Biblical Interpreters* (Downers Grove/Leicester: Inter-Varsity Press, 1998), pp. 526-31

Davies, P.R, 'Male Bonding: A Tale of Two Buddies', in *idem, Whose Bible is it Anyway?* (JSOTSup, 204; Sheffield: Sheffield Academic Press, 1995), pp. 95-113. An ingenious suspicious reading of the Abraham narrative.

Driver, S.R., *Introduction to the Literature of the Old Testament* (Edinburgh: T. & T. Clark, 6th edn, 1897). For many years a standard exposition of a modern critical approach.

Emerton, J.A., 'Wisdom', in G.W. Anderson (ed.), *Tradition and Interpretation* (Oxford: Clarendon Press, 1979), pp. 214-37. Emerton surveys the debate about wisdom literature, including reference to the Joseph story.

Endres, J.C., *Biblical Interpretation in the Book of Jubilees* (CBQMS, 18; Washington, DC: Catholic Biblical Association, 1987). A recent study of early biblical hermeneutics.

Fokkelman, J.P., *Narrative Art in Genesis* (The Biblical Seminar; Sheffield: JSOT Press, 2nd edn, 1991 [orig. pub. Assen: Van Gorcum, 1975]). A controversial pioneering literary study of selected stories.

Gottwald, N.K., *The Hebrew Bible: A Socio-Literary Introduction* (Philadelphia: Fortress Press, 1985).

Green, A., *Devotion and Commandment: The Faith of Abraham in the Hasidic Imagination* (Cincinnati, OH: Hebrew Union College Press, 1989). A fascinating study in Jewish theology and spirituality.

Gunn, D.M., 'New Directions in the Study of Hebrew Narrative', *JSOT* 39 (1987), pp. 65-75. Gunn discusses the shift from historical to literary approaches to the text.

Gunn, D.M., and D. Fewell, *Narrative in the Hebrew Bible* (Oxford: Oxford University Press, 1993), ch. 4. The interpretation of Abraham depicts him as a man of unfaith.

Hals, R.M., 'Legend', *CBQ* 34 (1972), pp. 166-76; repr. in G.W. Coats (ed.), *Saga, Legend, Tale, Novella, Fable* (JSOTSup, 35; Sheffield: JSOT Press, 1985). A helpful discussion of the varied uses of 'legend'.

Heine, R. (ed.), *Origen's Homilies on Genesis and Exodus* (Fathers of the Church, 71; Washington, DC: Catholic University of America, 1982).

Hendel, R.S., *The Epic of the Patriarch: The Jacob Cycle and the Narrative Traditions of Canaan and Israel* (HSM, 42; Atlanta: Scholars Press, 1987). Chapter 1 offers a useful survey of the history of modern interpretation of the Jacob material.

Humphreys, W. Lee, 'A Life-Style for Diaspora: A Study of the Tales of Esther and Daniel', *JBL* 92 (1973), pp. 211-23. Humphries notes links of the Joseph story with Esther and Daniel.

Jowett, B., 'On the Interpretation of Scripture', in *Essays and Reviews* (London: Longman, 1860), pp. 330-433. Page 338 has the famous proposal to 'read Scripture like any other book'.

Kirkpatrick, P.G., *The Old Testament and Folklore Study* (JSOTSup, 62; Sheffield: JSOT Press, 1988). Kirkpatrick doubts whether oral tradition can preserve an accurate account of events.

Koch, K., *The Growth of the Biblical Tradition: The Form-Critical Method* (London: A. & C. Black, 1969 [ET from the German edn of 1964, 1967]), pp. 111-32. An extensive source-critical and traditio-historical study of Gen. 12.10-20; 20.1-18 and 26.5-11.

Köckert, M., *Vätergott and Väterverheissungen* (FRLANT, 142; Göttingen: Vandenhoeck & Ruprecht, 1988). Köckert criticizes the consensus view of patriarchal religion built upon the work of Alt.

Lemche, N.P., *Ancient Israel: A New History of Israelite Society* (BibSem, 5; Sheffield: JSOT Press, 1988). Lemche proposes a view of Israel's history that departs radically from the outlines of the Old Testament.

Levenson, J.D., *The Death and Resurrection of the Beloved Son: The Transformation of Child Sacrifice in Judaism and Christianity* (New Haven: Yale University Press, 1993). A ground-breaking historical and hermeneutical study.

Long, B.O., *Planting and Reaping Albright: Politics, Ideology, and Interpreting the Bible* (University Park, PA: Pennsylvania State University Press, 1997).

McKane, W., *Studies in the Patriarchal Narratives* (Edinburgh: Handsel, 1979). Focusing on traditio-historical study, McKane shows how purported development of the tradition varies according to the literary type assigned to the material.

Magonet, J., *A Rabbi's Bible* (London: SCM Press, 1991). An entertaining approach to the problems of biblical interpretation from a Jewish perspective.

Mann, T.W., *The Book of the Torah: The Narrative Integrity of the Pentateuch* (Atlanta: John Knox Press, 1988), pp. 29-77. A sophisticated reading of Genesis 12–50.

Mare, W. Harold, *The Archaeology of the Jerusalem Area* (Grand Rapids: Baker Book House, 1987).

Miller, J.M., and J.H. Hayes, *A History of Ancient Israel and Judah* (London: SCM Press, 1986), ch. 2. Miller focuses on methodological problems involved in any historical work on Genesis 12–50.

Miller, W.T., *Mysterious Encounters at Mamre and Jabbok* (BJS; Chico, CA: Scholars Press, 1984). Useful for its discussion of early Jewish and Christian interpretations of Genesis 18 and 32.

Moberly, R.W.L., 'The Earliest Commentary on the Akedah', *VT* 38 (1988), pp. 302-23. A study of Gen. 22.15-18.

—*The Old Testament of the Old Testament* (Overtures to Biblical Theology; Philadelphia: Augsburg–Fortress, 1992). The thesis of this book is that Genesis 12–50 stands in relation to the Mosaic Yahwism of Exodus 3 onwards as a kind of Old Testament.

—*The Bible, Theology, and Faith: A Study of Abraham and Jesus* (Cambridge: Cambridge University Press, 2000). Locates Genesis 22 and some of its interpretations within a wider proposal for reading Old and New Testaments as Christian scripture.

Nicholson, E.W., *The Pentateuch in the Twentieth Century: The Legacy of Julius Wellhausen* (Oxford: Clarendon Press, 1998). Argues for the retention of the Documentary Hypothesis as 'alone...the true perspective' for study of the Pentateuch.

Noth, M., *A History of Pentateuchal Traditions* (Chico, CA: Scholars Press, 1981 [ET from German]). The major modern traditio-historical study of the Pentateuch.

Otto, R., *The Idea of the Holy* (London: Oxford University Press, 1924 [ET from German]). A classic modern study.

Pagolu, A., *The Religion of the Patriarchs* (JSOTSup, 277; Sheffield: Sheffield Academic Press, 1998). Comprehensive recent discussion.

Pearl, C., *Rashi* (Jewish Thinkers; London: Weidenfeld & Nicolson, 1988). An introduction to Rashi's life and work.

Rad, G. von, 'The Form-Critical Problem of the Hexateuch', in *idem, The Problem of the Hexateuch*, pp. 1-78. This essay proposed fresh categories for Pentateuchal criticism.

—'The Beginnings of Historical Writing in Ancient Israel', in *idem, The Problem of the Hexateuch*, pp. 166-204 (ET from the German edn of 1944). Von Rad argued in this essay for a change in Israelite writing during the 'Solomonic Enlightenment'.

—'The Joseph Narrative and Ancient Wisdom', in *idem, The Problem of the Hexateuch*, pp. 292-300 (originally in VTSup, 1 [1953], pp. 120-27). A ground-breaking proposal to interpret the Joseph story in the categories of the wisdom literature.

—*The Problem of the Hexateuch and Other Essays* (London: SCM Press, 1984).

Rendtorff, R., *The Problem of the Process of Transmission in the Pentateuch* (JSOTSup, 89; Sheffield: JSOT Press, 1990 [ET from the German edn of 1977]). This work helped bring about a rethinking of pentateuchal criticism.

—'The Paradigm is Changing: Hopes—and Fears', *Biblical Interpretation* 1.1 (1993), pp. 34-53. Argues for P shaping the Pentateuch by analogy with D shaping the Deuteronomistic History.

Silbermann, A.M. (ed.), *Pentateuch with Rashi's Commentary: Genesis* (Jerusalem: Silbermann, 1972). With text, translation and notes of the great Jewish commentator.

Soggin, J.A., *A History of Israel* (London: SCM Press, 1984 [ET from the Italian edn of 1985]), pp. 89-108. A cautious survey of recent debate.

Spiegel, S., *The Last Trial* (New York: Behrman House, 1979). An introduction to history of Jewish interpretation of Genesis 22.

Sternberg, M., *The Poetics of Biblical Narrative: Ideological Literature and the Drama of Reading* (Bloomington, IN: Indiana University Press, 1985). A demanding but worthwhile literary approach. The first three chapters give the essence of the approach advocated.

Thompson, R.J., *Moses and the Law in a Century of Criticism since Graf* (VTSup, 19; Leiden: E.J. Brill, 1970). A useful survey of the development of modern Penta-teuchal criticism prior to recent rethinking of many issues.

Thompson, T.L., *The Historicity of the Patriarchal Narratives* (BZAW, 133; Berlin: W. de Gruyter, 1974). Thompson criticizes the consensus view of the Albright school.

Trible, P., *Texts of Terror: Literary-Feminist Readings of Biblical Narratives* (Overtures to Biblical Theology; Philadelphia: Fortress Press, 1984). Chapter 1 offers a close reading of the story of Hagar in Genesis 16 and 21.

Turner, L.A., *Announcements of Plot in Genesis* (JSOTSup, 96; Sheffield: JSOT Press, 1990). A literary analysis from the perspective of the 'first-time reader'.

Van Seters, J., *Abraham in History and Tradition* (New Haven: Yale University Press, 1975). Van Seters criticizes conventional views of Pentateuchal criticism.

—'The Religion of the Patriarchs in Genesis', *Bib* 61 (1980), pp. 220-33. An argu-ment against the supposed antiquity of patriarchal religion.

—*Prologue to History: The Yahwist as Historian in Genesis* (Louisville, KY: West-minster/John Knox Press, 1992). A distinctive thesis about the nature of Israelite historiography.

Weeks, S.D.E., *Early Israelite Wisdom* (Oxford: Oxford University Press, 1994). A sharp critique of much conventional modern wisdom about Israelite wisdom.

Weiser, A., *Introduction to the Old Testament* (London: Darton, Longman & Todd, 1961 [ET from German]).

Wellhausen, J., *Prolegomena to the History of Ancient Israel* (Gloucester, MA: Peter Smith, 1973 [repr. from German]). The work that fixed the categories for modern Pentateuchal criticism.

—*Die Composition des Hexateuchs and der Historischen Bücher des Alten Testaments* (Berlin: Georg Reimer, 3rd edn, 1899). This work provides the detailed analysis underlying the documentary hypothesis.

Wenham, G.J., *Genesis 16–50* (WBC, 2; Waco, TX: Word Books, 1994).

Whitelam, K., *The Invention of Ancient Israel: The Silencing of Palestinian History* (London: Routledge, 1996). A suggestive and provocative approach to the work of Albright and others.

Whybray, R.N., *The Making of the Pentateuch: A Methodological Study* (JSOTSup, 53; Sheffield: JSOT Press, 1987). The most telling critique of the documentary hypothesis, although it deals only with narrative and not with law and is weak on positive alternatives.

Wiles, M.F., 'Origen as Biblical Scholar', in P.R. Ackroyd and C.F. Evans (eds.), *The Cambridge History of the Bible* (Cambridge: Cambridge University Press, 1970),

I, pp. 454-89. A useful introduction to one of the great patristic biblical scholars.

Winton Thomas, D., *Documents from Old Testament Times* (New York: Harper & Row, 1961). A useful collection, more condensed than Pritchard.

Part III
EXODUS
William Johnstone

INTRODUCTION

The books of the Old Testament from Genesis to 2 Kings tell how in the space of a thousand years or more a small family of ancient Semites, the descendants of Israel, grew from humblest beginnings as wandering shepherds on the fringes of the civilizations of the ancient Near East to become a nation, a kingdom and even an empire before tragically succumbing to division, dissolution and the loss of the land which had made their nationhood possible. Exodus, as the second book of that collection, tells part of the story of the early promising years, which even then were shadowed with the threat of disaster.

The book of Exodus falls into clear sections:

1.1–15.21 relates how the twelve sons of Israel and their households, who had been forced by famine to leave Canaan and settle in Egypt, increased in such numbers that the Egyptians began to fear for their own security. They subjected the Israelites to slavery and sought to slaughter all their sons at birth. Remarkably, however, one of these, Moses, was saved alive by the king of Egypt's own daughter and, ironically, was adopted into the royal household. When Moses grew up, he was forced, after impetuously murdering an Egyptian who was maltreating an Israelite, to flee from Egypt to the neighbouring deserts of Midian. There he was commissioned by God to return and lead his people out of slavery. After ten plagues culminating in the death of all the Egyptian first-born, the obdurate Egyptians were finally prevailed upon to let Moses and his people go. But no sooner had they left, than the Egyptians changed their minds and pursued after them as far as the Red Sea. There the Israelites were miraculously saved by the parting of the waters, while the pursuing Egyptians were all drowned.

15.22–18.27 begins the account of Israel's long march through the wilderness towards the land of Canaan, murmuring and rebelling as they went but always miraculously preserved. The story of that march is continued in Num. 10.11 and is completed only at the beginning of the book of Joshua.

19.1–40.38 is the initial part of the record of events at Mt Sinai, the central section of the whole Pentateuch, which continues down to Num. 10.10. The chapters in Exodus describe the making of a covenant between the Israelites and their God on the basis of the 'Ten Commandments' and the 'Book of the Covenant' (19.1–24.18); the revelation to Moses of the specification of the Tabernacle, where God will dwell in the midst of his people, and of its furnishings and personnel (25.1–31.17); the breaking of the covenant by the people of Israel in the 'golden calf' incident and the re-making of the covenant (31.18–34.35); and the construction of the Tabernacle, on which the glory of God indeed descends (35.1–40.38).

But what kind of a work is Exodus? The answer to the question may appear to be self-evident: it is a history-book. After all, it is couched in the form of a narrative which tells the story of events dated from the beginning of Israel's stay in Egypt to the first day of the second year after their exodus from it.

Exodus, however, is not only a history-book. Interwoven with the thread of the narrative and, in the end, dominating it are stipulations for religious observances, legal practices and cultic institutions. Exodus is thus also in part a calendar and liturgical handbook for religious festivals and in part a law-code.

Even more remarkable, as history books go, is its account of the self-disclosure of God. As in the rest of the Old Testament, the course of Israel's history is interpreted theologically. God's all-pervasive purpose in the life of this people is overtly recognized. The family of seventy are, in fact, children of a promise once pledged by God in covenant to their forefather Abraham; they are the heirs of the further promises of freedom and land. It is God who sees the affliction of those who are thus 'his people'. It is he who commissions his 'servant' Moses to rescue them, equipping him with a wonderworking staff to perform miraculous signs. The escape from Egypt is a miraculous deliverance performed by God. The people thus created by God's initiative and saved by his intervention are formally constituted as his people at his mountain in Sinai by a covenant with himself. The climax of the book is the construction of the Tabernacle, a dwelling-place for God himself in the midst of his people.

The contents of the book thus require the consideration not only of historical but also of institutional and theological questions. Since such disparate materials have all been brought together into one presentation, it is appropriate also to look at the literary formation and formulation of the book: if, as already seems likely, it is a theologian who has finally put the work together, with what purpose did he write, what sources did he use and how did he set about his task? In the light of these discussions it may be possible to come to a clearer appreciation of the kind of work the book of Exodus is.

Chapter One

MATTERS HISTORICAL: CLEARING THE GROUND

Exodus begins with the story of how the enslaved Israelites gained their freedom from their Egyptian oppressors. The narrative format of the story has prompted the seemingly natural assumption that it recounts historical events. Is this assumption correct? If so, how far is it correct?

In order to write history the historian needs primary sources as nearly as possible contemporary with the events to be portrayed. These sources may be official documents, such as annals, monumental inscriptions or decrees, or the often still more revealing occasional or private documents, such as letters, diaries or ledgers. Do such primary sources exist for the writing of the history of this early period of Israel's life?

This chapter will begin with the modern search for sources contemporary with the times of Israel's early encounters with Egypt. It will then outline a number of reconstructions of events, which have been offered on the basis of these sources in combination with biblical material, and indicate areas where problems remain. Finally, in the light of these inquiries, it will raise the question of the nature of the biblical material and ask whether, in fact, historiographical method can by itself do justice to the character and content of this material.

I. *The Biblical Chronology*

First a word about the Bible's own chronology is necessary. If material inside the Bible is to be correlated with material outside, then it is vital to know the relevant period on which comparable data are to be sought in the world of Israel's environment. The problems besetting the establishing of an 'absolute' chronology for the biblical data (i.e., one which dates the inner-biblical 'relative' chronology by means of cross-reference to datable external events or named persons) are, however, notorious even for periods which stand more fully in the broad daylight of history than does the exodus.

For example, a fixed point for settling the chronology of later Assyrian history is provided by the eclipse of the sun dated to 15 June, 763 BCE. The reference to this eclipse in the Assyrian annals enables the dates of the Assyrian kings mentioned in 2 Kings to be established with certainty. But it is extremely difficult to relate the data in 2 Kings on the reigns of the kings of Israel and Judah to this information. The length of time given from the accession of Jehu to the throne of Israel in the mid-ninth century until the fall of Samaria in 721 is some 119 years, according to the Assyrian king-list from Khorsabad. For the same period 2 Kgs 10–18 allows about 143 years for Israel and 165 years for Judah.

If difficulty in correlation is encountered even for periods which are relatively well documented, from both biblical and extrabiblical sources, it is compounded for the period before the ninth century, from the reign of Solomon back into earliest times, when correlations between the figures named in the Old Testament and historical figures known from contemporary ancient Near Eastern sources cease.

The biblical chronology for the exodus and related episodes thus hangs in the air. It begins from the biblical data, especially 1 Kgs 6.1, 'In the four hundred and eightieth year after the people of Israel came out of the land of Egypt, in the fourth year of Solomon's reign over Israel...' Assuming Solomon's first year to be c. 960 BCE, the exodus must have taken place c. 1436 BCE. If one adds to that the data of Exod. 12.40, 'The time that the people of Israel dwelt in Egypt was four hundred and thirty years', the descent of Jacob and his sons must have been c. 1866, with Abraham's migration from Haran 215 years earlier (Gen. 12.4; 17.1ff.; 25.26; 47.9), that is, c. 2081 BCE. The fragility of this chronology is indicated by the fact that in Gen. 15.13 the length of the sojourn in Egypt is reckoned to be not 430 but 400 years, while in Gen. 15.16 it is merely three generations. It is also part of that overall biblical chronology which led Archbishop Ussher in the mid-seventeenth century to date creation to the year 4004. It is possible in any case that '480' in 1 Kgs 6.1 represents the schematic assignment of 40 years to each of the twelve generations assumed to intervene between the exodus and Solomon. If one were to apply the figure of, say, 25 years as the more normal length of a generation, the date of the exodus would be brought down by some 180 years. But even the figure twelve may be schematic.

Further Reading

The most comprehensive collection of relevant extrabiblical sources published in English is *ANET* (for the Assyrian king-list mentioned above see p. 566 [cf. pp. 280f.]).

Specifically on the question of chronology, see, e.g., J. Finegan, *Handbook of Biblical Chronology* (Oxford: Oxford University Press, 1967).

There are many *Histories of Israel* (e.g., among those available in English, M. Noth [2nd edn, 1960], J. Bright [3rd edn, 1981], S. Herrmann [1975], H. Jagersma [1982], J.A. Soggin [1984], J.M. Miller and J.H. Hayes [1986], J.A. Soggin [2nd edn, 1993]).

A comprehensive attempt to treat the biblical material on the exodus as historical is to be found in R. de Vaux, *The Early History of Israel* (London: Darton, Longman & Todd, 1978).

A useful discussion of approaches and issues is to be found in J.H. Hayes and J.M. Miller (eds.), *Israelite and Judaean History* (London: SCM Press, 1977); see also G.W. Ramsay, *The Quest for the Historical Israel: Reconstructing Israel's Early History* (Atlanta: John Knox Press, 1981); L.L. Grabbe (ed.), *Can a 'History of Israel' be Written?* (JSOTSup, 245; Sheffield: Sheffield Academic Press, 1997).

II. *Ancient Near Eastern Sources*

Apart from the Bible itself, the historical status of which is the very point at issue, the potential sources of knowledge about ancient Egypt are two-fold: (1) literary, that is, references in authors whose works have been preserved from antiquity; (2) archaeological, including epigraphical.

1. Until the dawn of Egyptology, the beginnings of which are conventionally dated to the decipherment of the bilingual hieroglyphic-demotic Egyptian/Greek inscription on the Rosetta Stone pioneered by J.F. Champollion in 1822, the only basis outside the Bible itself for reconstructing Israel's relationships with Egypt was surviving ancient literary texts. But these are late, inconsistent and often tendentious. Among the Alexandrian writers, for example, Manetho (early third century BCE, now preserved in Josephus, first century CE) assigns Moses to the reigns of Amenophis and his son Ramesses of the XVIIIth and XIXth Dynasties, while Artapanus (second century BCE, now preserved in Eusebius) assigns him to Chenephres of the Vth Dynasty, and Lysimachus (second–first centuries BCE, also in Josephus) to Bocchoris of the XXIVth. Anti-Jewish feeling is evident in Manetho's account of Moses as a deposed priest of the god Seth, leader of a band of leprous mine-workers in Sinai and ally of the Hyksos invaders from Jerusalem who controlled Egypt for thirteen

years. The expulsion of alien leprous Jews recurs in Hecateus of Abdera (about 300 BCE), Lysimachus, and Apion (first century CE). Equally propagandistic are the pro-Jewish accounts in Philo (first century CE), where Moses is presented as an idealized Hellenistic philosopher-king, or in Josephus himself where the antiquity and nobility of the Jews are portrayed for the benefit of his Roman audience.

Scholars were thus left to guess at the nature and significance of the historical encounter of the Israel of the exodus period with contemporary Egypt. For example, on the basis of Acts 7.22 ('Moses was instructed in all the wisdom of the Egyptians'), the early biblical critic Alexander Geddes could state, citing the Deist John Spencer, 'It is not now a question among the learned, whether a great part of their [the Israelites'] ritual were not derived from that nation [Egypt]' (*Holy Bible*, 1792, I, p. xiii).

2. The new discipline of Egyptology was accordingly enthusiastically encouraged, not least by biblical specialists. The aims of the Egyptian Exploration Fund (later Society), set up in 1882, were soon defined as including 'illustration of the Old Testament narrative, so far as it has to do with Egypt and the Egyptians', in particular, the illumination of the four hundred and thirty year period of Israel's sojourn (Exod. 12.40). Bricks made without straw were shipped at vast expense back home to London irrespective of whether the Israelites had, or could have had, any hand in their manufacture. Since then, Egyptology has properly established itself as an autonomous discipline and the marginal significance of the biblical connection has become manifest: thousands of texts have been recovered, hundreds of sites have been excavated but nowhere in Egypt is there evidence of a specific individual 'Moses' or even of a group identifiable as the 'people of Israel'. The one seemingly unambiguous mention of Israel occurs in a victory stela of the Pharaoh Merneptah, dated to c. 1230 (*ANET*, pp. 376ff.); the reference there, however, is to Israel as a people encountered by the Egyptians in Canaan. As far as their descent, sojourn and exodus as portrayed in the Old Testament are concerned, there can be at most only suggestions of plausible periods and backgrounds.

Further Reading

On 1., a palatable review is to be found in D.J. Silver, *Images of Moses* (New York: Basic Books, 1982), ch. 2.

On 2., see T.G.H. James (ed.), *Excavating in Egypt: The Egypt Exploration Society 1882–1982* (London: British Museum Publications, 1982).

III. *Evidence for the Relations between Semites and Egypt in the Second Millennium BCE*

The Old Testament narrative tells how Israel's relations with Egypt in this period passed through three phases, descent, sojourn and exodus. These episodes, though vaguely dated in the biblical chronology, are most likely to have occurred at some time in the second millennium BCE and it is, therefore, the Egyptian records of this period which have been combed for evidence of contacts with Israel's forebears. In the event, while no specific evidence has been found in Egyptian sources, it has proved possible to identify parallels to the biblical data. The following are among the most frequently cited.

1. For the *descent* of Semites into Egypt:
   (i) the Beni Hasan mural (*ANET*, p. 229, dated about 1890 BCE);
   (ii) the Hyksos invasion in the Second Intermediate Period (c. 1720–1570);
   (iii) the captive lists of Amenophis II (*ANET*, pp. 245ff., third quarter of the fifteenth century).
2. For the *sojourn* of Semites in Egypt:
   (i) a text naming Asiatics employed in a Theban household (*ANET*, pp. 553f., mid-eighteenth century), where the Asiatics received Egyptian names as did Joseph (Gen. 41.45);
   (ii) a text of Ramesses II from the thirteenth century mentioning the '*apiru* in building operations ('*apiru* is a term probably related in some way to 'Hebrew', as its Babylonian form *ḫabiru* in, e.g., the Amarna letters, makes more plain) (Galling, *Textbuch*, pp. 35f.);
   (iii) a text of Ramesses IV from the twelfth century, mentioning the '*apiru* in the army (*ibid.*).
3. For the *attainment by Asiatics* like Joseph *to high office*:
   (i) the position of Dod as chamberlain at the court of Amenophis IV in the early fourteenth century (*EA*, pp. 158, 164);
   (ii) the rule by a Syrian between the XIXth and XXth Dynasties (*ANET*, p. 260, end of the thirteenth century).
4. For the *exodus* of Semites from Egypt:
   (i) the Tale of Sinuhe (*ANET*, pp. 18ff., twentieth century);
   (ii) the expulsion of the Hyksos (*ANET*, pp. 233f., sixteenth century);

(iii) the pursuit of two runaway slaves (*ANET*, p. 259, copy
of text from the end of the thirteenth century).

What is striking about these parallels is the width of period which
they cover. If they show anything at all, it is that many of the events
described in the Old Testament are entirely typical of relations
between Egypt and their eastern Semitic neighbours, both nomad and
settled, at many times throughout the second millennium BCE. If
pressed, they would suggest that Exodus describes specific and, it
must be said, largely commonplace moments within great historical
processes—military invasion, colonization, imperialism, decline of
empire and, particularly important so far as herdsmen are concerned,
transhumance, the annual interchange of pasture-grounds from desert
to Delta and back again (cf., especially, the 'Prophecy of Nefer-rohu',
dating from the twentieth century BCE [*ANET*, pp. 444ff.] and the
'Report of a Frontier Official', copy of text from thirteenth century
BCE [*ANET*, p. 259])—which are far vaster than Israel's relations with
Egypt. Of these complex processes the Exodus narrative, considered
historiographically, provides a drastically over-simplified account
written from Israel's point of view. What the parallels do not prove is
the specific historicity of any of the events recorded in Exodus: none
of them can be identified with an incident referred to there. More
damagingly, if they are true parallels, they actually detract from the
biblical record: the attempt to understand it as historical and to
enhance it by historiographical means destroys its uniqueness and
threatens, rather, to relativize it.

IV. *Some Historical Reconstructions*

The inconclusiveness of these parallels coupled with the vagueness of
the Exodus narrative about chronology—not to mention the high incidence of the miraculous within the narrative—should give fore-
warning that standard historiographical methods are unlikely to do
full justice to the biblical material. Nonetheless, scholars have been
challenged to relate the biblical record to knowledge of ancient Near
Eastern, in particular Egyptian, history and have pursued this aim
with enormous, if at times misdirected, energy. Because of the difficulties, however, scholars are divided about even the basic question
of 'absolute' chronology. Three broad chronologies can, with variations, be found within scholarly discussion: the 'long', the 'short' and
the 'part long, part short'.

1. *The 'Long' Chronology*

(i) This chronology starts from the biblical data noted in Chapter 1.I above, which suggest that the exodus must have taken place c. 1436, the descent of Jacob c. 1866 and the migration of Abraham c. 2081 BCE. On the assumption that these are indeed chronological data in the strict historiographical sense, search has been made for suitable corroborative evidence in ancient Near Eastern history.

(a) On the side of ancient Near Eastern literary texts, appeal has been made to Josephus' interpretation of Manetho's tradition of the invasion and expulsion of the Hyksos as the descent and exodus of the Israelite 'shepherd-kings'.

(b) On the archaeological side, the references in Babylonian texts at the end of the third millennium to the arrival of the Amorites ('westerners') were felt by many (see Chapter 1.IV.3 below) to be corroborated by the findings of field archaeology that city life had gradually revived inland from the coast of Canaan after a period of decline at the end of the Early Bronze Age (EBA). The migration of Abraham was related to this phenomenon. Details in the patriarchal narratives have been compared with cultural practices evidenced from ANE texts of the second millennium: for example, E.A. Speiser has compared Abraham's passing his wife Sarah off as his sister (Gen. 12.10f.; 20.1f.; cf. Isaac and Rebekah in Gen. 26.6ff.) with Hurrian texts from Nuzi. More recently J.J. Bimson has argued that archaeological evidence (especially the destruction levels marking the transition from the Middle to the Late Bronze Ages [MBA/LBA] and the incidence of Bichrome Ware) can be interpreted to support an incursion of Israel into Canaan in the fifteenth century. Bimson's position has been given wider currency in the 'coffee-table' presentation of Ian Wilson, who himself links the exodus with the ash cloud and tidal wave unleashed by the volcanic eruption of the island of Santorini in the Aegean c. 1450 BCE.

(ii) The problems with such an early chronology (even granting that the biblical data can be appropriately interpreted in a strictly chronological sense) include the following.

(a) In the Old Testament the Hebrew patriarchs are not equated with but distinguished from the Amorites, who are regarded as among the indigenous inhabitants of the land (cf. Gen. 10.16).

(b) The detailed archaeological argumentation for the migration of Abraham in the transitional EBA/MBA period and the arrival of the Israelites in Canaan after an exodus near the beginning of the LBA (the LBA is usually dated c. 1560–1200 BCE), involves a high degree of selectivity and a substantial amount of special pleading in the use of the evidence. Had it not been for the biblical chronology, no archaeologist would have thought of dating the end of MBA later than the mid-sixteenth century, nor the introduction of Bichrome Ware later than the sixteenth century. Such phenomena are far too widespread in Canaan, Syria and Cyprus to be specifically related to an Israelite incursion, even assuming that to have been marked by armed conflict, and have links with other pottery typologies, especially Cypriote and Helladic, which provide additional chronological controls. The Santorini eruption does not fit the biblical record very well: volcanic ash, however reinterpreted in terms of darkness or as causing skin irritation, does not figure among the plagues in Exodus 7–11; a tidal wave, even assuming it reached the south eastern Mediterranean coast, accords ill with the narrative of the crossing of the Red Sea.

(c) More recent archaeological interpretation by, for example, M. Kochavi and A. Mazar, links the arrival of the Israelites in Canaan to much later phenomena. Intensive archaeological excavation and surface exploration in the 1970s and '80s find evidence for the coming of the Israelites in the growing number of rural settlements spreading from the region of Gilead into the areas labelled by the Bible 'Manasseh' and 'Ephraim' from the beginning of the Iron Age (IA 1, c. 1200–1000 BCE) with gradual encroachment south into 'Benjamin' and 'Judah'. This, in rather general terms, matches the biblical picture in Numbers 32, Deuteronomy 1–4 and Joshua of Israel settling first in Trans-Jordan in the form of Reuben, Gad and Half-Manasseh before the main drive of the settlement of the remaining tribes on the West Bank.

(d) A disconcerting feature of recent archaeological investigation in the 'wilderness' of Sinai south and south east of the coastal strip has been the absence of evidence of occupation, Israelite or otherwise, from the beginning of MBA to the beginning of IA or even later, at sites plausibly identified as those featuring in the exodus narrative, for example, Baal-zephon (occupation not resumed till the Persian period, 539–331 BCE) and, especially, Kadesh-barnea (no Israelite occupation until the time of Solomon). If Israel's settlement took place from the east, as archaeological evidence and biblical tradition suggest, this absence of evidence occasions little surprise but leaves the wilderness wandering period archaeologically unsupported.

(e) This absence of evidence for the presence of Israel in the wilderness in the LBA has led some, for example, E. Anati, to affirm a still longer chronology: the wilderness wandering is to be associated with the increasingly copious evidence of occupation dated from the EBA to the beginning of MBA at numerous sites in the Negev and Sinai, including Kadesh-barnea and Baal-zephon themselves. In support of his argument, Anati, like many another scholar, links the problems of dating the exodus and wilderness wandering to those of the immediately following period, the conquest of Canaan under Joshua. Matching the gap in occupation in the Negev, which poses problems for an exodus and wilderness wandering in MBA/LBA, is the gap in occupation from about 2200 until IA 1 at Ai, which, according to Joshua 7f., was destroyed by Joshua and the Israelite invaders. If Ai was destroyed by Joshua, then the conquest, and, therefore, the preceding wilderness wandering and exodus, must be dated towards the end of the EBA. Anati compares also Jericho, where, according to K.M. Kenyon (its excavator in the 1950s), the LBA town ceased to exist by the third quarter of the fourteenth century and thus could not have been destroyed by Joshua in a thirteenth-century invasion but only in an earlier one.

The chief difficulty in Anati's theory—even on its own terms—is that, in order to account for the long gap in the biblical record between an exodus and conquest at the end of the third millennium and the subsequent history of Israel, he has to assume that 'an entire period' (more like a thousand years!) has been omitted.

(f) If Israel settled in Canaan or even 'conquered' Canaan in the LBA, it would have encountered the Egyptian imperial power there. But of such an imperial presence there is no evidence in the account of the settlement in Joshua or of the post-settlement period in Judges. The more recent archaeological picture of Israel's settlement in the period after 1200 (cf. (c) above) fits the historical evidence for the social, political and military conditions of the time. A fifteenth-century date also leaves too large a gap between settlement and monarchy to be filled by the material in Judges. The conditions which made it possible for Israel to settle (the progressive impoverishment of Canaan by centuries of Egyptian exploitation and the incursions of the Sea Peoples from the west) only developed with the decline of the Egyptian empire in Syria and Canaan at the end of the LBA (cf. e.g. the division of Syria and Canaan between the Egyptians under Ramesses II and the Hittites after the battle of Qadesh c. 1296; the Syrian interregnum between the XIXth and XXth Dynasties c. 1200 and the engagement of Ramesses III against the Sea Peoples c. 1188 [*ANET*, pp. 255ff.]).

(g) A general point may be added. In the discussion of archaeological data as such from the ancient Near East from EBA to LBA, terms like 'the patriarchal period' or 'the period of the exodus' are inappropriate: these impose on the vast range of evidence for the peoples of the ancient Near East, of whom the patriarchs and early Israel were at most a fringe group, a biblical pattern that is of highly marginal relevance. Even the term 'biblical archaeology', widely current (e.g. in the 'Albright school'), if it leads to such misapplication, is better avoided. Near eastern archaeology is an autonomous cluster of disciplines which have to evolve their own patterns of interpretation of all the evidence, appropriately including, but not dominated by, the biblical.

2. The 'Short' Chronology

(i) The criticism of the 'long' chronology has already provided part of the case for the 'short'. Because conditions in the Egyptian empire in Canaan at the end of LBA were apparently more advantageous for Israel's conquest, most scholars in recent times, for example, H.H. Rowley, have dated the exodus in the thirteenth century. The stele of Merneptah (cf. Chapter 1.II, above) mentioned Israel as already one of the peoples subjugated in Canaan; it is assumed, therefore, that the exodus must have taken place some time during the reign of Merneptah's father, Ramesses II (1304–1237). If Ramesses II is the Pharaoh of the exodus, then his father Seti I (1318–1304) must be the Pharaoh of the oppression and of Moses' flight to Midian. That it is this, the XIXth Dynasty, called 'Ramesside' after its founder Ramesses I (1320–1318), which is responsible for the oppression, seems to be confirmed by the name of one of the store-cities, Raamses, where the Israelites were employed as slave labourers (Exod. 1.11). If oppression and exodus are thus to be dated to the XIXth Dynasty, the descent must have taken place earlier. The suggestion is made that the 'heretic' king of the XVIIIth Dynasty, Amenophis IV/Akhenaten (1379–1362), who espoused the 'monotheistic' cult of the Aten, the solar disc, would have welcomed the monotheistic Joseph as his secretary of state (cf. the Joseph cycle, Genesis 37; 39–50). This kind of scenario has been associated by S. Herrmann with migrations of the Aramaeans, to whom, according to biblical tradition, the Patriarchs are indeed related (e.g., Gen. 11.28; Deut. 26.5).

(ii) At first sight, this identification of the Egyptian context of Israel's descent, sojourn and exodus may seem more probable. Its uncertainty and arbitrariness should not, however, escape notice.

(a) The reference to Raamses in Exod. 1.11 is complicated by the references to the consonantally identical place Rameses (Gen. 47.11; cf. Exod. 12.37; Num. 33.3, 5), where Jacob and his sons were installed at the time of the descent, which ought equally to imply the XIXth

Dynasty. If one is forced to plead anachronism in the case of Genesis, why not also in the case of Exodus?

(b) 'The way of the land of the Philistines', the name of the route to Canaan forbidden to the escaping Israelites (Exod. 13.17), is most probably also an anachronism, since the Philistines as one of the 'Sea Peoples', who were part cause and consequence of the collapse of the entire LBA civilization in the eastern Mediterranean, only properly settled post-1200.

(c) Even the place name Raamses, though pointing to the XIXth Dynasty, was known until Ptolemaic times (i.e. post-323 BCE) and is, thus, non-specific as regards dating. It is perfectly possible that knowledge of atrocious working conditions for labourers in the grandiose building operations of Ramesses II, to whose reign some half of the surviving monuments of Egypt belong, became as notorious as the plagues of Egypt (already known to the Hittites; cf. *ANET*, pp. 394ff.). Quite detailed knowledge about conditions in Egypt is displayed by Old Testament writers who had not necessarily been there (cf. e.g. Amos 8.8; 9.5; Isa. 19; Jer. 46; Ezek. 29ff.).

(d) The sole historical point of reference is the Merneptah stele, but how much does it in fact prove? It provides a chance piece of information about a situation that may have long endured: that roving bands of marauding habiru, among whom Israelites were indistinguishable, were in the region is already known from, for example, the Amarna letters of a century and a half earlier. All else is supposition. As already noted, there are several alternative possibilities for the descent, sojourn and exodus of Semites. On the basis of the historical evidence it is more plausible to argue for recurrent processes than for a single event. It may then be better to consider the biblical material in another light and not assume (as, e.g., H.H. Rowley tends to) that its data and the data from ancient Near Eastern archaeology are, so to speak, mathematical digits of the same order which can be added up more or less congenially.

(e) There is no evidence that the wave of Aramaean wanderers reached the Delta of Egypt; the Egyptian records speak rather of the Shosu, the bedouin population of the Sinai peninsula.

3. *The 'Part Long, Part Short' Chronology*

This chronology associates the patriarchs with the Amorites but also places the exodus in the thirteenth century. It reflects something of an international and inter-faith 'consensus' reached in the 1960s and held in a variety of forms by, for example, W.F. Albright, K.M. Kenyon and B. Mazar, and has been eloquently advocated by, for example, J. Bright and R. de Vaux in their respective *Histories of Israel*. The approach, however, merely combines the difficulties and uncertainties of both the 'longer' and 'shorter' chronologies.

Further Reading

The literature on the archaeological and historical matters dealt with in Chapter 1.IV is vast. The following provides bibliographical information on works of some of the scholars referred to above in order of citation.

Galling, K., *Textbuch zur Geschichte Israels* (Tübingen: J.C.B. Mohr, 2nd edn, 1968).

Speiser, E.A., *Genesis* (AB, 1; New York: Doubleday, 1964).

Bimson, J.J., *Redating the Exodus and Conquest* (JSOTSup, 5; Sheffield: JSOT Press, 1978). An interesting controversy has been conducted between Bimson and B. Halpern (the latter championing a 'short' chronology for the exodus) in the *Biblical Archaeology Review*, 13 (1987). *BAR* in general, with its lively format and lavish illustrations, provides highly accessible information on questions concerning current archaeological research and the Bible; other vols. (e.g. 1981, 1982, 1994, 1998) contain further articles on the exodus. The *Biblical Archaeologist* provides a similar service at, generally, a rather more technical level.

Wilson, I., *The Exodus Enigma* (London: Weidenfeld & Nicolson, 1985).

Thompson, T.L., *The Historicity of the Patriarchal Narratives* (BZAW, 133; Berlin: W. de Gruyter, 1974).

A conservative response to Thompson has been edited by A.R. Millard and D.J.

Wiseman, *Essays on the Patriarchal Narratives* (Leicester: Inter-Varsity Press, 1980).

Kochavi, M., and A. Mazar, 'The Israelite Settlement in Canaan in the Light of Archaeological Excavations', in *Biblical Archaeology Today: Proceedings of the International Congress on Biblical Archaeology, Jerusalem April 1984* (Jerusalem: Israel Exploration Society, 1985).

Oren, E., 'Ancient Military Roads between Egypt and Cana'an', *Bulletin of the Anglo-Israel Archaeological Society* (1982), pp. 20-24.

Cohen, R., *Kadesh-barnea: A Fortress from the Time of the Judaean Kingdom* (Jerusalem: The Israel Museum, 1983).

Anati, E., *Har Karkom: The Mountain of God* (New York: Rizzoli, 1986).

Rowley, H.H., *From Joseph to Joshua* (London: The British Academy, 1950).

Herrmann, S., *Israel in Egypt* (Studies in Biblical Theology; London: SCM, 1973)

Additional Bibliography

Shirun-Grumach, I. (ed.), *Jerusalem Studies in Egyptology* (ÄAT, 40; Wiesbaden: Otto Harrassowitz, 1998).

V. *Other Problems Encountered by the Historical Approach*

When the material in Exodus is treated as though it were a historical source, two further major problems, besides that of dating the exodus, are encountered: the numbers involved and the location. These problems are typically solved by rationalization: scaling down of the numbers; localization of the event. But the presence of these embarrassments should merely confirm the nature of the biblical material as not primarily historiographical, and underline the need for an appropriate method of interpretation. If the true nature of the material is appreciated, such embarrassments are needless.

1. *The Numbers Involved in the Exodus*

Exodus 12.37 gives the number of Israelites involved in the exodus as 'about six hundred thousand men on foot, besides women and children'. On the assumption that most of these adult males were married with families, the total must have been some two or three million. As if that were not enough, the text adds, 'A mixed multitude also went up with them, and very many cattle, both flocks and herds'. Commentators have felt compelled to concede that numbers of this magnitude could not possibly have crossed any ordinary stretch of water by a — presumably — narrow path in the space of one night. Equally impossible to envisage is how for forty years a host of such a size could have been sustained with food and water and its flocks and herds provided with pasture in the inhospitable deserts of Sinai. Modern census figures suggest a total of c. 40,000 Bedouin in the whole Sinai peninsula. In 1882 CE the figure was as low as 4,179.

Some means of reducing the biblical number has been sought. One way is to assume that the word for 'thousand' (*'elep*) means here 'family', as apparently in Judg. 6.15; 1 Sam. 10.19. But, if so, why would the women and children be mentioned in addition? In any case, that 600,000 is intended by the biblical writer as a genuine number is confirmed by the census lists in Numbers 1–4. It is, therefore, assumed that the number must be a mere exaggeration, as frequently occurs in other statistics in the Old Testament (cf. e.g. 1 Chron. 19.18, where 7,000 is read for the 700 of the parallel in 2 Sam. 10.18) and in texts from the ancient world. It then becomes a matter for arbitrary speculation how many could have been involved in such a desert trek, for example, Bimson's 72,000. The suggestion of P. Weimar and E. Zenger that the number might have been as few as 150 is the *reductio ad absurdum* of this approach.

2. *The Location of Crossing of the Red Sea*

Since so vast a host could not have crossed the 10–30 km of the Gulf of Suez of the actual Red Sea in one night, alternative locations have been sought. Once again, a modification is proposed for the accepted sense of the Hebrew. The Hebrew expression *yam suph* (Exod. 13.18

etc.) has traditionally been rendered 'Red Sea' on the basis of the Greek translation in the Septuagint. But, since *suph* means 'reeds' (as, e.g., in Exod. 2.3, 5), the Hebrew, so the argument runs, should be translated 'sea of reeds'. Various suitable expanses of reed beds have then been suggested by various scholars at points roughly along the line of the modern Suez Canal from the Bitter Lakes in the south to Sabkhat al-Bardawil (classical Lake Sirbonis) just below the Mediterranean coast in the north. Quite a plausible case can be made out for the narrow strip of sand which separates Sabkhat al-Bardawil from the Mediterranean: at times no more than a few metres across, it is easy to envisage how a company might pass over it on foot while its pursuers in heavy chariots could get bogged down. There are even classical parallels of troops being trapped in this area (Diodorus, 16.46; 20.73f.; cf. Strabo *Geographica* 1.58). On the other hand, *yam suph* does clearly refer elsewhere in the Old Testament to the Red Sea (unambiguously even to the Gulf of Aqaba, 1 Kgs 9.26) and must be so intended in Exod. 10.19.

3. *Further Geographical Problems*

(i) *The geography of the sojourn in Egypt.* Only three localities are mentioned. Some biblical passages (Gen. 46.28) imply that 'land of Goshen', where the Israelites were settled (Gen. 45.10ff.), lies between the southern boundary of Judah and the eastern Delta. But this seems to accord ill with other features in the narrative, especially a settled community of some 2–3 million. It has, accordingly, been conventional to identify Goshen with the Wadi Tumilat, which runs east to Ismailiya from Zagazig (so, e.g., E. Naville, the Egypt Exploration Fund's first excavator). A modern parallel to the sudden departure of nomads settled in this area, when threatened with an oppressive regime, has been popularized by A.H. Sayce (*History of the Hebrews*, 1897, p. 153).

There is no unanimity on the location of Pithom and Raamses (Exod. 1.11): Pithom is variously identified as Tall al-Maskhutah (Naville), Tall al-Rutabah (A. Gardiner); Raamses as Tall al-Rutabah (W.M.F. Petrie, Naville), Tanis (P. Montet), Qantir (M. Hamza), Tall al-Dab'a (M. Bietak).

(ii) *The location of Sinai.* The location of Sinai, the immediate goal of the escaping Israelites, is as uncertain as their point of departure on the Red Sea. Three main areas have been canvassed among the score or so of proposals that have been offered.

(a) The south of the Sinai peninsula, in the vicinity of St Catherine's monastery, where granite peaks of impressive grandeur rise to a height of more than 2,500m (Jabal Musa, 'the mountain of Moses', e.g., is 2,285m high). The name of the Wady Firan ('the water-course of the rats') in the south-west of the peninsula has been thought to retain an echo of the biblical 'Paran'. The objections to this location include the fact that it is based only on a Christian tradition derived from refugees from Egypt fleeing Roman persecution in the third century CE. St Catherine's itself, so named after the Alexandrian martyr, was fortified in the sixth century by the Byzantine emperor Justinian. Further, it lies within the region of southern Sinai, where, because of the turquoise mines, Egyptian interests were at their keenest and the presence of Egyptian patrols was to be expected.

(b) The region of Kadesh-barnea, in the vicinity of which Israel spent much of the forty years of the wilderness period. The most probable identification for the site is Ayn al-Qudayrat, the most fertile oasis in N. Sinai, near the intersection of the 'Way of Shur' and the 'Way of Gaza'; about 10km to the SE there is the oasis of Ayn Qudays, which may preserve an echo of the biblical name. Accordingly, suitable mountains in the vicinity have been sought, for example, Jabal Hallal (B. Mazar), Har Karkom (E. Anati). The biblical tradition, that Horeb (understood in the Bible as a synonym of Sinai; in the modern tradition as the range of which Sinai is the southern peak) is eleven days' journey from Kadesh-barnea (Deut. 1.2) is, however, to be noted.

(c) It is held by, among others, M. Noth, that the description of the theophany at Sinai in Exod. 19.18 implies volcanic activity. The nearest volcanic region is in the north-west of the Arabian peninsula (cf. the traditions linking Moses with the Midianites).

(iii) *The route of the wilderness wandering*. Given the dubiety about the locations of the crossing of the Sea and of Sinai, the route between the two can hardly be plotted with certainty. Pihahiroth, Migdol and Baal-zephon (Exod. 14.2) have Semitic names ('mouth of the channels', 'tower', 'lord of the north') and probably lay on or near the coast of the Mediterranean to the east of the Delta. But Israel is then forbidden to traverse the obvious route along the coast to Canaan. When they turn inland to Succoth and Etham, then to the wilderness of Shur (Heb. 'the wall'; cf., perhaps, the wall 'to crush the Sand-Crossers' in the Tale of Sinuhe, *ANET*, p. 19), with the watering-hole of Marah and Elim, and thence to the wilderness of Sin, with the watering-holes of Massah, Meribah and Rephidim, before, finally, reaching the wilderness of Sinai, they follow a route to the south, the north or through the centre of the Sinai peninsula, according to the views of the interpreter about the location of Sinai.

Further Reading

P. Weimar, E. Zenger and their school have published widely on Exodus. Their estimate of the number of participants in the exodus is to be found in their early work, *Exodus – Geschichten und Geschichte* (Stuttgart: KBW, 1975), p. 114.

For a brief statement of a view rather similar to that given here – but still essentially linear in its conception – see

Giveon, R., 'Archaeological evidence for the Exodus', *Bulletin of the Anglo-Israel Archaeological Society* (1983–84), pp. 42-44.

For reviews of the geographical questions, see

Davies, G.I., *The Way of the Wilderness* (Cambridge: Cambridge University Press, 1979).

Har-El, M., *The Sinai Journeys: The Route of the Exodus* (San Diego: Ridgefield, 1983).

As an example of the eccentricities to which the question gives rise, see

Salibi, K., *The Bible Came from Arabia* (London: Cape, 1985).

VI. *How Far Should the Book of Exodus Be Regarded as a Historical Work?*

This inconclusive outcome of historical research invites a re-examination and clarification of the nature of the biblical record. How far is it appropriate to regard Exodus as a work of historiography, in the conventional sense that its chief purpose is to provide explanation for the course of events at the mundane level in, say, social, political or economic terms, using as far as possible only primary sources?

Perhaps even to ask this question is to begin to answer it. However much the material in Exodus is related to historical events – and it will be argued below that it does relate to events marking fundamental historical change – that relation subserves a still more far-reaching objective: to portray to the people of Israel in terms which describe their origins, yet which also encapsulate their whole continuing life, the truths of their enduring relationship with God. To use Exodus to recreate the past as one historical event or series of events, however laudable the motive, is to overlook the nature of the narrative as a statement of the accumulated and summated significance of all past experience focused on, but not exhausted by, the primal events. The thrust of the biblical materials is not backwards to recover an original, but forwards from a presupposed, but not precisely reconstructed, original, which absorbs recurring experience within itself and imposes pattern on it, towards the ultimate goal to which the relationship with God strives.

Because the whole is couched as a narrative of the past, the elements within it have, under the exigencies and impetus of the narration, to take on the character, which may or may not be foreign to them, of being past events and be suitably formulated as incidents. The narrative itself is not a sober historiographical analysis and reconstruction, seeking merely to satisfy the antiquarian interest of the intellect, but an artistic work which seeks also to appeal to the imagination and win the commitment of readers or hearers of all ages and abilities. It employs suitable devices of narrative art to capture and intrigue the audience.

It needs little more than a first run through Exodus to see that narration has taken over and supplanted historiography, and that, under the impetus of the narrative portrayal of basic truths as events, there are many features which, as events, are improbable or even impossible. Only if historiography is given supreme valuation can this be regarded as unfortunate, and only then is there anything to be gained by trying to explain away any of these features: it will be the view taken here that only by giving these features their full value can the true significance of the material be appreciated. The negative task of seeing what the narrative is *not*, perhaps most clearly appreciated where the historical and historiographical are at issue, should help in that task.

The narrative as a whole is not historiographical. It is unilinear in form with little development of policy and counterpolicy by the protagonists. The characters are 'stock': the obdurate Pharaoh; the impotent advisers; even Moses, after his colourful infancy (since H. Gressmann, legendary elements are commonly identified here) and youth, fades as a personality behind the persona of the mediator.

The setting is also non-historiographical. The almost complete lack of interest in the geography of Egypt has already been noted. Geographical vagueness is matched by temporal. Three Pharaohs are mentioned (the one who welcomed Joseph, the one of the time of Moses' birth, youth and flight from Egypt and the one of Moses' return to Egypt) but none is identified by name or dynasty. The biblical chronology is equally obscure. One set of calculations (T. Nöldeke) places the exodus at 2,666 years after creation, at the 2/3 point of a period of 4,000 years, which may suggest eschatological, if not apocalyptic, speculations. The whole is set in primal time within a primal context: it is Israel's 'myth' of national origins but set within a recognizably real world where, however, the jagged and fragmented complexion of actual events has been smoothed down to the essential profile.

The surrealist (i.e., the real portrayed in terms beyond the actual) atmosphere is heightened by the marvellous and the miraculous; mundane possibilities or impossibilities are ignored. Two midwives suffice for the fecund wives of the 600,000 Israelite menfolk; Pharaoh's daughter gives Moses an Egyptian name which she explains by means of a Hebrew popular etymology; Moses turns all the water of Egypt into blood, then Pharaoh's magicians prove that they can do the same; in the fifth plague all the cattle of the Egyptians die but are smitten with boils in the sixth, killed by hail in the seventh and their firstborn perish along with all the other firstborn of Egypt in the tenth; from midnight on the night of the tenth plague there is time for news of the catastrophe to reach the Pharaoh from all over the land of Egypt, for Pharaoh to summon Moses and Aaron and for 2–3 million Israelites, including infants and children, to be driven out of the land carrying all their possessions and driving their flocks and herds.

It must be clear that it is wholly inappropriate to apply the canons of historiography to these and other materials in Exodus. Such points are not to be made in a cheap way to deride its content. It is only when the material is allowed to discharge its proper function, and not one which is largely foreign to it, that it can be respected for what it is. It exploits lore of many kinds, legend, folk-tale, religious and social institution, all set within a broadly historical context, in order to embellish the fundamental affirmation that the LORD alone directs the course of events. The high incidence of miracle (signs, plagues, deliverance at the sea, preservation in the wilderness, theophany at Sinai) is intended to convey that the action takes place not through inner-worldly causality but in accordance with the LORD's direction and intervention.

But what, then, *is* the relationship of the narrative in Exodus to history? It seems to me wholly compatible with the evidence to find that Exodus, within the limits imposed by its narrative form, reflects the general trend of history at the end of the LBA and the beginning of IA—the destruction of Egypt's West Asiatic empire, the confining of Egypt within its eastern borders and the emergence of new nation states in Syria and Canaan. Exodus is the Israelite version of these events. The Exodus narrative is part of Israel's confession of faith and of the vehicle of the continuing affirmation of the enduring significance of that faith. This is an astonishing outcome of events: the armed imperial might, which had dominated and impoverished the area for centuries, has been neutralized in a way far beyond human expectation or agency to achieve. Israel confesses that this is the work of none other than their God: 'This is the LORD's doing and it is marvellous in our eyes'. It is, thus, a fundamental mistake to attempt to explain away the miraculous elements in the narrative or to decode them into a series of mundane, rationally comprehensible events: the function of the miraculous is to portray, in terms of a narrative related to—but not bound by—history and to many other elements, the unsuspected continual presence and the unimagined active power of God in the detail, as well as in the general trend, of events.

In the light of these considerations one can more dispassionately review the historical and geographical problems which typically confront the interpreter (the 'date' of the exodus, its 'location', the numbers involved in it and so on). In the narrative of the exodus the Bible epitomizes, in Israelite terms, prevailing conditions of subjugation and escape throughout the Egyptian empire:

1. The contact between the Egyptian imperial might and the Semitic semi-nomads and *habiru*, of whom Israel's forebears were a part, took place in the desert fringes from Syria to Sinai and in the frontier zones of the Canaanite city-states. This centuries-long process is expressed in the dynamics of the narrative as a 'descent' into metropolitan Egypt and a 'sojourn' there.

2. All the forebears of later Israel knew at first hand, whether in metropolitan Egypt or in the Egyptian empire in Canaan, what it meant to confront an imperial power and to be 'enslaved' by that power. It is totally beside the point rationalistically to seek to reduce the number of those participating in the exodus.

3. Building operations under the least favourable conditions conceivable in the searing heat of the plague-ridden Delta in the time of Ramesses II, the last most successfully self-assertive Pharaoh known, whose name lived on in the colossi, temples and towns he constructed, provide the ultimate expression for subjection. But whether any of Israel's forebears were ever in fact slaves in metropolitan Egypt itself is not of prime concern and the Egyptian evidence need not be forced to provide support.

4. The plagues of Egypt and the exploitation of subject peoples in the Asian provinces of the empire were constants of experience known to all. Within the Old Testament, being overtaken by the Egyptian plagues is held up as a recurrent threat—as is, indeed, being subjected once more to Egyptian bondage (e.g. Deut. 28.60-68). As in Second Isaiah, release from bondage in Egypt is a paradigm for release from captivity.

5. The geography of the desert route provides a clear example of ideological use of the data. The line of escape is not the rational direct route into Canaan—or even into the wilderness. This is particularly

clear in Exodus 14: there is a provocative 'turning back' (v. 2), motivated not by human considerations of military strategy or of eluding
pursuit, but by the desire to demonstrate definitively by the miracle at
the Sea that it is Israel's God who is the sole agent of the deliverance
of his people and of the destruction of their enemies (cf. e.g. the
'recognition formula' in vv. 4, 18, 'the Egyptians shall know that I am
the LORD', and the believing response of Israel, vv. 30f.).

It is again as futile, therefore, to attempt to locate this theological
affirmation in geographical detail as it is to date the exodus to a precise historical moment. There is no reason to deny that by 'Sea' the
biblical writer has in mind the Red Sea. The collocation of place-
names from the sand-bar north of Sabkhat al-Bardawil and the Red
Sea itself is motivated by his wish to make through the well-known
physical features of the landscape—influenced, one need not absolutely exclude, by his knowledge of the strategic possibilities of the
sand-bar—a statement about the definitive line where Egyptian
encroachment is cut off. Rationalistically to replace the 'Red Sea' by
the 'reed sea' is entirely beside the point and one hopes that it may be
dropped from scholarly discussion. Much more relevant are those
interpretations which find in the motif of the Sea a reflection of
Israelite polemical appropriation of the ancient Near Eastern cosmic
myths of the battle between the creator god and the great deep (cf.
Exod. 15.5, 8, 10). Speculation about the most favourable oases where
Israel could have found food and water and pasture for their flocks
and herds (cattle in the desert!) is equally irrelevant.

6. One may make again the general point about rationalizations
about date, numbers, location and so on, that, even accepting the
validity of the grounds on which they are based, they carry little
conviction. The criterion by which they seek to evaluate the Exodus
narrative is the historically possible, or as nearly credible as possible.
But, quite apart from the subjectivity of the view about what is historically credible, the more historically credible the exodus becomes
the less remarkable it becomes and the more difficult it is to account
for the impression which it has left on the traditions of ancient Israel.

In the light of the foregoing discussion, it seems to me appropriate
to maintain that the writer of Exodus (what might be meant by
'writer' is the subject of Chapter 3) is concerned to portray religious
institutions and beliefs in terms of a narrative which reflects historical
realities only in broad outlines and is concerned only in so far as is
necessary to present a verisimilitude of conditions of the general
period while being quite eclectic in its choice of detail.

Israel's religion is not founded on historical events; rather, Israel's religious writers are using a narrative form of presentation in which history provides the general framework; for the filling in of the detail, historical circumstances are only one source among many. This complex narrative is the medium for expressing a prior religious tradition: the historical events in Exodus are not the source but the vehicle, not the basis but the confirmation, not the proof but the proving-ground.

Further Reading

Batto, B.F., 'Red Sea or Reed Sea?', *BAR* 10.4 (1984), pp. 57ff.
—*Slaying the Dragon: Mythmaking in the Biblical Tradition* (Louisville, KY: West-minster/John Knox Press, 1992).
Kloos, C., *Yhwh's Combat with the Sea: A Canaanite Tradition in the Religion of Ancient Israel* (Leiden: E.J. Brill, 1986).

VII. *The Figure of Moses as Illustration of the Issues*

As with the exodus as a whole, so with Moses the question of historicity has bulked large in discussion. Support for the 'essential historicity' of Moses has been sought in the general consideration that Judaism, like Christianity and Islam, needs a founder. As R.H. Charles has put it, 'A great religious and moral revelation is not the work of a moral syndicate, but is due to the inspiration of some great outstanding personality' (*The Decalogue*, p. lii). The same point often appears in the more popular form, 'If Moses did not exist, he would have to be invented'. His Egyptian name ('Moses' is the Hebraized form of the Egyptian element 'is born' in such names as Thut-mosis, Ra-meses) is added as further proof.

The latter point is not very strong. The name 'Moses' may provide little more than plausible colouring or Hebraic polemic ('[he, i.e. the LORD] draws out'): knowledge of Egyptian personal names in ancient Israel is evidenced by a number of figures in the Old Testament who bear Egyptian names but who, or whose parents, may never have set foot in Egypt (e.g. Eli's son Phinehas, 1 Sam. 1.3). It may be but a further example of general knowledge of matters Egyptian in ancient Israel.

As for the general point, one might well reply, 'Just so!' In the light of the discussion in Chapter 1.I–VI, the narrative is to be regarded as a confession of faith which presents a broadly generalized and drastically oversimplified picture of historical processes taking place in the ancient Near East in the centuries of transition from LBA to IA; it is primarily a theological statement cast into the form of a linear narrative which exploits lore of many kinds, historical, folk, institutional, liturgical and legal. As will be suggested in Chapter 2, much of this lore has been secondarily attracted to the exodus and Sinai as the supreme foci of experiences of deliverance and revelation. It is not likely, then, that one individual, even a Moses, can, historically speaking, have been associated with the inception of all of these practices or even with all the historical processes to which they are related in the biblical narrative. But for the sake of coherence and accessibility the biblical narrative focuses them on one figure.

The quest for the historical Moses, however well-intentioned, thus runs counter to the thrust of the biblical source: a preoccupation with the biography of the great man can only distract attention from the purpose of the narrative. One may speculate that, historically, Moses was, like Joshua, Samuel or Ezra, a significant local figure. He may have been associated with the semi-nomads of the northern Negev, who were threatened by the Egyptian power in the region, whether these nomads were 'Israelite' or 'Kenite'. He may even have intermarried with the latter. As a Levite, he may have functioned at some local sanctuary; Kadesh-barnea would be an attractive possibility were it not for the lack of archaeological evidence there before the tenth century (cf. Chapter 1.IV.1[ii][d]). The brazen serpent, Nehushtan (2 Kgs 18.4), associated with him, sounds like a genuinely primitive feature. It is this local figure who has been extended under the impetus of the unilinear narrative into an idealized pan-Israelite leader.

Even such a reconstruction remains perforce speculative and leaves the reader perplexed as to what is ultimately gained thereby. If this is true of attempts to reconstruct the life of Moses on the basis of historiography (whether minimalist, as by, e.g., M. Noth [cf. Chapter 3.II], or maximalist as by, e.g., E. Auerbach), it is still more the case with accounts based, for example, on psychoanalysis, as notoriously by Sigmund Freud, or, more recently, on political science by A. Wildavsky. Any validity which such essays possess, as some of their authors indeed recognise, arises not from the recreation of the actual experience of one historical figure but from the perception of a more all-embracing—in fact, fundamentally theological—truth focused on that figure.

The main thrust of the narrative is theological. The LORD is the sole agent of deliverance. It is only in his service that the human agent receives any, and then only reflected, significance. Moses is the 'diminished hero' (D.J. Silver); the excellency is of God not of man. The point is admirably caught in the *Seder* of the annual celebration of the Passover to this day: Moses plays no role in it.

Further Reading

Auerbach, E., *Moses* (Wayne State University Press, 1975).

Bokser, B.M., *The Origins of the Seder: The Passover Rite and Early Rabbinic Judaism* (Berkeley: California University Press, 1984).

Coats, G.W., *Moses: Heroic Man, Man of God* (JSOTSup, 57; Sheffield: Sheffield University Press, 1988).

Van Seters, J., *The Life of Moses: The Yahwist as Historian in Exodus–Numbers* (Contributions to Biblical Exegesis and Theology, 10; Kampen: Kok Pharos, 1994).

Wildavsky, A., *The Nursing Father: Moses as a Political Leader* (University of Alabama, 1984).

Chapter Two

MATTERS INSTITUTIONAL: THE RELIGIOUS CORE

In Chapter 1 it has been argued that the genre of the book of Exodus is confession of faith expressed in a narrative of origins. This narrative exploits lore from many sources, folk, institutional and legal, and is set within a framework which views from an Israelite perspective — and drastically oversimplifies — the historical conditions of the period of transition from Late Bronze Age to Iron Age 1. The purpose is not to reconstruct the past for its own sake but to express the constants of Israel's experience of life under God. Religious institution, as one of the chief ways of expressing and experiencing life under God, provides congenially one of the mainsprings of this narrative.

There are six main institutions or complexes of institutions articulated in narrative form in Exodus: the Festival of Passover, the Festival of Unleavened Bread, the Offering of Firstlings, Theophany, Covenant, and Law. These institutions are some of the most important means whereby Israel lived out its community life under God in the annual cycle of worship and in the daily round of affairs. Through them hope for the future was affirmed in the light of origins over against the often bitter experience of present reality. These actualities of life expressed through shared institutional practice are in Exodus gathered up into a coherent narrative. In mutual interaction, this narrative draws from these institutions and imparts to them definitive interpretation.

In Exodus, these six institutions appear in two groups of three: Passover, Unleavened Bread and Firstlings are dealt with in chs. 12–13 within the wider context of the exodus (chs. 1.1–15.21); Theophany, Covenant and Law in chs. 19–24 within the wider context of revelation at Sinai (Exod. 19.1–Num. 10.10). It will be argued below that in each case, surprisingly enough perhaps at first sight, an institution, which has in origin nothing whatever to do with either exodus or Sinai, is secondarily associated with one or the other ('historicized' is the usual term, but, in the light of Chapter 1, that places too high a premium on 'history' to the exclusion of all else). The purpose of this secondary association is that each institution, which has in all probability been observed from time immemorial and has, thus, imparted to all participants a shared expression of communal life, may receive definitive interpretation and become a fully appropriate vehicle for expressing corporate understanding and identity in terms of Israel's faith.

I. *Passover*

Exodus 12.1–13.16 is both legislation (12.1-27, 43-49; 13.1-16) and account of putting legislation into effect (12.28-42, 50f.). But of the three practices legislated for, Passover, Unleavened Bread and First-lings, it is only Passover (12.1-13, 21-27, 43-50) that could have been practicable, and then only partially, on the original occasion as envisaged by the narrative—Unleavened Bread (12.14-20; 13.3-10), a seven-day pilgrimage festival held at the sanctuary (Exod. 23.14f.), could not be observed while the Egyptians were in hot pursuit; Firstlings (13.1f., 11-16), offered on the eighth day after birth (Exod. 22.30 [Heb. 29]), depended on the season of birth and are obviously quite different from the yearling lamb/kid chosen for Passover (12.5). Thus, despite the initial impression of uniformity in these chapters, where legislation on Passover-Unleavened Bread-Passover-Firstlings-Unleavened Bread-Firstlings is interwoven, only Passover is relevant to exodus and the other two have been brought secondarily into association with it in order to receive added justification (13.8, 14f.). This secondary association with the exodus of practices which have in origin nothing whatever to do with it, in order to impart additional warrant or significance to them, is not uncommon in the Old Testament: thus, for example, circumcision (Josh. 5.9), sabbath (Deut. 5.15), the Festival of Tabernacles (Lev. 23.43), the whole sacrificial system (Lev. 22, climaxing in v. 33), the jubilee (Lev. 25.55) and, even, just weights and measures (Lev. 19.35ff.).

But is even the Passover quite at home in the context of the exodus as portrayed in Exod. 12f.? The historical implausibility of certain features of that account has already been noted in Chapter 1. Nor could the complete range of stipulations concerning the Passover have been kept on the night of the exodus: any part of the Passover lamb left till the following morning was to be burnt (12.10) and no Israelite was to leave his house until the morning (12.22)—but Moses and Aaron were summoned to audience with Pharaoh that night (12.31) and the people of Israel were hustled out of the land, seemingly forthwith. There is, thus, a certain tension between the legislation on the Passover and the account of its first observance: the narrative is created to provide an aetiology for the Passover but, once launched, has to follow a course dictated by its own momentum.

Is it possible, then, that the Passover also, like Unleavened Bread and Firstlings, was an independent institution, which had in origin nothing to do with the exodus, yet has been secondarily associated with it and, indeed, has provided the decisive mould within which the narrative of the exodus has been cast? Writers on the Passover, for example, J.B. Segal or J. Henninger, have drawn attention to anthropological parallels among the Bedouin of Sinai or among pre-Islamic Arabs to elements within the exodus narrative: the Bedouin custom of smearing the blood of a slaughtered animal at the entrance to a house threatened with cholera, the flesh being eaten in a common meal called a *fidyah* (cf. Hebrew *pādâ*, 'redeem', used, e.g., in Exod. 13.13, 15). Similar rites are practised on many occasions of new beginnings: the breaking-in of new ground, the opening of a new well, the building of a new house, at betrothal and marriage. The purpose of these rites is apotropaic, that is, to ward off any malign influence that may lurk to harm the participants. The similarity to the Israelites' daubing the lintel and two doorposts of their houses to ward off 'the destroyer' (Exod. 12.23) is surely striking. Among the Bedouin and the pre-Islamic Arabs there is also evidence of a spring rite of offering a blood-sacrifice of the first-born of the herd, which must be without blemish and, preferably, male, followed by a communion meal often with the sprinkling or anointing with sacrificial blood. The purpose of the rite is again to secure protection for the community, their possessions and their herds in the ensuing year.

These parallels can be linked, following the suggestions by L. Rost, still more dynamically to the biblical material. It is striking that the selection of the Passover lamb/goat falls on the tenth day of the first month inasmuch as it is precisely on the tenth day of the seventh month, the Day of Atonement, that the 'scapegoat' is driven out into the wilderness to Azazel, in Jewish tradition the desert demon. The two halves of the pastoral year of the nomad are thus matched by two corresponding rites: the Passover lamb/goat is slain in the first month around the time of the spring equinox, which marks the seasonal change from the winter months with their modest grazing in the wilderness pastures, to the aridity of summer, when the shepherd is driven with his flocks into the stubble fields of the peasant for meagre forage; correspondingly in the seventh month, around the time of the autumn equinox, when the early rains are expected, allowing agriculture once more to begin and the pastures of the wilderness once again to flourish, the scapegoat is driven off into the wilderness. It is difficult not to see in these institutions the vestige of immemorial nomadic rites aimed at warding off malevolent forces as the shepherd and his troupe set off into the potentially threatening environments of the agricultural lands in the spring and of the desert fringes in the autumn. Passover and Day of Atonement both have roots in the rhythms of transhumance, the seasonal migration of stock in search of grazing, which have belonged to pastoral life since time began.

It may even be that the exodus narrative reflects this primordial spring rite in Moses' request to Pharaoh for permission to go three days' journey into the wilderness to hold festival to Israel's God (Exod. 3.18 etc.). Moses' request would then not be simply an *ad hoc* device to secure the release of his people but would correspond to age-old custom now about to be invested with revolutionary significance. The practice of transhumance is referred to in Egyptian texts (cf. *ANET*, pp. 259, 446, cited in Chapter 1).

It is in the light of such a nomadic pastoral background that details of Passover observance can be appreciated. The victim is selected from the small cattle, the sheep and goats, of a pastoral community. Alone of all the festivals of Israel, the Passover was held at night, the appropriate time after the heat of the day when the flocks had finished their foraging and the shepherds had returned to camp. It had to be finished before daybreak, when the flocks would set out once more to seek pasture, hence the preparedness for the swift departure ('your loins girded, your sandals on your feet, and your staff in your hand', Exod. 12.11). As would befit a nomadic society, the animal was not sacrificed at a sanctuary nor offered by a priest; the head of the family himself was the officiant, roasting the flesh of the victim as on the Bedouin's improvised spit over an open fire on the domestic hearth. The victim was eaten with the unleavened bread of travelling folk and the uncultivated wild herbs of the wilderness.

The original separateness of even Passover from the exodus is, thus, a lively possibility. One circumstance makes this even more likely. If the association of Passover with transhumance is correct, it should have been observed as a spring rite of passage from the desert to the sown. Departure *from* the land of Egypt into the wilderness is exactly the opposite of what is to be expected at this season. There is, however, another passage in the Old Testament where the spring rite of transition from the desert into the sown is observed in consonance with the seasonal realities: the narrative of the entry into the land of Canaan in Joshua 1–6 places the event precisely at the time of

Passover (Josh. 5.10) and, furthermore, at the time of the barley harvest (Josh. 3.15), in connection with which the festival of Unleavened Bread was observed at the sanctuary at Gilgal (Josh. 5.11). It may be that it was from the resources of age-old observances such as at Gilgal that some of the ideas, which lie at the base of the exodus narrative, were nurtured in Israel's consciousness. It is equally striking that the narrative of crossing the Jordan in Josh. 3.14ff. contains distinct parallels to the narrative of crossing the Red Sea in Exodus 14. Institutional considerations can thus support the archaeological findings noted above: Israel's forebears belong to the wave of Aramaeans encroaching from north-east Transjordan, whose contact with Egyptian oppression was in the imperial provinces of Canaan, not in the metropolitan Egypt of the Nile valley and Delta.

The argument which seems to be developing is, thus, the following. In the exodus narrative Israel's immemorial religious institutions, in particular the Passover, are secondarily associated with historical processes. On the one hand, they receive new and definitive significance from these processes; on the other, they become the means whereby the continuing significance of these historical processes is expressed and reappropriated by the celebrating community. Israel's institutions in their definitive interpretation are unfolded as story in terms of the realities of experience, using lore of manifold kinds. The Passover (also in its Christian guise of Lord's Supper), as the still continuing annual celebration thus definitively interpreted in terms of God's deliverance of his people from slavery in Egypt, is clearly the most potent single force for expressing and reinforcing identity as a family of the people of God. But the secondariness of the association of Passover, as of Unleavened Bread and Firstlings, with exodus should not be overlooked. It is not inappropriately expressed by the phrase which recurs in the legislation for the observance of each: it is only 'when you come to the land/when the LORD brings you into the land' that 'you shall keep this service/set apart to the LORD...' (Passover, Exod. 12.25; Unleavened Bread, 13.5; Firstlings, 13.11).

Further Reading

The standard textbook on Israel's religious institutions is

Vaux, R. de, *Ancient Israel: Its Life and Institutions* (London: Darton, Longman & Todd, 1961).

As in his *History*, de Vaux presents somewhat more 'conservative' views than those offered here.

Henninger, J., *Les fêtes de printemps chez les Sémites et la pâque israélite* (Paris: Gabalda, 1975).

Rost, L., *Das kleine Credo* (Heidelberg: Quelle & Meyer, 1965), pp. 101ff.
Segal, J.B., *Hebrew Passover* (London: School of Oriental and African Studies, 1963).

II. *Unleavened Bread*

The impossibility of observing the seven-day pilgrimage festival of Unleavened Bread on the occasion of the exodus (Exod. 12.14-20; 13.3-10) has been noted in Chapter 2.I and provides a *prima facie* case for the secondariness of associating this festival with it. This second-ariness may be confirmed by the clear separateness of Unleavened Bread and Passover in the legislation on the festivals in Exod. 23.14-19 and its parallel in Exod. 34.18-26. While the Passover was a pastoral rite, celebrated by the family in the household, Unleavened Bread, which marks the beginning of the barley harvest, was one of the three annual harvest festivals of the farming community, when all the males went on pilgrimage to the sanctuary (the other two harvest festivals were Weeks, which was held seven weeks after the beginning of barley harvest and marked the end of wheat harvest, and Ingathering/Tabernacles, at the autumn equinox, which celebrated the bringing of the winnowed grain from threshing-floor into granary, and the vintage). While in the present form of the legislation in Exod. 12.14ff. Passover is celebrated on the night of the 14th and Unleavened Bread from the 15th till the 21st, this association may be secondary: the timing of Unleavened Bread may in earlier days have depended on the date of the ripening of the barley, which must have varied from locality to locality and from season to season (cf. Deut. 16.9).

The original separateness of Passover and Unleavened Bread is probable also on sociological grounds: Unleavened Bread, as the festival which marks the inauguration of the harvest season, is clearly a farmers' festival; as argued above, Passover is, by contrast, a shepherds' festival. Passover and Unleavened Bread thus represent the rites observed in the two distinct 'morphemes' of Israelite society, the pastoral and the peasant.

Unleavened Bread has, however, been brought into association with Passover in order to give it normative interpretation. This association is facilitated by the coincidence of two features between the two festivals: both are spring rites; in both unleavened bread is eaten. The need for such a normative interpretation of an indigenous farmers' rite in terms of Israel's faith as expressed in the narrative of an 'exodus from Egypt' is suggested by such an incident as 2 Sam. 21.1-14, where entirely heterodox rites are practised from the beginning of the barley harvest. These heterodox rites are further illumined by the beliefs of the indigenous Canaanite population in the dying of Baal in the ripened and winnowed grain in the drought of summer, and his rising again in the springing grain with the coming of the autumn rains, as expressed in the myths of ancient Ugarit. This normative interpretation of Unleavened Bread is also found in the hortatory additions to the legislation on the festival in Exod. 23.15; 34.18.

Further Reading

For two 'morphemes' in Israelite society, see the works of M.B. Rowton, e.g. 'Dimorphic Structure and the Problem of the *'apiru- 'Ibrim'*, *JNES* 35 (1976), pp. 13ff.
For the Ugaritic texts, see
Gibson, J.C.L., *Canaanite Myths and Legends* (Edinburgh: T. & T. Clark, 2nd edn, 1978), e.g., p. 77.

III. *Firstlings*

If Passover and, to a more limited extent, Unleavened Bread are thus unfolded as story as part of the narrative of Israel's deliverance from Egypt, how far is this also true of Firstlings? Firstlings and Firstfruits were offered from time immemorial (cf. Gen. 4.3f.). The reason for the offering was, presumably, the self-evident one of rendering tribute to God as the giver of fertility in flock and field; by this token — the offering of the first-born and the firstfruits — the whole progeny and produce were hallowed and, at the same time, the remaining progeny and produce were desacralized and made available for ordinary human purposes (cf. Exod. 22.29f. [Heb. 28f.]; Deut. 26.1-11).

But the first-born son of the human family is to be redeemed. Elsewhere it is the Levites who vicariously bear the cost of the redemption of the Israelite first-born sons (Num. 3.11ff., 40f.). By contrast, in Exodus 13 the institution of Firstlings and the redemption of Israelite first-born sons (vv. 1f., 11-13) are brought into association with the exodus and thus given secondary justification (vv. 14f.): it was at the cost of the first-born males throughout Egypt, both of human and of beast, that Israel's dedication to the LORD and freedom were purchased. The exodus now provides the aetiology not only for Israel's freedom but for the offering of the Israelite Firstlings, whereby that freedom was symbolized. The freedom once purchased at the cost of the Egyptian first-born is not merely a far-off, once-for-all event; it is not only sacramentally reappropriated once per year by the celebrating family and community in the conjoint festival of Passover-

Unleavened Bread; it is reaffirmed throughout the year on the eighth day after the birth of every first-born male, whether of human or of domestic animal, and constantly made present in every family by the continuing presence of the redeemed eldest son.

The whole narrative of the exodus (Exod. 11.1–13.16) is thus contained within the framework of the death of the Egyptian firstborn. But, since the death of the Egyptian first-born—as the tenth, climactic, plague—links up with the complete plague cycle beginning in 7.14, and, even further back, with the motif of Israel as the first-born of the LORD in 4.22, the literary impact of the elaboration of Firstlings has been very considerable (many commentators link the tenth plague to Passover rather than Firstlings, hardly correctly). Other motifs, like the hardening of Pharaoh's heart and the despoiling of the Egyptians, confirm the link still more widely back to ch. 3.

It is not unlikely that the elaboration of many of the first nine plagues is dependent again on commonplace general knowledge of conditions in Egypt. It is not difficult to imagine that the first plague, the turning of the waters of the Nile into blood, is a popular version of the annual Nile flood, when the waters are heavy with suspended silt. The unfailing regularity of the phenomenon must have been well known (cf. again Amos 8.8; 9.5; the night of 17th June is still known in Egypt as *laylat al-nuqṭah*, 'the night of the drop', because it is believed that annually on that night the first drop, which causes the Nile flood, falls from the heavens). The immediately following plagues are then not difficult to understand: the frogs, which swarmed throughout the land from the flood-waters; the gnats and flies which multiplied from their dead bodies; the spread of disease on animal and human. The remaining plagues of hail, locusts and darkness 'that could be felt' (eclipse[?]/sirocco[?]) are equally stereotyped as divine visitations.

The secondary association of Firstlings with the exodus has thus had a dynamic effect on the presentation of the narrative. As the basis for the introduction of the tenth plague, its influence extends back to the motif of the hardening of Pharaoh's heart in ch. 3; in the process it has gathered to itself a wide selection of materials drawn from popular lore.

IV. *Theophany*

Theophany—the self-disclosure of God—must be regarded as the central theme of Exodus. Though God is everywhere and can appear anywhere, yet within Exodus, as generally within the Old Testament as a whole, theophany is not mere sporadic mystical encounter with the numinous—though it can be that—but usually has its institutional counterparts. The fundamental institutional counterpart to theophany is the sanctuary.

It may be helpful to sketch the concept of the sanctuary which appears to have been current in the North-West Semitic world of Israel's origins, for the distinctive features of the Israelite conception of the sanctuary can perhaps best be seen as modifications of that model. The primary element of a sanctuary was the *bāmâ*, the 'high place', the local counterpart of the cosmic mountain on which the Deity was conceived as dwelling and where he sat enthroned as cosmic king. An essential element of the *bāmâ* is the altar (the 'horns' of the altar may themselves have been regarded as models of the cosmic mountain), the meeting-place between the physical and the spiritual realms, symbolized by the fire on the altar, which transposed the material sacrifice into the smoke ascending into the heavens. A temple as such is not essential; it is in principle merely a *bēt bāmâ*, a 'house of a high place'. But where a temple is built, it too is regarded as the local counterpart of the cosmic dwelling-place of God, which in its plan and furnishings symbolizes elements of the cosmic realm.

These features and concepts enable one to link together a number of elements in the Exodus narrative. It is naturally at a mountain, seemingly already known as the 'mountain of God', equated with Sinai/Horeb, that Moses encounters God (Exod. 3.1): the LORD, too, has his mountain, whence he exercises his dominion even over Egypt and, thus, the destinies of nations (this concept is greatly developed in connection with Mount Zion; cf. the 'Enthronement Psalms' 47, 93, 96–99 and the Psalm in Exod. 15, already noted in Chapter 1.VI in connection with the conflict with the Sea). (The fire of the burning bush [Exod. 3.2ff.] is best understood as the symbol, not of theophany as so often in the Bible, e.g., in Exodus itself at 19.18, but of persecution despite which God's people Israel, symbolized by the bush, is not consumed. Here God appears not *as* fire, but *in* the fire.) The mountain where God had appeared to Moses becomes the rendez-vous after the exodus: the place of theophany becomes a sanctuary—where God has appeared once, he may be expected to appear again. It is here that Jethro, priest of Midian, encounters Moses his son-in-law again (Exod. 18). The fact that Jethro takes the lead in the sacrifice at God's altar may suggest that this mountain had already been a Kenite shrine (assuming one can derive such historical data from the chapter); it at least lends confirmation to the view that here Israel was participating in generally recognized rites. The climactic theophany and revelation follow in Exodus 19ff.

Numerous details in Exodus 19ff. are of significance for the Israelite conception of theophany. The description of the theophany is, in part, metaphorical in order to express in the most impressive terms available the awesome grandeur of God's self-manifestation: thus the meteorological imagery of storm-cloud, thunder, lightning, with the appropriate geophysical response of volcanic eruption and earthquake (19.16, 18). But the mythological overtones of the imagery should not be overlooked: in the Ugaritic texts Baal 'rides the clouds' and manifests himself in the thunder and lightning (cf. the stele from Ugarit in The Louvre with Baal brandishing the mace [thunder] in his right hand and the spear with zigzag shaft [lightning] in his left). At Sinai the God of Israel is portrayed with the stock North-West Semitic accoutrements of deity.

In part, however, Exodus uses the institutional symbolism of the temple cult: the descending fire is suggestive of the altar-fire, which in principle descends from God himself (Lev. 9.24; 1 Kgs 18.24). It is this fire which provides the pillar of cloud by day and of fire by night rising from the perpetual burnt-offering on the altar. Rationalistic considerations about the improbability of a perpetually burning transportable altar which guides Israel through the wilderness should not blind one to the source of the imagery: as in the surrealist history and geography of the exodus, so in the religious institutions an ideal theological statement is being made. The altar with its continual burnt offering expresses the universal—and, therefore, omnipresent—reality of the unbroken communion between God and people and is, thus, the appropriate symbol for the presence of God, whether guarding his people from the pursuing Egyptians or guiding them through the wilderness.

There is a further element in the symbolism of the cloud. It is from the altar-fire descending from God himself that the coals are taken for the firepan on which incense is burnt. The incense cloud, kindled from God's own altar-fire and wreathing the sanctuary, thus symbolizes the mystical presence of God among his people and veils the mystery of God from human gaze.

What is true of the mountain of Sinai is true also of the tabernacle. The tabernacle is the local, physical, counterpart of the dwelling of God; every detail of it is in accord with the plan as revealed by God to Moses on the mountain (Exod. 25.9, 40; 26.30; cf. Heb. 8.5; so for the Jerusalem temple, 1 Chron. 28.19). It is doubtless for this reason that the detail of the tabernacle and its furnishings is given exhaustively in Exod. 25.1–31.17 (if, on occasion, confusingly: e.g., in 27.9-18 to have the curtains round the court hung on sixty poles one must assume

they are hung as on yard-arms) and that the execution of the tabernacle in accordance with this specification is minutely and with
apparently redundant repetition recorded in Exodus 35–40. As the
mountain is the place where the LORD descended in his theophanic
cloud, so in the cloud his glory fills the tabernacle (40.34ff.).

But characteristic features of the Israelite concept of the sanctuary
prevail. Alongside the tabernacle the tent of meeting (Exod. 33.7-11)
somewhat confusingly remains: revelation in communicable terms
continues alongside the ineffability of the mysterious glory of God in
the tabernacle. The sanctuary is no localized temple but a movable
shrine which dictates the movements of the people. While much of
the detail of the structure and furnishings of the tabernacle (and especially of its model the Jerusalem temple, e.g., the tripartite structure of
holy of holies, holy place, court corresponding to the 'three decker'
universe) probably reflects cosmic symbolism, the presentation,
beginning with the ark for the stones of the 'testimony' (25.10ff.) and
ending with the stipulations for the observance of the sabbath (31.12-
17), emphasizes distinctively Israelite beliefs.

Further Reading

Biran, A. (ed.), *Temples and High Places in Biblical Times* (Proceedings of the Col-
    loquium in Honor of the Centennial of Hebrew Union College, Jerusalem,
    1977; Jerusalem: Hebrew Union College/Jewish Institute of Religion, 1981).
Otzen, B., 'Heavenly Visions in Early Judaism: Origin and Function', in W.B.
    Barrick and J.R. Spencer (eds.), *In the Shelter of Elyon* (Festschrift G.W.
    Ahlström; JSOTSup, 31; Sheffield: JSOT Press, 1984), pp. 199ff.

V. *Covenant*

'Covenant', by which the relationship between God and people is
formally defined in Exod. 19.1–24.11; 34.1-28, provides yet another
example of the process whereby an institution practised widely in the
ancient Near East in both space and time has been secondarily associated with exodus/Sinai in such a way that exodus/Sinai is presented as the original and supreme instance, which thereby provides
that institution with its necessary aetiology. Because of the demands
of the Exodus presentation of Israel's history in a linear narrative,
covenant is focused on Sinai as if it were an event which happened
once for all time. It is, on the contrary, the institutional commonplace
in the ancient world whereby parties not related to one another by the
immediate natural family tie of blood bind themselves to one another

by ties of reciprocal obligation. As such, covenant belongs to the immemorial customs of the world of Israel's origins. Only secondarily has it been applied in the Old Testament theologically to denote the relationship between God and Israel.

That 'covenant' at its most elemental is primarily an inter-human contract can be seen from a number of instances of its usage in the Old Testament itself. Marriage is obviously one of the simplest forms of covenant between parties not previously linked to each other by family ties (Mal. 2.14). A solemn agreement between two friends can, equally, be termed a covenant (1 Sam. 23.15-18). Two passages in particular, Gen. 31.43-54 and Jer. 34.8-22, provide information about the rites involved in covenant-making between human parties and their significance. Both concern parties not linked to each other by ties of immediate family: Jacob and Laban, though related to each other as nephew and uncle, belong to separate households (Gen. 28.2); the slaves of the people of Jerusalem (Jer. 34.8ff.) have been bought by them into their households. In both cases the two parties have been thrown into a relationship which requires regulation. There is an objective token that an agreement has been made: the pillar/heap of witness in Gen. 31.45ff. presumably implies that the terms of the agreement between Jacob and Laban are oral; in Jeremiah 34 there may have been an objective document containing the terms of the agreement. The terms are agreed between the two contracting parties and commitment to the terms of the agreement is sworn on oath (Gen. 31.53) or solemnly pledged by a rite of self-imprecation Jer. 34.18f.). The fact that this commitment is sworn or pledged before God makes God witness to the agreement (Jer. 34.15); his surveillance is now the sanction securing adherence to the terms of the agreement, even in secret, when no human witness is present (Gen. 31.49f., 53); he is the agent of the punishment of the partner who is guilty of breach of the stipulation of the covenant; Jer. 34.17). The agreement is capped, at least in Gen. 31.54, by a common meal at the sanctuary. If table fellowship is the supreme expression of the solidarity of the independent household, the communion sacrifice (the *zebaḥ šᵉlāmîm*) at the sanctuary performs that function for the covenant community. In it the offering is divided between three parties, the offerer, the priest and God (e.g. Lev. 7.11ff.). Through participation in the body and blood of the one sacrificial victim (the formulation is that of W. Robertson Smith), God, his mediators and his people are bound together in the new solidarity, the new blood-tie of the one covenantal relationship, which transcends the old one of the mere kin group.

The background of the covenant ceremony in Exodus, especially

Exod. 19.3-9; 24.1-11, is thus a practice of immemorial antiquity, to which many of the details conform—situation to be regulated, conditions, promise, stipulation, oath, record, witness, communion sacrifice, new bond in the body and blood of the one sacrificial animal, meal. It is, therefore, not in the least surprising that parallels to the covenant at Sinai have been found in ancient Near Eastern treaties of the second and first millennia BCE. G.E. Mendenhall was the first to popularize the view that the LBA Hittite vassal treaties provide close parallels to covenant texts in Exodus and thus support the Mosaic date of the covenant at Sinai. It is now generally acknowledged, however, that because of the wide diffusion of the treaty form, no straightforward conclusion about the date of the covenant material in the Old Testament is possible. As before, one is struck both by the arbitrariness of the argument (vassal treaties are evidenced among the Hittites in the period of Moses; therefore, the covenant at Sinai understood as a vassal treaty can be defended as Mosaic—but in fact vassal treaties from many other epochs are known) and by the fact that it serves to undermine the uniqueness of the institution, the historicity of which it seeks to defend. Without, then, any compulsion to use the parallels as ammunition in the debate about date, one may be grateful for the enhanced appreciation now available of the six-part structure of the typical ancient Near Eastern treaty: introduction of the speaker; historical prologue; stipulations; the document clause; the gods as witnesses; the sanction of curse and blessing. Against this pattern the individuality of specific texts, not least biblical texts, can be the more clearly perceived. It is evident that, for example, the Deuteronomy material adheres much more closely to this pattern than does that of Exodus.

Much more interesting than the question of date, insoluble as it is by this means, is the observation of the adjustments the category 'covenant' had to undergo in the Old Testament when it was transferred from the normal 'horizontal' inter-human contract *before* God as witness to the 'vertical' axis, to a covenant *with* God as partner. Like all analogies, 'covenant' eventually breaks down. Exodus presents a thorough-going attempt to apply the full rigour of the category to the relationship between God and Israel. Israel is repeatedly given the option of undertaking its side of the agreement; repeated assurances are given that they regard themselves as able to keep the agreement (Exod. 19.8; 24.3). But no sooner is the covenant concluded by the people on the plain (Exod. 24.3-8) and by its representatives on the mountain (Exod. 24.1f., 9-11), than, when the covenant-mediator Moses' back is turned (Exod. 24.12–31.18), the people fall away in the worship of the 'golden calf' (Exod. 32). The covenant is, nonetheless, remade by God on the identical terms as before (Exod. 34.1-28) to declare that though all men should be false yet he will remain faithful. The covenant unilaterally abrogated by man is unilaterally reinstituted by God (see further Chapter 4.II.2[iii]).

Further Reading

McCarthy, D.J., *Treaty and Covenant* (Analecta Biblica, 21A; Rome: Biblical Institute Press, 1978).

Mendenhall, G.E., 'Ancient Oriental Law and Biblical Law', *BA* 17 (1954), pp. 26ff.; 'Covenant Forms in Israelite Tradition', *ibid.*, 50ff.

Nicholson, E.W., *God and his People: Covenant and Theology in the Old Testament* (Oxford: Clarendon Press, 1986).

Niehaus, J.J., *God at Sinai: Covenant and Theophany in the Bible and the Ancient Near East* (Carlisle: Paternoster, 1995).

VI. *Law*

Within the framework of the covenantal ceremony in Exod. 19.1–24.11 there is embedded a law-code (Exod. 20.22–23.19), conventionally termed the 'Book of the Covenant' ('B'), on the assumption that it is the document referred to in Exod. 24.7. It will be argued below that it seems relatively clear that this law-code illustrates yet once more the association with Sinai of a long tradition of Israelite and ancient Near Eastern material which has, in its origin and development, nothing whatsoever to do with exodus/Sinai, in order to supply it with normative meaning, ultimate sanction and appropriate aetiology. The question about the processes whereby this material seems to have become associated with Sinai will conveniently provide a link to the next chapter, which will deal with the literary growth of the book of Exodus.

Even when no external texts were available for comparison, the connection of much of this law with the conditions of the Mosaic age seemed open to question. The legislation concerns, indeed presupposes, a settled community living in houses (22.2, 7f. [Heb. 1, 6f.]), frequenting fixed sanctuaries (23.17, 19), possessing cattle as well as sheep (21.28f.), fields with their crops, vineyards and olive groves and the necessary installations for pressing the grapes and olives (22.29 [Heb. 28]; 23.10f.). Because there is no reference to a king, a favourite date ascribed to B has been the twelfth–eleventh centuries BCE between the settlement and the rise of the monarchy.

The response that Moses was by divine inspiration legislating for future conditions was countered not so much by the view that such prospective legislation was necessarily impossible—though it was regarded as unlikely—as by the observation that, even granting the biblical sequence, before the legislation in B could be put into practice it was already modified, ostensibly forty years later on the eve of the settlement, by new legislation in Deuteronomy (e.g. on slavery, Exod. 21.2-11; cf. Deut. 15.12-18). In the light of such evidence, it is more likely that law in Israel passed through the same gradual process of development and periodic compilation in response to changing conditions as in other cultures and as in later Judaism itself (cf. the compilation of the Mishnah c. CE 200 and of the Talmud c. CE 500 and the continuing development of the 'law of Moses' to the present day).

Since the rediscovery of ancient Near Eastern law-codes, especially the publication in 1902 of the law-code of the Babylonian king Hammurabi (c. 1700 BCE; cf. *ANET*, pp. 159ff., 523ff.), it has become clear that there is a long and widespread legal tradition in the ancient Near East with which the Old Testament material shows distinct affinity. The law of retaliation, 'an eye for an eye and a tooth for a tooth' (Exod. 21.24), so often held up as an example of Old Testament barbarism but in fact a means of restricting revenge and of ensuring that punishment fits the crime (in any case in Rabbinic interpretation the punishment is commutable into monetary compensation), has its parallel in Hammurabi 196: 'If a citizen has destroyed the eye of one of citizen status, they shall destroy his eye'. Such evidence, once more, does not prove the historicity of the Mosaic revelation at Sinai: rather, it shows that that legislation is the gathering up in Israelite terms of a long legal tradition, which is in the Old Testament secondarily focused on Sinai. There, by that theological shorthand, it receives ultimate warrant. Later Jewish tradition, which focuses not only the written law but also the oral law on Sinai, can again be compared (cf. e.g. *'Abot* 1.1ff.).

To place the 'date' of B somewhere between settlement and monarchy is simply to be deceived by a misapprehension of the unilinear biblical narrative, as though, if the material cannot be ascribed to the Mosaic period, it must be assigned to a later. Certainly its compilation may be dated to such a period (and there is the tradition in Josh. 24.25 of promulgation of law by Joshua, as there is by Moses, apart from Sinai, in Exod. 15.25). But the roots of the material are to be traced long before the time of Moses in the ancient Near Eastern society of the third and second millennia BCE.

The secondariness of the association of the law-code B with Sinai can, in fact, be relatively clearly established. Within B there is a remarkable variety in the formulation of different blocks of material, and these blocks of material have evidently been brought together by redactional activity with a particular purpose in mind. There are four main types of formulation in B:

1. The 'when..., if..., then...' type, for example, 21.18f. This is a discursive variety of law which begins with a general situation ('When men quarrel...'), introduces particular circumstances ('if the man rises again...') and concludes with the appropriate legal sentence ('then... he... shall be clear...'). The whole is expressed in the third person ('men... the man... he') and thus adheres to the standard form of legal formulation in the ancient Near East (cf. *ANET*, pp. 159ff., 523ff.). As belonging to this type there may be identified 21.1-11 (the second person formulation, 'you', in vv. 1f. is wholly exceptional in the context and has come in by attraction from the preceding material in 20.26) and 21.18–22.17[Heb.16]. The technical term for this type of legislation is given in the heading of 21.1: *mišpāṭ*, 'ordinance'. This is the variety of law identified by Albrecht Alt as 'casuistic [i.e. case] law'.

2. The 'whoever' type, for example, 21.15. This is terse in formulation. It begins with a participle (in the example 'whoever strikes...' [Heb. *makkēh*]) and is expressed in the third person. 21.12-17 and 22.18-20 [Heb. 17–19] belong to this type (21.13f. seems to be a secondary qualification separating manslaughter from murder; the second person 'you' in 22.18 [17] is again a secondary contamination from the surrounding context; cf. 22.21 [20]). It may be surmised that the technical term for this type of legislation (assuming it had one) is *ḥōq*, 'statute', inasmuch as 'statute' is frequently paired with the above class, 'ordinance', in the Old Testament (e.g. Exod. 15.25b; Josh. 24.25). 'Statute and ordinance' are tantamount to the Hebrew for 'law-code'.

3. The 'you (masculine plural) shall not...' type, for example, 20.23, that is, a prohibition addressed to the second-person plural. A possible technical term for this type would be *miṣwâ*, 'commandment'.

4. The 'you (masculine singular) shall not...' type, for example, 20.24, that is, a prohibition addressed to the second person singular. This is the same form as the Decalogue, or 'ten words' (e.g. Exod. 34.1; Deut. 4.13), hence the technical term for this variety might be *dābār*, 'word'.

Types (3) and (4) are intermingled with one another and stand as blocks at the beginning and end of B. They thus provide B with its outer framework (20.23-26; 22.21[Heb.20]–23.19). Alt combined types (2)–(4) under the term 'apodeictic [i.e. unconditional] law', but it is probable that they should be distinguished from one another in some such way as will be attempted below.

The interrelationship of these blocks of material can be presented diagrammatically as follows:

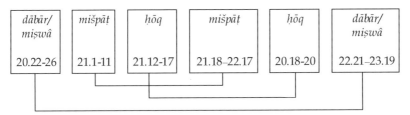

dābār/ miṣwâ	*mišpāṭ*	*ḥōq*	*mišpāṭ*	*ḥōq*	*dābār/ miṣwâ*
20.22-26	21.1-11	21.12-17	21.18-22.17	20.18-20	22.21-23.19

What accounts for the arresting fact that the *ḥōq ûmišpāṭ* ('statute and ordinance') material, formulated objectively in the third person, is held within a framework of *dābār/miṣwâ* ('word/commandment'), couched as direct second person address? The suggestion may be offered that by the imposition of this framework an original lawcode, *ḥōq ûmišpāṭ*, is being secondarily subordinated to the form of a covenant-code, *dābār/miṣwâ*, and thereby incorporated within 'covenant at Sinai'.

The *mišpāṭîm*, 'ordinances' (21.1-11; 21.18–22.17[16]), are wholly at home in the age-long legal practice of the ancient Near East. *Mišpāṭ* means both 'custom' and 'precedent' as well as the judgement based thereon. The *mišpāṭîm* thus cover a wide range of civil and criminal cases (slavery, personal injuries, goring oxen, theft, damage to crops, deposits, loans, seduction etc.), on which there is established practice. It is striking that in this range of inter-human, mundane, communal issues there is a prevailingly secular tone: there is not a single reference to God as the source of revelation. Neither is it surprising that such issues are not unique to Israel and that the legislation on them has parallels in other ancient Near Eastern law. Jurisdiction in these cases is vested with the 'elders in the gate', that is, the council of the heads of household within the community alluded to in Exod. 21.22 and more fully described in Deut. 16.18-20; 17.2-7. There is thus an affinity between *mišpāṭ* and wisdom, both in its internationalism and in its chief exponents, the wise men/elders. It is only when the requisite two or three witnesses are lacking that the case must be referred to the sanctuary for decision by the drawing of the sacred lots or affirmation by oath before God (Exod. 22.7-13 [Heb. 6–12]). There is here no primary connection with covenant, let alone Sinai.

The *ḥuqqîm*, 'statutes' (21.12-17; 22.18-20[Heb.17–19]), concern actions which threaten the established order of society — the sanctity of the life and freedom of the individual and duty to parents and to God. Infringements of these are absolutely prohibited and necessarily incur the death penalty. Jurisdiction in these matters again belongs to the 'elders in the gate', as the parallel legislation in Deuteronomy on the case of the unruly son makes clear (Deut. 21.18-21; cf. Exod. 21.15, 17). These seven *ḥuqqîm* have their counterparts in anathemas pronounced in the curse liturgy in Deut. 27.15-26 but it is clear that that passage is concerned with the prevention of such practices even 'in secret', that is, when there are no witnesses to bring a case to court. Again there is no necessary link with covenant.

The outer framework elements of *dābār* and *miṣwâ* (Exod. 20.22-26; 22.21[Heb.20]–23.19), however, introduce a completely new factor: they are expressed not in the objective third person formulation of the law-code but as direct address by God to Israel, both individually and corporately. They are thus cast in the form of the code of the covenant between God and Israel. Naturally, therefore, the stipulations refer to matters directly concerning the divine–human relationship. The opening part of the framework (20.22-26) states the exclusiveness of Israel's relationship to its covenant partner, God, and prescribes the appropriate mode of constructing the altar, the means by which that relationship is expressed and maintained. The materials in the concluding part of the framework (22.21[Heb.20]–23.19) are more miscellaneous in character and are disposed in four sections. Sections one and three (22.21-27[Heb.20–26]; 23.1-9) concern a variety of interpersonal relationships: the care for the weak in society, the stranger, the widow, the orphan, the poor and, even, the domestic animal; the safeguarding of the judicial process—the discharge of *ḥōq ûmišpāṭ*—is here taken up into the covenantal obligations. Sections one and three are linked together by the prohibition 'you shall not oppress a stranger', with which section one begins and section three ends (22.21 [Heb.20]; 23.9), and by interweaving the humanitarian concern for the domestic animal (23.4f.) with the demand for the upholding of justice. These humanitarian concerns are held within the context of the specific duties of Israel towards God enjoined in sections two and four (22.28-31[Heb. 27-30]; 23.10-19): the prohibition of cursing God; the acknowledgment of God the giver by the offering of Firstlings and Firstfruits; the eating of flesh only if offered according to the approved sacrificial rites; the observance of the sabbatical year, the sabbath and the three annual pilgrimage festivals.

Although all of these are couched in the *dābār/miṣwâ* form, there are vestiges of the *mišpāṭ* 'when..., if..., then...' formulation in the regulations for the building of the altar in 20.24f., for lending to the poor in 22.25-27[Heb. 24-26] and for the care of the straying or overburdened beast in 23.4f. These traces may provide valuable evidence for the process here being proposed: material originally a law-code, couched in *ḥōq ûmišpāṭ* form, is in B being taken up and incorporated secondarily into a covenant-code in the *dābār/miṣwâ* formulation. If the commonplace institution of covenant itself, within the context of which law is thus placed, is secondarily focused on Sinai as the supreme example from which all other examples derive their significance, then *a fortiori* the focusing of all law on Sinai is still more secondary.

That a process of assimilation of law-code to covenant-code was indeed taking place in the presentation of the Pentateuch is confirmed by a comparison of the Book of the Covenant with the code in Deut. 12.1–26.15. The introduction to the code in Deut. 12.1 is very revealing: there the contents about to follow are termed *ḥuqqîm* and *mišpāṭîm*, 'statutes' and 'ordinances', though they are almost uniformly cast in the form of second person address, that is, what has begun life as a law-code is now presented as a covenant-code. Thus material which appears in Exodus in the third person *mišpāṭ* formulation of the law-code is reformulated in Deuteronomy in the second person *dābār/miṣwâ* of the covenant-code (cf., e.g., the legislation on slavery in Exod. 21.2-6 [third person *mišpāṭ* form] and Deut. 15.12-18 [second person *dābār* form]). Exod. 22.21-27 [Heb.20-26]; 23.1-9 thus represents an intermediate stage of development in the reformulation of law-code as covenant-code, between the pure *mišpāṭ* form and its full-scale assimilation to the *dābār/miṣwâ* form in Deut. 12.1–26.15. The basic character of B as a law-code remains essentially unchanged: it has been transformed into a covenant-code by the addition of the outer framework and some small consequential adjustments (especially the second person address which has crept in at 21.1f., and 22.18[Heb. 17]). By contrast, Deuteronomy represents a large-scale transformation of law-code to covenant-code, appropriately enough in a book which is widely regarded as the covenant document *par excellence* in the Old Testament.

It would not be surprising if, therefore, the material in Exodus proved itself to be of earlier date than that in Deuteronomy. It is, accordingly, to the question of the comparative date of this material that attention must now be turned. The question of date inevitably involves questions about the origins of the material, the processes of its composition and compilation, the people involved in these processes and the purposes with which they set about their work.

These are the questions which have traditionally in scholarship been gathered together under the heading 'literary criticism'.

Further Reading

The 'classical' study of law in the Old Testament is

Alt, A., *Essays on Old Testament History and Religion* (Oxford: Basil Blackwell, 1966; repr. Sheffield: JSOT Press, 1989), pp. 79ff.

The user should be warned that there are a number of mistakes in this translation of the 1934 German original, e.g., the extent of 'casuistic' law in B should read xxi:2–xxii:16 on p. 88 nn. 15 and 16; in the discussion of the protasis of 'casuistic' law the Hebrew conjunctions *kî* and *'im* have been transposed on p. 89.

Boecker, H.J., *Law and the Administration of Justice in the Old Testament and Ancient East* (London: SPCK, 1980).

Clements, R.E., *Deuteronomy* (Old Testament Guides; Sheffield: JSOT Press, 1989).

Patrick, D., *Old Testament Law* (Atlanta: John Knox Press, 1985).

Paul, S.M., *Studies in the Book of the Covenant in the Light of Cuneiform and Biblical Law* (VTSup, 18; Leiden: E.J. Brill, 1970).

Chapter Three

MATTERS LITERARY: THE CREATIVE SYNTHESIS

In the light of the foregoing discussion, it is clear that the book of Exodus represents an extraordinarily rich amalgam of the most diverse materials. It must now be our task to try to trace the literary growth of this collection; our particular concern will be to understand the intentions of those responsible for the various stages of its compilation and redaction. But because Exodus is integrally connected with the other books of the Pentateuch, discussion of its origins and growth cannot be separated from the wider problems of Pentateuchal study.

To open up a way into these questions and the myriad discussions of them, three major contributions to the study of Exodus will first be looked at, those of S.R. Driver, M. Noth and B.S. Childs. Each comes from the hand of a scholar who has written (among his many other works) not only a commentary on Exodus itself but also a work of 'introduction' on the wider issues of Pentateuchal composition and who represents, or has even pioneered, a distinctive approach. Thereafter, two further approaches to the interpretation of Exodus will be looked at: the history of redaction and the literary approach. The chapter will conclude with a study of the Decalogue, as a comprehensive illustration of the issues.

Further Reading

Among the 'myriad discussions' available in English, besides those to be studied more closely below, the following may be noted.

Introductions
O. Eissfeldt (1965), R.K. Harrison (1970), G. Fohrer (1970), O. Kaiser (1975), J.A. Soggin (2nd edn, 1980), W.H. Schmidt (1984), R. Rendtorff (1985).
    For a review of the issues involved in such works see
Barton, J., *Reading the Old Testament* (London: Darton, Longman & Todd, 1984).

Clements, R.E., *A Century of Old Testament Study* (Guildford: Lutterworth Press, 2nd edn, 1983).

Hayes, J.H., and C.R Holladay, *Biblical Exegesis: A Beginner's Handbook* (London: SCM Press, 2nd edn, 1987).

Nicholson, E.W., *The Pentateuch in the Twentieth Century: The Legacy of Julius Wellhausen* (Oxford: Clarendon Press, 1998).

Whybray, R.N., *The Making of the Pentateuch: A Methodological Study* (JSOTSup, 53; Sheffield: JSOT Press, 1987).

For a review of the critical issues as they concern Exodus see

Johnstone, W., *Chronicles and Exodus: An Analogy and its Application* (JSOTSup, 275; Sheffield: Sheffield Academic Press, 1998).

Vervenne, M. (ed.), *Studies in the Book of Exodus: Redaction–Reception–Interpretation* (BETL, 126; Leuven: Leuven University Press/Peeters, 1996).

Commentaries

Further technical commentaries on the Book of Exodus (leaving aside smaller ones of a more confessional, devotional or homiletical nature) include

Hyatt, J.P. (New Century Bible; London: Oliphants, 1971), conceived largely in traditional 'literary-critical' terms (cf. Chapter 3.I).

Durham, J.I. (Waco, TX: Word Books, 1987), an essay in 'final form' interpretation (cf. Chapter 3.V).

Houtman, C. (Historical Commentary on the Old Testament; 3 vols.; Kampen: Kok, 1993, 1996, 2000), a judicious 'final form' commentary with very full review of the secondary literature. Houtman's Introduction (Der Pentateuch: Die Geschichte seiner Erforschung neben einer Auswertung, Contributions to Biblical Exegesis and Theology, 9; Kampen: Kok Pharos, 1994) should also be noted.

For an evaluation of selected recent commentaries on Exodus, see

Rodd, C.S., 'Which is the Best Commentary? VIII. Exodus', *ExpTim* 98 (1986/7), pp. 359ff.

The large commentary by W.H. Schmidt (1974ff., of which only the first fascicles have so far appeared) in the full-scale German series, Biblischer Kommentar, must also be mentioned. It is cast in the 'form-critical/history of tradition' mould (cf. Chapter 3.II). Cf. his

Exodus, Sinai und Mose (Erträge der Forschung, 191; Darmstadt: Wissenschaftliche Buchgesellschaft, 1983).

I. *S.R. Driver and 'Literary Criticism'*

Driver's *Introduction to the Literature of the Old Testament* was first published in 1891 and passed through nine editions. It became the standard work in English on the subject for two or three generations and helped to secure the ascendancy of a view of the composition of Scripture which had been developing, particularly on the Continent, since the end of the eighteenth century and even earlier. His commentary on Exodus appeared in the Cambridge Bible for Schools and Colleges (Cambridge University Press) in 1911.

1. *The Literary Criticism of the Hexateuch*

Because the view of the whole affects the understanding of the part, it is necessary to begin by outlining Driver's general argument in support of the conclusion that it was perhaps not until the fourth century BCE that the Hexateuch (he includes Joshua along with the Pentateuch) after a long literary history finally reached its completion and cannot, therefore, have been written in its final form by Moses.

The book of Deuteronomy (on which Driver as joint editor wrote the first International Critical Commentary in 1895) provides the clearest evidence of this, for example:

(i) Deut. 34.5f. records the death of Moses;

(ii) Deut. 1.1; 2.12; 3.8 imply that the settlement in Canaan has already taken place—but Moses, according to Deuteronomy 34, died before the settlement;

(iii) the unprecedented measures of Josiah's reformation in 621 BCE (especially the centralization of the cult and the mode of celebration of the Passover, 2 Kgs 22f.) match Deut. 12; 16.1-8;

(iv) by contrast, the plurality of altars in the pre-monarchic and early monarchic period, at which Israel's accredited religious leaders functioned uncondemned, shows that the legislation in Deut. 12.1ff. on the one legitimate altar was not yet in existence;

(v) the legislation in Deut. 17.14-20 on the post-Mosaic innovation of the monarchy reflects the account of the reign of Solomon in 1 Kgs 10.28f.; 11.1ff.;

(vi) other laws in Deuteronomy (tabulated in *Introduction*, 9th edn, pp. 73ff.), for example on slaves and Levites, stand midway between the Book of the Covenant in Exod. 20.22ff. and legislation in Leviticus and Numbers.

On the basis of these and many other observations, Driver espoused the 'New Documentary Hypothesis', which had been finally put forward in magisterial synthesis by J. Wellhausen in the 1870s. According to this, the Hexateuch comprises four main literary documents: J (which uses the Divine name 'Jahweh', comes from Judah and is dated in the ninth century), E (which uses the Divine name 'Elohim', comes from Ephraim and is dated somewhat later), D (i.e. Deuteronomy, dated seventh century) and P (the priestly document, dated sixth–fifth centuries). These documents were progressively integrated by three redactors, R^{JE}, R^D and R^P, in the early seventh, later seventh and fifth/ fourth centuries respectively. In anticipation of the discussion in Chapter 3.IV, it may be noted that these four 'sources' are not identified with equal certainty: D and P are clear in language, content and date, but J and E are less so.

2. *The Literary Criticism of the Book of Exodus*

Driver's account of the literary growth of Exodus itself is, accordingly, in terms of the Documentary Hypothesis. But it must be noted that equal weight is by no means given to each document, nor is there equal certainty about their delimitation. In effect there are essentially two: P, the more certain, and JE in combination. Only a few verses, especially in the Decalogue, are recognized as belonging to R^D (though, as noted below, Driver does regard R^{JE} as akin to Deuteronomy).

Driver's identification of P, the framework for his discussion, may be reproduced: 1.1-5, 7, 13-14; 2.23b-25; 6.2–7.13, 19-20a, 21b-22; 8.5-7, 15b-19; 9.8-12; 11.9-10; 12.1-20, 28, 37a, 40-51; 13.1f., 20; 14.1-4, 8-9, 15-18, 21a, 21c-23, 26-27a, 28, 29; (15.19;) 16.1-3, 6-24, 31-36; 17.1a; 19.1-2a; 24.15-18a; 25.1–31.18a; 34.29-35; 35–40. I shall register substantial agreement with this delimitation of P in Chapter 3.IV.

Virtually the remainder of the material is apportioned by Driver between J and E. But he has to concede that reliable criteria are not always available for making the discrimination between these two sources. His analysis of, for example 19.3–24.18 and 31.18–34.28, key passages which will occupy our attention in Chapter 3.IV and VI, is acknowledged by him to be provisional: the Decalogue (20.1-17) and the Book of Covenant (20.22–23.33), though derived from pre-existing written sources, are ascribed to E. 34.18-26, because it is parallel to 23.15, 12, 16-19, is attributed to J. 34.1-4, 10-28 must, then, in Driver's view, be regarded as J's original account of the *establishment* of the covenant at Sinai, which once followed 19.20-25; 24.1-2, 9-10, but which has now been displaced to ch. 34 by the insertion in its place of the parallel material from E in 20.22–23.33; 24.3-8. In its new position it is used by the compiler to describe the *renewal* of the covenant: the terms of this 'renewed' covenant in 34.11-26 are described as 'ten words' (34.28); 'hence', Driver cautiously notes, 'it has been supposed that these verses, though now expanded by the compiler, consisted originally of ten commands forming a "ritual Decalogue" (as opposed to the "moral Decalogue" of ch. 20)' (*Introduction*, 9th edn, p. 39).

Driver regards J and E as 'akin to the writings of the great prophets'. The work of the redactor is estimated positively: 'R^{JE} approximates in both style and character to Deuteronomy' (*Exodus*, p. xi). There is a convergence here towards the position which will be argued for in Chapter 3.IV, below.

3. *'Tradition' — An Unanswered Question*

Though Driver does not claim to write as a historian, he does wish to defend the historicity of at least the outline of the events portrayed in

the narrative. The link which he proposes between the events themselves and the relatively late literary sources JE and P is tradition:

> 'The date at which an event, or institution, is first mentioned in writing,
> must not…be confused with that at which it occurred, or originated: in
> the early stages of a nation's history the memory of the past is preserved
> habitually by oral tradition; and the Jews, long after they were
> possessed of a literature, were still apt to depend much upon tradition'
> (*Introduction*, 9th edn, p. 125).

But Driver has left us little indication about how these traditions
might have been preserved. One is left with guesses and intuitions as
to what the basis and historical content of these traditions might have
been. Of Exodus 15, for example, he writes, 'The hyperboles in v.[5b.8.10b]
are too great for an eye-witness, even though a poet, if the crossing
took place…not in deep water, but in some shallow spot where the
wind drove the water aside' (*Introduction*, 9th edn, p. 30). His rational-
ism cannot be held at bay: progressive tracing of the tradition of the
crossing of the Red Sea back through the literary sources leads to progressive naturalistic explanation. 'In…E the wonders are greater than
in J…in P they are still greater than in E' (*Exodus*, p. liii). But what is
gained by reconstructing a less miraculous narrative that is still five
hundred years or so after the event? It is precisely in connection with
the attempt to trace the history and transmission of traditions from
their very origins through to their literary dress that attention now
turns to Martin Noth.

Further Reading

Driver, S.R., *Introduction to the Literature of the Old Testament* (Edinburgh: T. & T.
Clark, 1891).
—'Exodus', in *Cambridge Bible for Schools and Colleges* (Cambridge; Cambridge Uni-
versity Press, 1911).
Friedman, R.E., *Who Wrote the Bible?* (London: Cape, 1988), despite its title, is con-
cerned throughout to answer the question, 'Who wrote the Pentateuch?',
using literary criticism.
Boorer, S., *The Promise of the Land as Oath: A Key to the Formation of the Pentateuch*
(BZAW, 205; Berlin: W. de Gruyter, 1992).

II. *Martin Noth and 'The History of Tradition'*

According to the New Documentary Hypothesis, the sources of the
Pentateuch, J, E, D and P, reached their definitive literary formulation
only in the first millennium BCE. But the publication in modern times
of thousands of texts from the ancient Near East (e.g. a version of the

Babylonian Flood in 1872, the lawcode of Hammurabi in 1902), including some from the second, and even the third, millennium BCE, encouraged comparisons with Pentateuchal materials and a reappraisal of the possible antiquity of the traditions lying behind them. It was now becoming clear that these Pentateuchal sources might contain much older written and oral traditions. The technique evolved for tracing these older stages of tradition back from their present literary formulation to their presumed original context in the life of the ancient Near East is broadly termed 'form criticism'. It was pioneered by Hermann Gunkel in the early decades of the twentieth century particularly in connection with Genesis and Psalms, for both of which comparative Babylonian material had become available.

'Form criticism' seeks to analyze the literary documents of the Bible into their constituent elements, the individual traditions, and to classify them according to type ('category', *Gattung*, or 'genre'). The social context (*Sitz im Leben*) of such genres can often be determined, and thus the appreciation of their function within their original social context enhanced (e.g. the Psalm is typically at home in the liturgy of the cult as an expression of national or individual joy or grief; certain types of law are in the hands of the 'elders in the gate'). Form criticism is thus a means of gathering together both biblical and extrabiblical materials of related type for appropriate comparison or contrast. The inner structure of each passage may by this means be the better appreciated, its conventionality or individuality perceived (cf. the discussion on covenant and treaty in Chapter 2.V). It may be possible to propose a 'typology' for a particular genre, that is, the stages in its historical evolution (*Formgeschichte*, 'the history of the form'), and to locate the individual example in question within that typology (e.g. does a particular Psalm still reflect a specific liturgical occasion or has it developed in form beyond the specifically cultic to become a more universally accessible expression of faith or piety?; is 'covenant' in the Old Testament rightly understood as 'treaty'?). It may thus be possible to trace how and by whom a particular example of a speech form has been transmitted from its original context in the life of the ancient Near East to its present literary formulation in the Old Testament (*Überlieferungsgeschichte*, 'the history of transmission').

The programme of form criticism may be summed up in Gunkel's dictum of 1906: 'Hebrew literary history is…the history of the literary types practised in Israel'. That is, the history of Israel's literature (say, the Pentateuch) must be written not merely by analyzing it into its constituent source documents (in this case, J, E, D and P) and arranging them in historical sequence, as in 'literary criticism'; a more complete account of the literary history of the material will be attained by analyzing these sources themselves still further into their elements and tracing these elements back to their original ancient Near Eastern contexts.

Martin Noth was a major exponent of the form-critical method, especially its history of transmission aspect. A wide-ranging discussion of the issues as they concern the Pentateuch is to be found in his book *A History of Pentateuchal Traditions*. His commentary on Exodus (he also wrote on Leviticus and Numbers) appeared in 1962. Noth was also the first editor of the massive Biblischer Kommentar—of which Schmidt's commentary, noted above, is a part—which began to appear in 1955 and will not be completed until well into the twenty-first century. The BK may be said to be the carrying through of Gunkel's 1906 programme: to provide a form-critical definition of every pericope of the Old Testament and to trace the history of transmission of the materials therein back to their original *Sitz im Leben*. The aim is to discern the contribution of each pericope of the Old Testament to the overall kerygma of the Bible by means of a thorough account of its origin and development. In this way, precision for the use of the term 'tradition' and as complete an appreciation as possible of the materials transmitted thereby are sought.

Noth, then, defines his task as 'to ascertain the *basic themes* from which the totality of the transmitted Pentateuch developed, to investigate how they were replenished with individual materials, to pursue their connections with each other and to assess their significance' (*History*, p. 3). Access to these materials perforce begins with analysis of the extant literary text of the Old Testament. Noth shows himself in this to be a faithful disciple of the Wellhausenian tradition: P, which is generally easily recognizable, is the basis of the Pentateuchal presentation and has been 'enriched' by JE, just as J, the basis of JE, has been enriched by E. He acknowledges that some passages defy literary critical analysis and cites specifically Exodus 19, 24 and 33 (cf. S.R. Driver). He does allow for a greater presence of D-type material. Since this question will be of some importance in Chapter 3.IV below, Noth's identification of D-style materials in Exodus may be noted: 12.24-27a; 13.1-16; 15.25b, 26; 16.4bβ, 28; 17.4-7; 19.3b-9a(b); 32.7-14; 33*. 34.1a, 4 are 'secondary'.*

But, following a suggestion of O. Procksch, Noth pushes back the development of tradition a stage earlier by postulating that J and E shared a basic text, 'G' (from *gemeinsame Grundlage*, 'shared basis'). He

---

* Text not to be attributed uniformly to one source.

does not decide whether G was written or oral: 'traditio-historically this is not of great consequence'.

In Noth's view, the content of the Pentateuch may be analyzed into five original 'themes': patriarchs, exodus, wilderness, Sinai and settlement. Of these, exodus must be given priority: the 'hymnic' participial phrase 'who brought [you] out [from the land of Egypt]' (Exod. 20.2) is the 'kernel of the whole subsequent Pentateuchal tradition'. The exodus is traced to the 'bedrock' of a historical event, the destruction of the Egyptians in the Sea (Exod. 15.21b). While not all Israel can have been involved in the exodus ('Israel' as an entity only came into being in Canaan), this tradition is so widely attested that many clan elements, later to become part of Israel, must have participated in it. The tradition, or 'saga', first 'emerged, developed and was transmitted' orally by narrators in the pre-state period 'within the anonymous totality of the tribes' when they gathered together on seasonal cultic occasions. On these occasions the hymnic affirmation was recited in the liturgy of the central sanctuary of the tribal league, whose focus was the ark. Thus both the *Sitz im Leben* and the history of transmission of the material have been defined.

In thus stressing the cultic context for the development of the basic Pentateuchal themes, Noth was clearly influenced by the form-critical work of Gerhard von Rad. According to von Rad, J, the writer of the earliest Pentateuchal document, based his work on an ancient Israelite confession of faith, 'the short historical credo' still to be found in Deut. 26.5-10, which had its origin in the liturgy of the festival of Weeks at the sanctuary at Gilgal. At that feast, the exodus from Egypt and the conquest of the land were celebrated. A significant point noted by von Rad is that in this confession of faith no mention is made of Sinai. Accordingly he concluded, following an observation already made by Wellhausen, that Sinai constituted a separate tradition (Exod. 19.1–Num. 10.10), preserved in the liturgy of a covenant festival celebrated at the festival of Tabernacles at Shechem. J used the 'credo' as the framework for his document; he was responsible for the *Einbau* ('inserting') of Sinai into his account of the exodus and conquest, as he was for the *Vorbau* ('prefacing') of the creation narrative of Gen. 2.4ff., and the *Ausbau* ('elaborating') of the patriarchal narrative in Genesis 12ff.

But Noth greatly widened and deepened the discussion. While he preserved the essential institutional dimension of the celebration of Israel's agricultural feasts at the sanctuaries, 'historicized' in terms of the exodus, he rightly criticized von Rad for linking the development of the material on exodus and entry into the land (for Noth they are, in any case, separate 'themes') so narrowly with the offering of first-fruits at just one sanctuary, Gilgal: 'throughout the territory in the pre-monarchic period the tribes had constantly to assert their claim to land... Thus the confession that Yahweh willed the possession of the land might have belonged in a rather general way to the presentation of first fruits' (*History*, p. 53).

Noth has thus traced the material back through literary analysis to G, and thence to the oral sources of the basic traditions in the *Sitz im Leben* of the festival celebrations at the sanctuaries. He then considers the subsequent development of the themes at the hands of narrators by the addition of materials of the most diverse character, the origin and growth of which he subjects to similar traditio-historical inquiry. Only a few examples from Noth's extended discussion can be given here. The plague narratives preceding the account of the Passover arose from 'the inventiveness of the storyteller...the narrator's impulse to multiply and enhance... Events specifically characteristic of Egypt are selected out of a rather general knowledge conveyed by caravan traders of the exotic and interesting in Egyptian life' (*History*, p. 69). The wilderness wandering was elaborated by the clans and tribes of the southern wilderness 'on the basis of their knowledge of the caravan routes...and of local traditions clinging to various stations along the way' (p. 116). Sinai is one of these southern traditions. The figure of Moses is linked most strongly to the wilderness tradition; the historical nucleus of the Moses material is the grave tradition in Deut. 34.6, in all probability 'the bedrock of a historical reality which is absolutely original' (p. 173). In these elaborations, 'what particularly stirred the interest of the Pentateuchal narrators was...not so much unique historical events in the course of living on the land, as the abiding everyday conditions of life' (p. 191). The basic themes and the individual traditions were then 'bracketed' together by such means as 'secondary' genealogies and itineraries, as well as by all-pervasive figures, pre-eminently Moses. Then, with the advent of written sources, 'the Pentateuchal narrative moved out of the sphere of the cult essential in the formation of the themes and out of the popular sphere essential in narrative elaboration and entered the *theological* sphere of reflection' (p. 228). Noth holds that each of the sources, J, E and P, constitutes a literary work of sustained theological discourse, attributable to an 'author'.

Finally, Noth considers the completed Pentateuch: 'Since the completed Pentateuch is what we have to interpret, and all literary criticism and traditio-historical investigation must be regarded only as a measure for the fulfilment of this task, so a history of Pentateuchal traditions is bound to end up again with the Pentateuch as a whole' (p. 248). And not only so in its own terms: 'the literary whole has been read as Holy Scripture and has been used in worship. Therefore it is also a task of scholarship to take into its purview this totality' (p. 250).

Further Reading

Noth, M., *A History of Pentateuchal Traditions* (Englewood Cliffs, NJ: Prentice-Hall, 1972; original German, 1948).
— *Exodus* (London: SCM Press, 1962; original German, 1959).
Gunkel, H., 'Fundamental Problems of Hebrew Literary History', in *What Remains of the Old Testament* (London: Allen & Unwin, 1928), pp. 57ff.
Rad, G. von, 'The Form-critical Problem of the Hexateuch', in *idem*, *The Problem of the Hexateuch* (Edinburgh: Oliver & Boyd, 1966), pp. 1ff.
Koch, K., *The Growth of the Biblical Tradition* (London: A. & C. Black, 1969).
Coats, G.W., *Exodus 1–18* (FOTL, 2A; Grand Rapids, MI: Eerdmans, 1999).

III. *Brevard S. Childs and 'Canonical Criticism'*

In the BK series the last section of the commentary on every pericope seeks to draw together the significance of the passage for biblical theology and thus achieve the aim, expressed by Noth but left, it must be said, rather undeveloped by him, of interpreting the Old Testament as part of Holy Scripture, the book of the believing and worshipping community. There can be little doubt that it has been B.S. Childs who has most vigorously pursued this goal. Childs's commentary on Exodus appeared in 1974. It has itself no introduction, for Childs has very accessibly set out his theory of interpretation with practical examples in an earlier study, *Biblical Theology in Crisis*. (The title refers to the perceived collapse during the 1960s of the 'Biblical Theology Movement', which emphasized to the point of exclusiveness the notion that God reveals himself through his mighty acts in history — preeminently, it is apposite to note in this context, the exodus.) The aims enunciated by Childs in *Crisis* have been exhaustively pursued not only in his commentary but in a further series of volumes including *Introduction to the Old Testament as Scripture*.

In *Crisis*, Childs makes it clear that he writes fundamentally as a Christian minister, who is concerned to give an account of the *Old Testament* as it actually functions in the church as Scripture, and to further that function. Childs rejects as inadequate the prevailing practice of 'historico-critical' exegesis — the tracing of the origin and growth of an Old Testament text within the life of ancient Israel and against its ancient Near Eastern background (cf. Chapter 3.II).

Interesting and illuminating though that often is, the *Old* Testament can be adequately interpreted only along with the New Testament within the context of the canon of the whole Christian Bible, that is, within a Christian *biblical* theology. He is scathing of modern commentators, for example on Psalms, who 'avoid scrupulously any reference to the New Testament while providing every conceivable Babylonian parallel' (*Crisis*, p. 144).

His argument may be indicated by the following loose catena of quotations. 'The Scriptures continue to point to a living God who spoke through his servants in the past, but who continues to confront the church and the world with his divine will. The Scriptures remain the vehicle through which he communicates afresh to his people by the activity of his Spirit' (*Crisis*, p. 131). The exegete is, therefore, no mere antiquarian: 'To do Biblical Theology within the context of the canon involves the acknowledgement of the *normative* quality of the Biblical tradition' (*Crisis*, p. 100). The exegete's task is only accomplished when the individual passage is seen in its theological interrelationship with the whole, that is, in its 'canonical intentionality' (*Introduction*, p. 79). The Testaments mutually interpret one another: the New Testament 'guards the Old Testament from distortion... God...is not the God of Israel alone, but of all nations. The physical blessings of this world—life, land, the people—are an inheritance that points to the ultimate reward which is God himself' (*Crisis*, pp. 218f.). The 'reverse move...has no historical rationale, but rests on the confession of a theological context' (*Crisis*, p. 109). It is this wider goal which opens the door to the recovery of the rich tradition of interpretation from 'pre-critical' times, especially the Fathers, the Rabbis and the Reformers.

Having stated these principles, Childs goes on to illustrate their application in the commentary (one of the examples in *Crisis* is reproduced directly from *Exodus*, then in process of preparation). The standard critical sections on textual, literary, form-critical and traditio-historical questions are executed with the utmost thoroughness and not a little innovation. But Childs regards his sections on the wider Old Testament and New Testament contexts, within which the passage now stands by virtue of the canon, and on contemporary theological reflection as the most significant for his overall aim.

The commentary provides a veritable feast of material. The major doubt rests on whether it is possible to achieve all this within the covers of one book. One need not doubt that tasks such as Childs envisages must be tackled in the discussion of the theology of the Old Testament and in biblical theology, as well as in systematic, moral and pastoral theology. The believer as believer must do the best possible within the limits of being an individual to work out a coherent personal stance using the resources of the Bible, tradition and experience to do so. But that is surely a co-operative enterprise. The exegete as exegete has a distinctive, if modest, part to play in that much wider inter-specialist task. The possibilities for relating Old Testament to New Testament alone fan out into an almost limitless range. Childs has laid down two principles for doing this (*Crisis*, pp. 114ff.): (1) following up the explicit citations of the Old Testament in the New Testament; (2) exploring passages which appear to be cognate in the semantic range of their vocabulary, especially where explicit quotation is lacking. The second of these may lead the interpreter in myriad directions. If that is true of the relation between Old Testament and New Testament, it is still more so of the relation of biblical theology to general theology. Indeed, one wonders whether Childs's model for the latter is wholly adequate. That the word of God, prevenient in his world, addresses the world and the church only through the canon as *'the'* vehicle of revelation seems inappropriately restrictive. Childs is in danger of substituting a new dominating biblical theology for the one he perceives as outmoded.

In the remaining sections of this chapter we return to the more restricted matters of run-of-the-mill 'introduction', not least to some questions still outstanding from those raised by Noth.

Further Reading

B.S. Childs, *Biblical Theology in Crisis* (Philadelphia: Westminster Press, 1970).
— *Exodus* (London: SCM Press, 1974).
— *Introduction to the Old Testament as Scripture* (London: SCM Press, 1979).
Childs's challenging proposals have been frequently subjected to appraisal, e.g., in *JSOT* 16 (1980) and
J. Barr, *Holy Scripture: Canon, Authority, Criticism* (Oxford: Clarendon Press, 1983, pp. 130ff.).
M.G. Brett, *Biblical Criticism in Crisis? The Impact of the Canonical Approach on Old Testament Studies* (Cambridge: Cambridge University Press, 1991).
  For a slightly different approach, emphasizing canon as organic growth and as model, see
J.A. Sanders, *From Sacred Story to Sacred Text: Canon as Paradigm* (Philadelphia: Fortress Press, 1987).

IV. *Redaction Criticism*

1. *Further Considerations Concerning the 'Form-Critical' Approach*

Childs finds that much critical work is preoccupied with analysis and the recreation of origins rather than with synthesis and the function of the 'final form' as canon of Scripture. Certainly, despite Noth's pro-testation about doing justice to the material, the great weight of his inquiry lies on the reconstruction of the earlier stages of the traditions.

(i) In Noth's historical reconstructions there is a high degree of the speculative and arbitrary. There is nothing in principle wrong with speculation: where evidence is sparse, it is essential and potentially creative. But to term Exod. 15.21b ('Sing to the LORD, for he has triumphed gloriously;/the horse and his rider he has thrown into the sea') and Deut. 34.6 ('[The LORD] buried him [Moses] in the valley in the land of Moab opposite Beth-peor; but no man knows the place of his burial to this day'), with their strongly theological character, the 'bedrock' of historical events is, viewed from a coldly historio-graphical standpoint, a confusion of categories.

(ii) Equally, Noth's (and von Rad's) account of the literary growth of the Pentateuch, impressive in its sustained argumentation though it is, remains speculative. He is obliged to concede, for example, 'we must deduce it [the growth of the exodus 'theme'] happened this way even without being able to give evidence in detail' (*History*, p. 51). There is, in any case, room for doubt about the status of the 'themes' in general. The wilderness traditions hardly stem from a basic 'theme' and Noth admits that it has no cultic rootage. It is more likely to be a conglomeration of elements of local knowledge about pilgrimage and caravan routes and desert conditions, combined at the literary level with ideological purpose. One may also question the originality of the theme 'promise to the patriarchs': it could be as well a reading back as a basic building-block. The so-called 'themes' may not be the original traditions which have grown by accretion and aggregation into 'G', but literary constructions formulated late in the history of the material to give narrative coherence to the normative theological account of Israel's origins.

(iii) Noth's contention for the existence of a pre-monarchical 'all Israel' central sanctuary, as the focal point for the gathering of tradi-tions and their normative spread throughout the tribes has also been heavily criticized: such unity may only have arisen with the Davidic monarchy, if then—or, indeed, if ever. The influences and institutions supplying cohesion to the traditions are likely to have been more diffuse: there was a shared history (freedom from Egyptian over-lordship, a brief period of autonomy, followed by Mesopotamian domination), a shared social background (the common and diverging interests of shepherd, peasant and urban dweller within an accepted legal and social framework) and a shared set of religious observances (sacrifice, festivals at local sanctuaries), which provided the necessary presuppositions for the construction of the national epic of origins in Exodus. But normative Yahwism, with its definitive interpretation of life during this history under these social conditions and expressed through these institutions, could hardly have prevailed without a hard-fought battle and creative work by dedicated theologians. And indeed it may only ever have prevailed among minority groups: how typical of the people as a whole were the gatherers of traditions during the Babylonian exile, with their interpretation of the past as a tale of the continuous breach of covenant by the community?

(iv) Perhaps there is an analogy between Exodus as a source for the reconstruction of the undoubted history of Israel's forebears in the transition between LBA and IA (see Chapter 1.VI) and Exodus as a source for the reconstruction of the literary history through which the traditions of Israel in their transmission have undoubtedly passed. The Israelites were in some sense 'slaves in Egypt'; but the resources for reconstructing that experience in historiographical detail are not available in Exodus. Similarly, multitudinous traditions were transmitted through multiple channels, no doubt formulated in conventional forms congenial to eventual integration. But one could as well hope to analyze one stream issuing from a vast reservoir into the constituent elements of the waters that have fed that reservoir as to retrace back to their sources the history of the individual elements that went to make up the narrative as it now stands. The task is the more impossible since the narrative represents a highly eclectic selection and combination of masses of commonplace information and institutional data. As Childs has stated, the motivation of the biblical sources is quite other than to give evidence for the reconstruction of the historical processes of their origin and development. The processes undoubtedly took place—and one is entitled to speculate about them to one's heart's content—but the evidence for them is no longer in any way complete, or even largely available, in this collection. This may seem a negative conclusion, but, I believe, as I shall argue below in Chapter 3.IV.2-3, there remains much that the critic can, with great certainty and usefulness, describe.

2. *The History of the Redaction of the Book of Exodus*

In the following sections an account of the history of the redaction of Exodus will be given which is more modest in its specific aim than either literary or form criticism, but more ambitious than canonical criticism.

Without denying the possibility of highly complex origins for the material such as literary and form criticism have suggested—indeed, while acknowledging the unfathomability of these origins—redaction criticism concentrates on the later levels of the text where editorial activity and intention can be more certainly discerned. The proposal will be made that it can be established with relative certainty that there are two main redactions to be found in the Book of Exodus. The later and final of these is essentially constituted by the material traditionally labelled 'P' by the literary critics, but understood not merely as a source so much as an edition, which has also provided its own input of material. The non-P material (cf. Driver's JE, R^{JE}, R^D) is also to be understood not simply as a source or series of sources but as an earlier edition with its own input of material. It will be argued that this earlier version is best affiliated to the movement which produced both Deuteronomy (the traditional 'D') and the material edited under the inspiration of that movement, conventionally called 'Deuteronomistic' ('Dtr'; cf. especially the 'Deuteronomistic History' [DtrH], which Noth defined as comprising Joshua–2 Kings). These two editions of Exodus will be referred to, in chronological order, as the 'D-version' and the 'P-edition'.

Redaction criticism will also want to hold its own against canonical criticism. It is not sufficient to interpret Exodus in its 'canonical intentionality' (to use Childs's phrase), that is, in the sense which is imparted to it by virtue of the fact that it belongs to Christian Scripture. Nor is it enough to concentrate on the 'final' form of Exodus. If it has indeed passed through two successive 'canonical' editions, the D-version and the P-edition, it can only be given its full value if the theological intention of the editors of *both* editions is fully appreciated.

It is thus an erroneous assumption that 'canonical' form is synonymous with 'final' form. The 'final' form of the Old Testament as it now stands has often involved the incorporation of successive 'canonical' forms, the earlier into the later, without abrogation and sometimes even without, or with little, change. The biblical canon is not the result of a single final decision about the canonicity of its contents late in the biblical period when all the materials lay ready to hand. Rather, as a 'rolling' canon, it grew in a complex manner by which collections of earlier materials provided the authoritative nucleus round which by interaction or innovation later materials developed. Simply by affirming 'canon' one does not obviate critical questions. Full appreciation of the content of Scripture must include appreciation of the intention of the editors who, step by step, promulgated authoritative Scripture, so far as that intention can be ascertained. It is that appreciation which redaction criticism aims to achieve.

3. *The Deuteronomistic Redaction of Exodus*
Since the existence of a final edition of Exodus (in my terms, the 'P-edition') is self-evident, and since its editorial intention will be studied in Chapter 4.III, this section will concentrate on the more controversial issue of the identification and delimitation of the penultimate 'canonical' version of Exodus, the 'D-version', before its editorial intention too is studied in Chapter 4.

The case for recognizing a D-version underlying the present 'final form' of the P-edition of Exodus may be built up as follows.

(i) There are striking parallels between Exodus and Deuteronomy which suggest that, protruding through the surface of the 'final form' of Exodus, there are outcrops of underlying D material. This is particularly the case in the account of the revelation to Moses on the mountain in Exod. 24.12–34.35. On the basis of the parallel in Deut. 9.7–10.11 one can make the following observations.

(a) The framework of the Exodus material is closely parallel to D (cf. Exod. 24.12, 18b; 31.18; 32.7, 8a, 9, 10, 15a, 19b, 20; 34.1, 4, 28 with Deut. 9.9, 10, 12-15, 17, 18a, 21a; l0.la, 2a, 3abβ, 4a). The standard literary-critical assumption (cf. e.g. Driver, *Deuteronomy*, p. 112, where these parallels are tabulated) has been that Deuteronomy is here dependent on an earlier JE narrative. But the question of the mutual relationship of these two sets of parallels is, in my view, no different from that, for example, between the Deuteronomistic History and Chronicles: that is, these parallel materials come from the same source.

(b) That this framework narrative in Exodus is in fact provided by D is supported by the number of occasions on which the version in Deut. 9.7ff. can be seen to supply *the original form* for the Exodus material, which has subsequently been modified by the final redactor, P. This seems to be particularly clear in the following instances.

(1) Exodus 31.18. The parallel in Deut. 9.10a suggests that the Exodus passage originally read, 'And the LORD gave Moses [1] the two [2] tables of stone written with the finger of God'. The final editor P has added at [1] 'when he made an end of speaking with him upon

Mount Sinai' (D uses 'Horeb', not 'Sinai') and at [2] 'tables of the testimony'.

(2) Exodus 32.15a. The parallel in Deut. 9.15 suggests that at the very least it was 'the two tables of the covenant', not 'the two tables of the testimony' which were in Moses' hands.

(3) Exodus 34.1-4. The parallel in Deut. 10.1-3 suggests that the Exodus passage originally read, 'The LORD said to Moses, "Hew two tables of stone like the first [and come up to me on the mountain, and make an ark of wood,] and I will write on the tables the words that were on the first tables, which you broke [1] [, and you shall put them in the ark]." So he [made an ark of acacia wood and] hewed two tables of stone like the first, [2] and went up the mountain [3] with the two tables in his hand'. P has suppressed the material in square brackets, the construction of the ark, at this point, since he gives it full coverage elsewhere (Exod. 25.10ff.; 37.1ff.). He has added material which matches his own preoccupations—at [1]: 'Be ready in the morning, and come up in the morning to Mount Sinai, and present yourself there to me on the top of the mountain. No man shall come up with you, and let no man be seen throughout all the mountain; let no flocks or herds feed before the mountain', at [2]: 'and Moses [N.B. that 'Moses' is misplaced here, a fact not apparent from RSV] rose early in the morning', at [3]: 'of Sinai, as the LORD had commanded him; and took' (the circumstantial clause 'with the two tables...' now modified as a verbal clause 'and took the two tables...').

(4) Exodus 32.20b, the account of P's rites consequent to the destruction of the golden calf, entirely replaces Deut. 9.21b.

(5) Exodus 32.25-29 gives P's entirely different account of and location for the vocation of the Levites from those in Deut. 10.8.

(6) These more certain cases make it likely that Deut. 9.9 supplies the original form of Exod. 24.12, 18b: 'The LORD said to Moses, "Come up to me on the mountain and wait there; and I will give you the tables of stone, [the tables of the covenant which I have made with them]." And Moses [remained] on the mountain forty days and forty nights'. P has turned the emphasis on covenant into one on law, hierarchy and theophany by the modification of Exod. 24.12b and the insertion thereafter of vv. 14-18a. (The figure of Joshua in Exod. 24.13 is Deuteronomistic.)

(ii) By a similar process of argument, Deut. 4.10-15; 5 enables the D-version of the theophany, revelation of law and covenant at Horeb (the name of the mountain is preserved in Exod. 33.1-6) to be recovered in Exod. 19.1–24.11.

According to the D scenario, Moses' task is to muster the people to the foot of the mountain, where the 'Ten Commandments' are spoken in their hearing out of the awesome fire and other accompaniments of theophany as the basis of the covenant relationship between God and people. Thereafter, Moses alone draws near to receive 'all the commandment and the statutes and the ordinances' (Deut. 5.31; cf. 4.14, 'statutes and ordinances'), which he then mediates to the people. Such a sequence of actions can be relatively easily (*pace* Driver and Noth!) recovered in Exod. 19.3-9, 16-17, 19; 20.1–23.33; 24.3-8).

This is not to say that all these materials were composed by the D-redactor, merely that they were compiled by him. As argued above in Chapter 2.VI, the law-code of the Book of Covenant (Exod. 20.22–23.33) has a long history behind it: but it can now be affirmed that it was the D-redactor's contribution to remould it as a covenant-code. The D-redactor has not only recast it in its present form but has provided it with its very name, 'the Book of the Covenant' (Exod. 24.7), and has set it and the theophany within the framework of covenant-making (Exod. 19.3-9; 24.3-8). Many characteristic turns of phrase confirm this framework as D (e.g. Exod. 19.5a, 'Now therefore, if you will obey my voice and keep my covenant'; cf. Deut. 11.13; 15.5; 27.10; for Exod. 19.5b, 'you shall be my own possession among all peoples', cf. Deut. 7.6; 14.2; 26.18). The unique altar rites of covenant-making in Exod. 24.3-8 may have some admixture of P-redaction in them, especially vv. 6 and 8a, which resemble P's consecration rites (cf. Lev. 8).

(iii) That the penultimate redaction of Exodus should be termed 'Dtr' (Deuteronomistic) rather than simply 'D' (Deuteronomic) is indicated in a number of places in the Horeb pericope (as we should now call it in the D-version; cf. the comment on Exod. 24.13 above).

(a) The promise (and implied threat) at the conclusion of the Book of the Covenant (Exod. 23.20-33), which corresponds to the blessing and curse of the covenant in the full-scale D presentation of covenant in Deuteronomy 27–28, includes that of the presence of the angel to lead the people into the land, if they will be obedient (cf. Exod. 33.1-6). This promise is explicitly taken up in thought and expression in Judg. 2.1-5, which is the epilogue precisely to DtrH's account of Israel's actual experience at the entry into the land.

(b) In the incident of the golden calf, the people acclaim their new idol as 'These are your gods, O Israel, who brought you up out of the land of Egypt!' (Exod. 32.4, 8). The odd plural 'gods', given that there was only one golden calf in the exodus narrative, is a deliberate cross-reference to the DtrH account of the golden calves set up by Jeroboam I at Bethel and Dan (cf. 1 Kgs 12.28, where the acclamation is repeated virtually verbatim). For DtrH 'the sin of Jeroboam son of Nebat which

he made Israel to sin' in setting up the schismatic and apostate northern kingdom was a fundamental factor in the ultimate exile of Israel
(cf. the veiled reference to the exile in Exod. 32.34). This signal and
emblematic apostasy, which by definition negated the entire history
of the northern kingdom (cf. 2 Kgs 17.16), is in the golden calf incident
in Exodus 32 foreshadowed by the D-redactor in the very origins of
the people themselves.

(c) As noted above, D in Deut. 4.10-15; 5 conceives that the covenant
was made primarily on the basis of the Decalogue, written by God
himself, and refers rather *en passant* to the additional 'statutes and the
ordinances'. The Dtr presentation in Exodus, however, gives this latter material full expression by incorporating the Book of the Covenant
(Exod. 20.22–23.33). This wider basis is recognized explicitly in Exod.
24.3f. by the reference to 'all the words of the LORD', written by
Moses. Similarly, whereas in Deut. 10.1-5, in the remaking of the covenant after the golden calf incident, the Decalogue again stands in the
forefront, in Exodus 34 both the Decalogue and the Book of the Covenant are reaffirmed as the conjoint basis of the renewed covenant:
Exod. 34.6-7, 14, 17 is a clear reference to the first 'commandment' of
the Decalogue in its D form (Deut. 5.7-10); Exod. 34.18-26 quotes some
three-quarters of the end of the Book of the Covenant (Exod. 23.12-19).
By the shorthand of a reference to the beginning of the Decalogue and
to the end of the Book of the Covenant, the Dtr-redactor in Exodus 34
asserts that all the legal material once given from Exod. 20.1 to Exod.
23.19 as the basis of the original covenant is reconfirmed as the basis
of the renewed covenant.

This difference in emphasis between D and the Dtr presentation in
Exodus as to the basis of the covenant, whether original or renewed
(Decalogue in the forefront in D; Decalogue and Book of the Covenant
in the Dtr edition of Exodus), holds the key to the understanding of
the much-disputed half-verse Exod. 34.28b; 'And he wrote upon the
tables the words of the covenant, the ten commandments'. In its present context, Moses appears to be the subject of the verb 'he wrote'.
Since elsewhere it is God who writes the Decalogue (Exod. 31.18, cf.
Deut. 9.10), it has been argued that either 'the Ten Commandments' is
an erroneous gloss here or that the reference is to a quite different set
of ten commandments which are to be sought in the previous verses.
It is for this reason that a 'Ritual Decalogue' has in classical literary
criticism been identified in Exod. 34.17-26, which, because it diverges
from the 'E' Decalogue of Exodus 20 (cf. 'Elohim' in Exod. 20.1), must
be attributed to 'J' (cf. Driver in Chapter 3.I.2). This, I submit, is
entirely erroneous. As far as content is concerned, there is no deca-

logue in Exod. 34.17-26, but a citation of the end of the Book of the Covenant. As far as formulation is concerned, once again the Dtr-redactor of Exodus is quoting a source recoverable from Deuteronomy: Exod. 34.1, 4, 28b // Deut. 10.1-4a. The parallel in Deuteronomy makes it quite unambiguous that God himself wrote the Decalogue and that 'God' is the subject of the verb 'wrote' in Exod. 34.28b. The Dtr-redactor of Exodus has, however, incorporated Exod. 34.27 ('Write these words; in accordance with these words I have made a covenant with you and with Israel'), which has no parallel in Deuteronomy, in order to include the Book of the Covenant—the conclusion of which has just been cited—as part of the basis of the renewed covenant. This incorporation referring to words which Moses wrote corresponds directly to the note in Exod. 24.3f. about Moses' writing 'all the words of the LORD', that is, the Book of the Covenant, as part of the basis of the original covenant. The 'Ritual Decalogue' is thus a chimera that must be laid to rest.

The modesty of the above proposals, despite their apparent complexity, should not go unnoticed: the D-version does not represent a 'source' as in classical literary criticism but a more or less visible redaction. As a redaction it no doubt incorporates earlier source materials (legal, historical, folk, institutional and the like); the search for these sources is a legitimate, if highly speculative, enterprise. As a redaction, that is, a full-scale finished edition, it is not merely combining sources as by a 'scissors-and-paste' method but, receiving and reconceiving the work of its predecessors, it seeks to write fluent sense. This may on occasion require large-scale modification of the source material, while at other times only the slightest touch. It is this fluent sense which justifies the stress on literary interpretations (particularly of the 'final form' of the Hebrew People) which have come into such vogue since the 1970s (see Chapter 3.V).

(iv) As for Exodus 1–18, it is once again possible to find in Deuteronomy's distinctive presentation of the topics of the two main sections of these chapters (plagues–Passover–exodus in Exod. 1.1-15.21; the itinerary of Israel through the wilderness to Horeb/Sinai in 15.22-18.27 and its associated chronology) a key which enables an earlier Dtr redactional level to be recovered beneath the final P-edition. It will be convenient (in order to link Exod. 1.1-15.21 to a study of the literary approach in the following section, Chapter 3.V, below) to begin with the latter, briefer, section.

(a) Exodus 15.22-18.27: The route from the Red Sea through the wilderness to Mt Sinai in Exod. 15.22-18.27 (plus the earlier notices in Exod. 12.37; 13.20; 14.2, 9b) corresponds, with some abbreviation, to the itinerary in Num. 33.1-15 (P), which summarizes the data of the final edition of the Pentateuch. Israel moves by stages from Marah to Rephidim. The stages are all marked by the 'murmuring' of the people (Exod. 15.24; 16.2, 7-9, 12; 17.3) and by responses from God in the form of miraculous acts performed by Moses. Chapter 18 then records the appointment of judges.

By contrast, in the historical retrospects in Deut. 1.6ff., Israel moves *straight* from the Red Sea to *Horeb*. It is only *after* Horeb that the choice of judges is made and that the sorry history of rebellion in the wilderness begins.

These differences in itinerary between D and P are matched by differences in chronology. According to 19.1 (part of the P itinerary), it has taken Israel at least six weeks from the exodus to reach Sinai. This contrasts with the direct journey of Deut. 1.6ff., which may be confirmed by Exod. 19.4 ('I bore you on eagles' wings and brought you to myself'), already identified as part of the D-version. This raises the question whether the 'three-day journey' to worship the LORD in the wilderness, for which Moses asked the Pharaoh's permission, also belongs to the D-version (Exod. 3.18; 5.3; 8.27[Heb. 23]; 15.22).

These observations present a *prima facie* case that the postulated original underlying D-version of Exod. 15.22–18.27 passes from the exodus directly to Horeb, and that its contribution to the history of rebellion in the wilderness is confined to the *post*-Horeb narrative in Num. 10.11f. The P-edition, by contrast, has disposed symmetrically around Sinai narratives of 'murmuring in the wilderness' associated with the miracles of the quails (Exod. 16.13; Num. 11.31f.), manna (Exod. 16.15ff.; Num. 11.6ff.), water from the rock (Exod. 17.1ff.; Num. 20.1ff.) and so on, partly reusing D-material in the process. Accordingly, while some of the material in Exod. 15.22–18.27 appears to be predominantly P, especially 15.22-25a; 16.1-36, other parts have an admixture of D-material more or less refashioned in this new location by the P-edition (15.25b-26; 17.1-16; 18.13-27). Exod. 18.1-12, the arrival of Jethro, has been transposed by the P-editor from its original position before Num. 10.29.

(b) Exodus 1.1–15.21: There is a lack in Deuteronomy of the sustained narrative retrospect parallel to material in Exod. 1.1–15.21 (such as is found, we have seen, in Deut. 4.10-15; 5; 9.7–10.11 // parts of Exod. 19–24; 31.18–34.29), which would assist in the recovery of the D-version beneath the final P-edition. But there are other indications.

(1) There are numerous more occasional references in the narrative retrospects of Deuteronomy (and in the wider DtrH, especially Josh. 24) to themes in Exodus which suggest the currency of these themes

in D/Dtr circles, for example the land sworn to the patriarchs and their descendants (Deut. 1.8, 35 etc.); the descent into Egypt as 70 persons (Deut. 10.22); Egypt as 'house of slaves' (Deut. 6.12); the LORD as the 'God of the fathers' (Deut. 1.21); the LORD hardening the heart of Israel's enemies (Deut. 2.30); the plagues as 'trials, signs, wonders, terror' (Deut. 7.8, 18f. etc.); the enquiry of the son (Deut. 6.20)/teaching to children (Deut. 4.9 etc.); the pillar of cloud by day and fire by night (Deut. 1.33); the drowning of the horses and chariots of the Egyptians in the Red Sea (Deut. 11.3f.; Josh. 24.6f.).

(2) Especially important is the D material on Passover/Unleavened Bread in Deut. 16.1-8 (and the account of its implementation under Josiah in DtrH in 2 Kgs 22–23) and on Firstlings, which immediately precedes it in Deut. 15.19-23.

(3) It is likely, as argued above, that, by the time of the postulated D-version, the material of B could be presupposed, in particular the final part (Exod. 23.12-19), which is cited in Exod. 34.18-26 as the conclusion of the terms of the remade covenant. This material includes legislation on Unleavened Bread, Passover and Firstlings.

It would seem, then, that a promising place to start in the search for the underlying D-version in Exod. 1.1–15.21 would be the material on Passover, Unleavened Bread and Firstlings in Exodus 12–13. In the light of the revolutionary nature of D's Passover, a rite at the central sanctuary which merges with and dominates Unleavened Bread (cf. Deut. 16.1-8; 2 Kgs 22f.; 2 Chron. 35), the account of the domestic observance in Exod. 12.1-28 is more likely to be P than D. This is supported by a large number of detailed observations: for example, v. 13 cannot be D; v. 9 may even be anti-D polemic; the referring to Israel as a 'congregation' (vv. 3, 6, 19); the echoes of the language of Leviticus, for example, in v. 10 (cf. Lev. 22.30) and v. 14 (cf. Lev. 23.41); the use of the spring calendar beginning with a month simply called 'the first' as opposed to 'Abib' (vv. 2, 18). Nonetheless, there are echoes of D material which suggest reuse by P of an underlying D-version, for example, the eating in haste (v. 11; cf. Deut. 16.3) and, especially, the instruction of the sons (vv. 25-28; cf. Deut. 6.20).

The material of Exod. 12.37-51 has also a distinctly P ring to it: for example, the itinerary (v. 37) matches that of Numbers 33, which, as has been noted above, contrasts with that implied by Deut. 1.6ff.; the chronology (v. 40) belongs to the final framework of the Pentateuch; the legislation on the Passover (vv. 43-50) again concerns domestic observance, which cannot be D. Nonetheless, again there may be echoes of an earlier D-version in the baking of unleavened cakes in v. 39 and the 'night of watching' in v. 42.

By contrast, Exod. 13.1-16 seems to be characteristically D in, for example, its echoes of the legislation of Deut. 15.19–16.8 and of B (Exod. 23.12-19 // 34.18-26); its catalogue of the indigenous population (v. 5; cf. Deut. 7.1); its instruction of the young (vv. 8-10, 14-16).

These observations suggest that the original D account comprised at least Exod. 12.29-36; 13.1-16; from the latter passage the P-redactor may have derived some materials in his refashioning of the account of the Passover as a domestic rite separate from Unleavened Bread.

This D material links closely with the preceding narratives of the plagues. The tenth plague, the slaying of the Egyptian Firstlings both human and animal, links directly to the D association of Firstlings with Passover/Unleavened Bread in Deut. 15.19–16.8. The centralization of the cult in D makes the D legislation on Firstlings as revolutionary as that on Passover: whereas in the Book of the Covenant (Exod. 22.30[Heb. 29]) they are offered on the eighth day after birth, presumably at a local sanctuary, in D they have to be saved up for annual offering at the central sanctuary as, in some cases, mature animals (cf. Deut. 15.19). These annual rites are here brought into association with the exodus to give them decisive interpretation; in Exodus these institutions are cast in narrative form for an aetiological purpose ('why do we practise this rite?', Exod. 13.5; cf. 12.25).

But the parallel to the D legislation extends even further: immediately preceding the legislation on Firstlings and Passover in Deut. 15.19–16.8, there is the legislation on the release of Hebrew slaves (Deut. 15.12-18). It is striking that the narrative sequence of Exod. 1.1–15.21 should thus parallel so closely the sequence of the legislation in Deut. 15.12–16.8 on release of Hebrew slaves–Firstlings–Passover. Deut. 15.12-18 (especially, v. 13) contains two key terms which recur in the presentation of the exodus in Exod. 1.1–5.21 as the release of the Hebrew slaves:

—'let go' (*šillaḥ*) is a thematic term in Moses' dealings with the Pharaoh throughout the plague cycle and links back before that to Moses' call narrative (Exod. 3.20; 4.21, 23; 5.1, 2; 6.1, 11; 7.2, 14, 16, 26, 27; 8.4, 16, 17, 24, 25, 28: 9.1, 2, 7, 13, 17, 28, 35; 10.3, 4, 7, 10, 20, 27; 11.1, 10; 12.33; cf. 13.15, 17; 14.5);

—'empty-handed' (*rêqām*): the Hebrew slave, having worked for nothing, is to be recompensed on his release. It is in this light that 'the spoiling of the Egyptians' is to be seen (Exod. 3.20-22, where both *šillaḥ* and *rêqām* occur; 11.1-3; 12.35f.): Israel is thus recompensed for their labour as slaves.

These observations vastly extend, then, the possible bounds of the D-version to embrace, as the historical references scattered throughout

Deuteronomy already largely imply, much of the material in Exod. 1.1–15.21. They match other inter-linkages: for example, the recurrent motif 'believing in Moses' (4.1-9, 31; 14.31; 19.9); the motif of the 'first-born' extends back to 4.21-23.

Certain blocks of material in Exodus 1–11 can, by contrast, be identified with a high degree of probability as 'P': for example, elements of the final chronological and genealogical schemata of the Pentateuch in 1.1-4; 6.14-27. The latter passage, with its interest in the genealogy of Aaron and the priesthood, raises the question of how far the figure of Aaron is integral to the D-version. That Aaron is essential for the Dtr presentation is clear from Exodus 32, cf. Deut. 9.20. But the role he plays in Chapters 1–11 is inconsistent: in 4.16 his task is limited to speaking to Israel, which he does in 4.30, whereas in 7.2 it is to speak to Pharaoh, which never, in fact, happens. One may suspect, then, that 6.28–7.6 is P's doublet of D's 4.13-17. There appear to be other doublets: the sign of Aaron's rod in 7.8-13 parallels Moses' rod in 4.15. The revelation of the name 'Yahweh' which precedes both (3.13-19; 6.2-9) is likely to be another such doublet (6.9 contrasts with 4.31). In summary, 1.1-4; 6.2–7.13, among other passages, may be assigned to P (cf. Driver in ch. 3.I.2). As before, this attribution may be confirmed by detailed usages, for example, 'acts of judgment' (*šᵉpāṭîm*) 6.6; 7.4; cf. 12.12; Israel referred to as 'hosts' (6.27; 7.4; cf. 12.17, 41, 51). But as before there is reuse of D-material (cf. *šillaḥ* in 6.11; 7.2).

(v) This discussion of the differences between the underlying D-version and the final P-edition in Exodus 1–24 permits far-reaching conclusions about associated religious festivals. It can now be seen that the D-chronology of the three-day journey into the wilderness (3.18; 5.3; 8.27[Heb. 23]; 15.22), plus the three days' preparation at Horeb (19.11, 15), culminating the next (i.e., seventh) day in the covenant in 24.3-8, matches the chronology of the seven-day Passover of Deut. 16.1-8. That is, Exod. 3.1–24.11 in the D-version is in part the narrative counterpart of the legislation on Passover in Deut. 16.1-8. The P-edition has radically transformed this scenario. By confining Passover to one night (Exod. 12) and by inserting six weeks of murmuring in the wilderness before Sinai (Exod. 19.1), it has now associated the revelation of the Torah at Sinai with the Festival of Weeks/Pentecost. A memory of that radical change is preserved in Jewish tradition: whereas in Deut. 16.8 the last day of Passover is called *'ᵃṣeret*, the Festival of Weeks is now known by that term, specifically *'ᵃṣeret šel pesaḥ*, 'the conclusion of Passover'.

(vi) Exodus 1–18 gives an excellent example of the complexity of redaction criticism and its difference from old-fashioned literary criticism. The literary critic would wish at this point to be able to include a summary diagram attributing the materials to the 'sources' JE and P. But the above discussion noting the extensive re-use of D-material by P shows that such a diagram is virtually impossible to produce, especially for chs. 12, 15 (from v. 22) and 16–18. These chapters all contain materials originally present in the D-version of Exodus and Numbers; but they cannot now be simply attributed to D because they have been extensively relocated by P in contexts where they were not present before in that earlier D-version. Yet in their reuse by P they still retain highly recognizable D features, so that to label them simply 'P' would be equally inappropriate to their intrinsic character. There is here both a striking respect for the older version and desire to utilize it and a radical freedom by which these older materials are reformulated to serve new purposes.

By such study the appreciation of the function of the redactor is greatly enhanced. He is no longer to be seen as a mere editor, more or less subserviently bringing pre-existing materials into as harmonious a whole as possible using the P-document as the base and fitting in as much of JE as he can (as—to take a favourite analogy of the old literary critics—Tatian in the second century CE in his Gospel harmony, the *Diatessaron*, used John's Gospel as base into which he fitted the Synoptics). The redactor is, rather, a creative theologian and hermeneut, who seeks through his faithfulness to tradition and his responsiveness to the demands of his people's predicament to set forth a definitive interpretation of their life before God in as accessible terms as possible. It is in the service of this theological creativity and popular access that he employs every appropriate literary art he can muster.

Further Reading

On the continuing controversy about the date of P and about its character, whether it is 'source', 'redaction' or both, see

Driver, S.R., *Deuteronomy* (ICC; Edinburgh: T. & T. Clark, 3rd edn, 1902), p. 112.

Noth, M., 'The "Priestly Writing" and the Redaction of the Pentateuch', Appendix to *idem*, *The Chronicler's History* (JSOTSup, 50; Sheffield: JSOT Press, 1987).

Vink, J.G., *The Date and Origin of the Priestly Code in the Old Testament* (Oudtestamentische Studiën, 15; Leiden: E.J. Brill, 1969), pp. 1ff.

Cross, F.M., 'The Priestly Work', in *idem*, *Canaanite Myth and Hebrew Epic* (Cambridge, MA: Harvard University Press, 1973), pp. 293ff.

Hildebrand, D.R., 'A Summary of Recent Findings in Support of an Early Date for the So-called Priestly Material of the Pentateuch', *JETS* 29 (1986), pp. 129ff.

Koch, K., 'P-kein Redaktor!', *VT* 37 (1987), pp. 446ff;

Blum, E., *Studien zur Komposition des Pentateuch* (BZAW, 189; Berlin: W. de Gruyter, 1990).

Dozeman, T.B., *God at War: Power in the Exodus Tradition* (New York: Oxford University Press, 1996), is much wider in scope that its title might suggest and contains much valuable discussion on matters of composition.

For a highly complex redactio-historical argument for a Dtr edition of the Pentateuch, see

Peckham, B., *The Composition of the Deuteronomistic History* (HSM, 35; Atlanta: Scholars Press, 1985).

V. *The Literary Approach*

It is perhaps this awareness of the skill and design of the final redactor as literary artist, coupled with a sense—justified or not—of diminishing returns in traditional criticism, that has awakened intense interest in the Bible as literature among interpreters especially since the 1970s.

A number of terms are applied to this literary approach. It is called 'synchronic'; that is, the text is considered as a whole, as a concerted literary work with its own artistic integrity, composed, as it were, contemporaneously under a unitary creative impulse. 'Synchronic' is opposed to 'diachronic', that is, the customary critical analysis, such as has been outlined in the earlier sections of this chapter, which seeks to trace the development of the text through time from its origin, through its manifold redactions to its present composite form. Since synchronic study is applied to the text in its completed form, it is also referred to as 'final form' interpretation. This synchronic study is often concerned with the 'text itself' as a literary creation or artefact. It is the 'text itself' which is the focus of interpretation, not the historical background, the author's intention, the objective realities to which it refers, nor the theological affirmations which it makes. The work is the bearer of, indeed *is*, its own meaning and can be appreciated without reference to the purpose or beliefs of the writer, who may become a figure of no more importance for the appreciation of the artefact than is the painter, sculptor or composer for the appreciation of other works of art.

The plague cycle in Exod. 7.14–11.10 provides within limited compass an interesting case-study for these issues (it has, as has been indicated above, interconnections with both preceding and succeeding materials, so that larger complexes up to and including the complete D-version of Exodus not to say the Pentateuch, not to say DtrH, not to say the final editions of all these, may equally legitimately be studied from this point of view).

Here the traditional literary-critical attribution of certain of the plagues or of their elaboration to 'P' rather than 'JE' (cf. Chapter 3.I.2, above) can hardly be said much to heighten understanding. It might be possible, for example, to begin from the problem of the role of Aaron in Exod. 1.1–15.21, which has been noted above. It could be argued that still more of the material on Aaron should be attributed to the P-edition: if the narrative of Aaron's rod and his contest with the magicians of Egypt in 7.8-13 is regarded as P-material, then all references to his rod and to such a contest might then be held to belong to the P-material; thus, the references to Aaron and the Egyptian magicians in 7.19ff.; 8.1ff., 12ff.; 9.8ff., that is, in plague narratives 1, 2, 3 and 6 (plague 9, because of the similarity of its formulation to plagues 3 and 6, is also likely to belong to the P-edition). The very phenomenon of this distribution may suggest, however, that there is an alternative, literary, explanation: the figure of Aaron and his rod is being deliberately introduced by the writer into the narrative for specific effect. It is this kind of literary question, which ponders the possibility of the deliberate construction of plot over an extended narrative, that has occupied increasing attention among interpreters.

A literary study of the passage taken as a whole discloses in the regular recurrence of narrative elements the artistry with which it has been structured so that its impact is heightened and its content enhanced. Because of the recurring elements of the drama of confrontation—between the Pharaoh and his officials, on the one hand, and God and his spokesmen and agents, on the other throughout the ten plagues, and of the stereotyped formulae in which it is cast, it is relatively easy to construct a table (tables and diagrams are recurrent features of the method) of the elements present in principle, and of the extent to which they are represented in each scene. A complete scene would include both the commissioning of Moses to unleash a plague, with instruction about the accompanying message of command and threat to be delivered to Pharaoh, and an account of the carrying out of the commission—the unavailing command and threat, the unleashing of the plague, the temporary relenting by Pharaoh followed by the hardening of his heart.

From such tabulation some obvious points on the subtle arrangement of the plot elements, scene by scene, can be made. No scene is in fact recounted in its required fulness: for example, there is never an account of both the commissioning and the implementation. Usually the commissioning does duty for both, except in plagues 8–10 where, at the climax of the series, the narrative rushes straight into the action. There is plot acceleration in the very short accounts of plagues 3 (gnats, 4vv.), 5 (plague on cattle, 7vv.), 6 (boils, 5vv.) and 9 (darkness, 9vv.), and retardation by the long accounts especially of plagues 2 (frogs, 15vv.), 4 (flies, 13vv.), 7 (hail, 23vv.) and 8 (locusts, 20vv.). The increasingly frantic concessions by the Pharaoh avail nothing against the inexorable hardening of his heart by the LORD. As for Aaron, he is a wholly subordinate figure. He appears as Moses' agent only when the magicians appear as Pharaoh's accomplices. When by plague 3 these have been outplayed by Aaron, both they and he disappear, except for their brief attempted come-back in plague 6, when they are finally outfaced by Moses himself. Yet only in plague 5 is there no mention at all of Aaron, even by implication.

Perhaps one can agree with those who favour a literary approach that in a passage like this on the ten plagues, the cumulative dramatic impact of the narrative 'as it is' renders highly marginal the question whether the material must have belonged as it stands to the D-version, or even earlier versions, or whether it has undergone limited expansion in the P-edition. Nonetheless, it is damaging to assume that, because of a method's clear success in one passage, it is to be absolutized as *the* method throughout. The full range of methods must still be tried passage by passage in order to benefit from any illumination which each may bring.

There is no need to polarize methods. For the community of synagogue and church, Scripture is used not merely for aesthetic satisfaction, though there is no reason why that should not bulk largely; it is read because it is assumed that it provides access beyond itself to theological truth and to religious experience. Authorial and editorial intention remains one, if not the sole, means by which theological significance is communicated. (Even in the appreciation of art, for example, knowledge of background, genre and artist's viewpoint may be vital: it is not unimportant for the appreciation of, say, Camille Pissarro's rural scenes to know that he was an Impressionist with left-wing political views.) Nor is there need to regard 'synchronic' and 'diachronic' study as mutually alien. They may function complementarily. The 'diachronic' analytical work outlined in Chapter 3.IV may succeed in establishing that there are at least *two* 'synchronic' levels within Exodus: the D-version and the P-edition, *both* of which are worthy of full appreciation, including aesthetic. Further, diachronic study may serve to confirm the confines of the compositional unit, the artistic integrity of which is under study. Without this confirmation, there can be as much of the speculative and subjective in 'final form' interpretation as in the attempt to reconstruct origins and development; one may be just as oppressed by the arbitrariness with which passages are delimited by this kind of study and by the impression-ism of the 'reading' offered by it as by the speculations of old-style literary and form criticism.

Further Reading

Essays on the narratives in Exodus 1–14:

Fokkelman, J.P., 'Exodus', in R. Alter and F. Kermode (eds.), *The Literary Guide to the Bible* (Cambridge, MA: Harvard University Press, 1994), pp. 56-65.

Isbell, C., A.M. Vater and D.M. Gunn in D.J.A. Clines, D.M. Gunn and A.J. Hauser (eds.), *Art and Meaning: Rhetoric in Biblical Literature* (JSOTSup, 19; Sheffield: JSOT Press, 1982).

Of more general works one might mention

Alter, R., *The Art of Biblical Narrative* (London: Allen & Unwin, 1981).

Brenner, A. (ed.), *A Feminist Companion to Exodus–Deuteronomy* (The Feminist Companion to the Bible, 6; Sheffield: Sheffield Academic Press, 1994).

—*Exodus–Deuteronomy* (The Feminist Companion to the Bible [Second Series], 5; Sheffield: Sheffield Academic Press, 2000).

Thompson, T.L., *The Origin Tradition of Ancient Israel.* I. *The Literary Formation of Genesis and Exodus 1–23* (JSOTSup, 55; Sheffield: JSOT Press, 1987).

VI. *The Decalogue as Illustration of the Issues*

The Decalogue provides a compendious example of the issues in Pentateuchal criticism and appropriately rounds off this chapter.

1. *Literary Criticism*

The existence of two recensions of the Decalogue (Exod. 20.2-17; Deut. 5.6-21), a 'doublet', makes possible that comparison of texts which is a staple element in literary criticism.

Between these two versions there are, in fact, some twenty-five variations. These range from mere alternative forms of writing, with no significance for meaning, to matters of considerable substance. Only the most significant variations can be noted here.

There is a difference between the two versions in the way in which the 'Ten Commandments' as a whole are counted: in Deuteronomy the MT supplies ten paragraph dividers (at the end of vv. 10, 11, 15, 16, 17, 18, 19, 20, 21a, 21b; so in Catholic and Lutheran usage), where-as in Exodus there are only nine (the equivalent of the divider between Deut. 5.21a and 21b is omitted; to recover 10 it is assumed that Deuteronomy's first commandment is divided into two; cf. Pro-testant usage). (Incidentally, a fundamental point for understanding the Decalogue is provided by the Jewish tradition which counts the so-called 'prologue' [Exod. 20.2] as the first 'commandment'. The objection that the prologue is a statement, not a commandment, makes the point admirably: who said they were 'commandments'?— the Hebrew calls them 'words', i.e., 'organizing principles', of which the fundamental one is God's act of liberating his people.)

Within the individual 'commandments' there are differences of detail (the 'commandments' are referred to below by the Roman numerals I–X, following the Exodus system):

II — Deut. 5.8 means 'an image, i.e., any likeness'; Exod. 20.4 reads 'an image *and* any likeness', in order to provide a referent for 'to *them*' (v. 5a), now that II is separated from I; in Deut. 5.9 'to them' refers to 'other gods' (v. 7).

— Deut. 5.9 means 'upon sons [i.e. those of the second generation], and upon those of the third generation, and upon those of the fourth generation'; Exod. 20.6 means 'upon sons [i.e. descendants], even of the third and fourth generation'.

IV — Deut. 5.12 'keep' stresses obedience to a command; Exod. 20.8 'remember' refers to the liturgical re-presentation of an original event.

— The phrase 'as Yahweh your God commanded you' (Deut. 5.12, 16) is added because Deuteronomy purports to be Moses' farewell address recalling the events at Horeb forty years earlier.

— The motive for the Sabbath command in Deut. 5.14f. is humanitarian and based on the mighty acts of God; that in Exod. 20.11 is based on the creation ordinance of Gen. 2.2-3.

VII–X — Deut. 5 adds 'and' at the beginning of vv. 18, 19, 20 and 21 and at 21b, thus not only making *two* prohibitions out of v. 21 but linking the series from v. 17 into a self-contained group of six.

IX — Deut. 5.20 reads 'witness of vanity', picking up the wording at the end of v. 11 on the misuse of the Divine Name; Exod. 20.16 reads 'lying witness'.

X — Deut. 5.21 a transposes 'your neighbour's wife' to the beginning of the list and makes of it an independent prohibition.

— Deut. 5.21b uses a different verb 'to covet', in order to mark the independence of the prohibition by its reckoning.

What is one to make of these divergences? The standard literary critical assumption has been that the variations between the two versions suggest that there has been secondary expansion of a common original, which was probably couched in the terse, uniformly negative, form of the present VI–IX, for example, Carpenter and Harford-Battersby, *The Hexateuch*:

I   Thou shalt have none other gods before me.
II   Thou shalt not make unto thee a graven image.
III Thou shalt not take the name of Yahweh in vain.
IV   Thou shalt not do any work on the seventh day.
V   Thou shalt not treat thy father and mother with disrespect.
VI   Thou shalt do no murder.
VII Thou shalt not commit adultery.
VIII Thou shalt not steal.
IX   Thou shalt not bear false witness against thy neighbour.
X   Thou shalt not covet thy neighbour's house.

A typical view (Carpenter and Harford-Battersby again) would be that, though the Decalogue in Exod. 20.2-17 now appears in the E document (cf. 'Elohim' in Exod. 20.1, 19), it is a secondary addition to it: E already has its own material parallel to I–IV (for I cf. 22.20[Heb. 19]; 23.13; for II cf. 20.23; for III cf. 22.28[Heb. 27]; for IV cf. 23.12). The Decalogue is thus likely to be later than E (just as it is later than J, which has its own equivalent to II in 34.17). But equally it is earlier than D, which presupposes it in Deut. 5.6ff. Nonetheless, it is a significant concession that even in its Exodus form the Decalogue has undergone D expansions in the prologue (original form, 'I am Yahweh which brought thee out of the land of Egypt'), in II ('a jealous God, visiting the iniquity of the fathers upon the children, upon the third and upon the fourth generation of them that hate me and showing mercy unto thousands'; cf. 34.7, 14), in IV (Exod. 20.9-10; Exod. 20.11 = R^P), in V and in X. *The Hexateuch* thus dates the basic form of the Ten Commandments in the seventh century, between JE and D.

This conclusion is thoroughly in line with the view of the history of Israel's religion in the classical literary criticism of the Wellhausenian type: the Decalogue is dependent on the work of the great eighth-century prophets, who were the founders of ethico-religious monotheism.

2. *Form Criticism*

The Hexateuch is notably vague in its account of the origins and social setting of the Decalogue. A number of attempts in the second and third quarters of the twentieth century to answer such questions more effectively by means of form criticism may be mentioned.

(i) S. Mowinckel, *Le Décalogue*: In the first two chapters of this work, Mowinckel considers the traditional literary-critical questions. He concludes that the Decalogue was composed in the latest pre-exilic period between Isaiah and Deuteronomy. It was incorporated into Deuteronomy about 600 BCE by a D redactor. It was then introduced about 500–450 BCE by R^{JEDP} into the framework of E, which originally passed directly from Exod. 19.19 to 20.18.

Mowinckel's third chapter, where he turns, expressly following Gunkel's method, to inquire into the form, function and *Sitz im Leben* of the Decalogue, marks a definite advance in the consideration of the historical and social questions.

Mowinckel has already argued that from Exod. 34.17-26 and 20.22–23.19 respectively one can identify J and E cultic Decalogues, which go back to a common original. The form of these Decalogues he identifies as the priestly *torah*, the ruling on who may enter to participate in the rites of the Jerusalem Temple (cf. the 'Entrance Liturgies' preserved in Pss. 15 and 24).

The particular occasion on which this type of material functioned as 'entrance liturgy' is the autumn new year (cf. e.g. Lev. 23.23ff.), which, Mowinckel argued, was a festival of covenant renewal. The evidence for this argument comes primarily from Psalms, especially Psalms 99, 81, 95, 50. Such Psalms, though late in their present form, arose as liturgical texts. Psalm 81 appears to be particularly significant: v. 3 [Heb. 4] refers to a pilgrimage festival, which, because of the mention of the sounding of the trumpet, must be the autumn festival (cf. Lev. 23.24); v. 6[Heb. 7] celebrates the exodus, v. 7[Heb. 8] the wilderness wandering to Kadesh, v. 8[Heb. 9] the giving of the law, v. 9[Heb. 10] echoes I and II (Exod. 20.3, 5), v. 10[Heb. 11] the prologue (Exod. 20.2), a reflection of ancient Near Eastern royal speech convention, which marks the 'epiphany' or 'parousia' of Yahweh. The priestly *torah* is thus 'brought into relation with the announcement made by a [cultic] prophet of the epiphany of God who comes to renew the covenant'.

The primary form of the present Decalogue, underlying the accretions of the D and P schools, is, according to Mowinckel, due to the circle of Isaiah's disciples (cf. Isa. 8.16). The Decalogue was the 'entrance liturgy' to their circle, made necessary because of their rejection of customary mores, both popular and official.

(ii) A. Alt's form-critical work has already been noted in Chapter 2.VI. He differs from Mowinckel in two important respects: (1) in his view, the Decalogue functioned not as 'Entrance Liturgy' but as the central text proclaimed by the Levites, on the basis of which the covenant was renewed; (2) these texts were proclaimed, not every year, but every seventh year, that is, the sabbatical year, when the ground was left fallow and debts were cancelled. But this kind of law is not limited to the cult: 'it displays an unrestrained...aggression which seeks to subject every aspect of life...to the unconditional domination of the will of Yahweh; it pursues the Israelite out of the sanctuary... into his daily life' (*Essays*, p. 132).

On the question of the date of such apodeictic material as the Decalogue, Alt is of the opinion that it goes back at least in form to the period when Israel's relation with the LORD was first understood in terms of a covenant, that is, to the desert period. Alt is unimpressed by the traditional literary-critical argument that the Decalogue is dependent upon the work of the eighth-century prophets. Nonetheless, he acknowledges that the present formulation of the Decalogue is likely to be much later: cf. its prosaic language, which has largely departed from a uniform pattern of terse prohibitions like those still preserved in VI–IX.

(iii) G.E. Mendenhall's argument has already been alluded to in Chapter 2.V and need be only briefly recapitulated here. He uses an essentially form-critical argument to push the potential origin of the Decalogue back to the Mosaic period. He points out that apodeictic law was not peculiar to ancient Israel: it was to be found in the LBA Hittite Vassal Treaty. Since this form of treaty was known in the Mediterranean coastal regions in the later second millennium BCE, Israel could have adopted this form to express its covenant with the LORD in that period. Shechem, with the Hittite associations of its indigenous population, the Bene Hamor (Gen. 33.18–34.31), and its tradition of covenant at the shrine of Baal-berith ('the lord of the covenant', Jud. 9.1-57), would have been a suitable place where Israel could have learned the pattern.

(iv) E. Gerstenberger, *Wesen und Herkunft*: Alt's form-critical discussion of the Decalogue, in particular, the category of 'apodeictic law' and the *Sitz im Leben* to which he assigned it, is the focus of attention.

Gerstenberger is sceptical of Alt's definition of the Decalogue as 'apodeictic law': only clauses which specify penalty as well as crime can properly be called 'law' and this is clearly not the case with the Ten Words. Most of them should, rather, be termed 'prohibitions'.

He also rejects Alt's ritual of covenant-making or renewal as the *Sitz im Leben* of the Decalogue. The terms of a covenant should relate to the relationship between the two covenant partners. But in the Decalogue only I and II, which expressly safeguard the exclusiveness of the relationship, would fit as the stipulations of a covenant between Yahweh and Israel. While the home of these stipulations in the cult might even be conceded, most of the other prohibitions (and com-

mandments), especially V–X, are concerned with the individual's
social responsibilities. Their presence in a liturgy of covenant-renewal
can at best be secondary.

What, then, is the primary setting of the prohibition? The prohibition 'don't do...' is an elemental and universal feature in human
speech, particularly related to the bringing-up of children within the
family. That might seem at first sight to be a truism of little value for
further elucidation of the question. But the chief example which Gerstenberger finds in the Old Testament carries some conviction, viz.
Jer. 35.6ff., the commandments which Jonadab son of Rechab imposed
as 'father' on his 'family' and which they then observed for at least
two-hundred years. The prohibition is expressed in second person
imperfect + the negative *lō'*, 'not', as in the Decalogue. The verb in
Jeremiah is in the plural as opposed to the singular of the Decalogue,
because the members are being thought of collectively; the singular
would be equally apposite for the individual. The commandments of
Jonadab are termed *dᵉbārîm*, 'words' (v. 14), precisely the term for the
clauses of the Decalogue in, for example, Exod. 20.1. The individual
prohibition appears not in isolation but in a series, in this case of four
(cf. the series of ten, or possibly sub-series of four and six, in the Decalogue; shorter series are in any case much more typical of the genre);
there are also positive commandments with result clause (v. 7, cf. V).
The reference of such prohibitions/commandments is to the preservation of family life (cf. V–X). They can thus be related to other such
lists, for example Lev. 18.7ff., which are concerned with safeguarding
the integrity of the family. The prohibition is comparable to the
instruction of wisdom literature, both Israelite (e.g. Prov. 1–9; 22.17ff.)
and international, and it is within the context of the wise that its *Sitz
im Leben* is to be placed. The chief exponents of the genre would then
be the head of the household, the hierarchy of brothers and sons
within the extended family and the elders within the community. The
authority of the father arose not simply because of his position in the
family but because of the sacral order of life which he represented. In
the course of time, aspects of this clan instruction were developed and
taken over by both the professional priest and the wise man and combined with other materials in cult, law and wisdom. This would suggest that the emergence of the Decalogue as a collection was later
rather than earlier.

3. *Canonical Criticism*

For the sake of the completeness of the illustration of the issues by
means of the Decalogue, brief allusion may be made to Childs's

typically perceptive comment on the function of the Decalogue in the 'canonical form' of the Exodus text. The Decalogue occupies a key position: the prologue, Exod. 20.2, summarizes the preceding chapters, Exodus 1–18; the 'ten commandments' in Exod. 20.3-17 provide the authoritative guide to all the succeeding legal material (*Introduction*, p. 174).

4. *The Literary Approach*

Equally briefly—for here, above all, the response of the individual interpreter is in play—possibilities for a literary interpretation may be noted. The unevenness in length of the individual 'commandments' is not to be regarded as an anomaly to be corrected by the imposition of a uniform pattern suggested by literary or form criticism. Disparity is of significance in itself. For example, it throws the sabbath commandment, IV, as the most elaborated, firmly into the centre of attention; duties to God and to man are then roughly symmetrically disposed on either side of it; the two positive commands, IV and V, which elicit active implementation, as opposed to the negative commands which merely require avoidance, are placed side by side.

5. *Redaction Criticism*

Redaction criticism is concerned with the process of the growing together of the elements which gradually produces the whole; 'redaction' strongly implies the final stages of editing *written* materials and 'redaction criticism' an interest in editorial intention and the function of a passage within its literary context, whatever prehistory it may have passed through in whole or in part.

Illuminating and legitimate though literary-critical and form-critical discussions may be, it must be abundantly clear that there is a strong element of the hypothetical within the reconstructions of the earlier phases reviewed in Chapter 3.VI.1 and 2. It is certainly more secure to ask redactio-historically about the function of the Decalogue in the virtually assured various stages of the evolution of the literary text, for which I have argued in Chapter 3.IV. The more modest redactio-historical aim of doing justice to the intention of the editors of the two levels of the D-version and the P-edition is more certainly attainable, and ensures that an appropriate degree of dialectic between canonical varieties of theology (the redemption of the firstborn, covenant and eschatology of the D-version and the presence of God, holiness and realized eschatology in the P-edition, as will be argued in Chapter 4.II and III) is preserved in the interpretation of the text.

There is no reason to doubt that the D-version of Exodus included

the Decalogue at precisely its present location (contra the views of
F.-L. Hossfeld): the parallels on the giving of the Decalogue in Deut.
4.10-15; 5, on which the argument in Chapter 3.IV.3 has largely
depended, indicate that this is so. The version of the Decalogue in
Deut. 5.6-21, shorn of its features as 'retrospect' (especially the recurring phrase, 'as the LORD your God commanded you', e.g., Deut.
5.12), is likely to give good evidence for the D-version of the Decalogue which once stood in Exod. 20.2-17 before the final redaction of
the P-edition. The major contribution of the P-edition's revision of the
D-version of the Decalogue is the motive for keeping the sabbath in
IV.

The D-version of Exodus provides the exilic account of Israel's origins. In its present context in the D-version the Decalogue ceases to be
(if it ever was) a reflection of particular historical and social conditions as at the end of the eighth century (as on the interpretation of
F. Crüsemann). Rather, the Decalogue can now be seen as an ideal,
eschatological, statement—however much it utilizes the social and
historical data of the past—looking towards the future realization of
Israel's life of freedom under the LORD. It is within this perspective
that some of the puzzling omissions of the Decalogue, for example,
the lack of reference to the care of the widow and the orphan and to
the other social concerns of the prophets, can be understood. For all
Israel in that eschaton will realize the perfect plan of the settlement
whereby every family, including its weakest members, each settled
inviolably on its own farmland, will have provision made for its support. Within that context full humanitarian consideration can be given
to the slave (whether voluntary [Deut. 15.16f.] or foreign prisoner of
war). The Decalogue in the D-version is, thus, a document full of theological pathos: the people of the LORD presently 'enslaved' in exile or
diaspora, lacking land, the basic condition of the freedom which is
God's gift, suffering perhaps even the loss of their former lands, prop-
erties and wives, not just at the hands of their enemies but even of
their rapacious former neighbours who have been spared the catastrophe (cf. Ezek. 11.14-21; 33.23-29), reaffirm their faith in their God
as redeemer, who, as once from Egypt so again from Exile, will one
day restore them to an ideal state of liberty.

In the final P-edition of Exodus, no doubt to be dated in the post-
exilic period of the 'return', the Decalogue becomes a document of
'realized eschatology'. The 'return from exile' may have been accomplished, but only to a partial degree. The definitive 'Return' is still
outstanding. The function of the Decalogue in the P-edition is thus to
portray how to live in the eschaton of an ideal that is not yet

historically fulfilled; how to make that eschaton 'proleptically present' in the time of waiting for the consummation; how to create the 'enabling environment' within which the realization of that day can be accomplished.

The differences of emphasis of D-version and P-edition focus conveniently on the sabbath. For D (Deut 5.15) it is for exiles a poignant reminder of freedom from slavery and its observance provides a proleptic experience of eschatological return to the freedom of the promised land. For P it is to participate in the ideal equilibrium of creation (Exod. 20.11; cf. Gen. 2.1-3), the rest of the perfection of creation on the seventh day, which provides a proleptic experience of the eschatological jubilee, when conditions in the land will return to their pristine ideal.

The overtly theological character of these observations on the purpose of the D-version and of the P-edition of the Decalogue lead appropriately into the final chapter.

Further Reading

A review of Decalogue research up to the mid 1960s is to be found in

Stamm, J.E., and M.E. Andrew, *The Ten Commandments in Recent Research* (Studies in Biblical Theology [Second Series], 2; London: SCM Press, 1967).

Gerstenberger, E., *Wesen und Herkunft des 'apodiktischen Rechts'* (The Nature and Origin of 'Apodeictic Law') (WMANT, 20; Neukirchen–Vluyn: Neukirchener Verlag, 1965).

I have given some account of two important studies:

Hossfeld, F.-L., *Der Dekalog: Seine späten Fassungen, die originale Komposition und seine Vorstufen* (OBO, 45; Freiburg: Universitätsverlag Göttingen: Vandenhoeck & Ruprecht, 1982).

Crüsemann, F., *Bewahrung der Freiheit: Das Thema des Dekalogs in sozial-geschichtlicher Perspektive* (Kaiser Traktate, 78; Munich, 1983), in 'The Decalogue and the Redaction of the Sinai Pericope in Exodus', *ZAW* 100 (1988), pp. 361ff., and 'The "Ten Commandments": some recent interpretations', *ExpTim* 100 (1988–89), pp. 453ff.

Carpenter, J.E., and G. Harford-Battersby (eds.), *The Hexateuch Arranged in its Constituent Documents by Members of the Society of Historical Theology Oxford* (London: Longmans, Green & Co., 1900).

Mowinckel, S., *Le Décalogue* (EHPR, 16; Paris, 1927).

Laarson, G., *Bound for Freedom: The Book of Exodus in Jewish and Christian Traditions* (Peabody, MA: Hendrickson, 1999), pp. 126-55.

Chapter Four

MATTERS THEOLOGICAL: THE PERVASIVE INTENTION

This final chapter assumes that the argument just presented about the literary formation of Exodus is tolerably sound. One may be rather sceptical about the possibility of tracing back by means of the analysis of *this* narrative the course of the evolution of the various materials which go to make up the book. Little time will be spent on inquiry into the theology of such hypothetical earlier stages. Out of the vast reservoir of traditions, the writers have produced in two main phases, the exilic D-version and the restoration P-edition, a verisimilitude of life at the time of Israel's origin. The purpose has not been to recreate the historical events in themselves so much as to illuminate the experience of their contemporaries and of succeeding generations.

I. *The Revelation of the Divine Name 'Yahweh'*

For the Hebrews a name could be held to express the nature of the person who bore that name (cf. 1 Sam. 25.25). The meaning of the name of God, with which the Decalogue itself opens, may thus be of fundamental importance for Israel's theology. Significantly, both the D-version and the P-edition base their presentations on the revelation of the divine name (Exod. 3.13ff. for D; 6.2ff. for P).

1. *The Form of the Divine Name: 'Yahweh', not 'Jehovah'*

The pronunciation of the proper name of God, except once annually by the High Priest on the Day of Atonement, was forbidden in Judaism. The prohibition was justified exegetically by appeal to Lev. 24.16, where the verb *nāqab*, rendered 'blaspheme' in RSV, was understood in the sense of 'pronounce distinctly' (as in its occurrence in Isa. 62.2). Where the divine name, Yhwh, stands in the written text of the Hebrew Bible, the practice was to *read* instead *ʾᵃdōnāy*, 'my Lord'. The traditional consonants, Yhwh, naturally could not be removed from the written text but, to mark the change of reading, they were provided with vowels equivalent to those in *ᵃdōnāy*. (The difference in the first vowel of the resulting combination, YᵉHoWaH, is explained by the fact that in Hebrew it is 'indistinct', pronounced as an 'a' with the glottal stop with which *ᵃdōnāy* begins, but as an 'e' with the Y of Yhwh.) The reading of the non-form 'Jehovah' is ascribed to Petrus Galatinus (CE 1460–1540), father-confessor of Pope Leo X.

Evidence of the vowels original to Yhwh comes from early Christian sources: for example, Clement of Alexandria (CE 150–215), 'Iaoue'; Epiphanius (CE 315–403), Theodoret (CE 393–466), 'Iabe'. These Greek forms suggest that the vowels in the first and second syllables of Yhwh were *a* and *e*, respectively, hence 'YaHWeH' (the variations in the consonants arise from the fact that the Attic/Koine Greek alphabet has neither Y̆, H nor W!). The probability of the resultant reading of the name as 'Yahweh' is confirmed by its being a recognizable Hebrew form—a third person singular masculine imperfect verb—and this is how the Hebrew Bible itself, especially Exod. 3.14f., certainly also understands it.

2. *The Meaning of the Name Yahweh*

The name 'Yahweh' occurs some 6,823 times in the Hebrew Bible and is attested outside the Old Testament, for example, in the Mesha' Stele (c. 840), at Kuntillat Ajrud (ninth–eighth century) and in the Arad and Lachish ostraca (sixth century).

Though the name is recognizable as a verbal form (and even that is not universally agreed), there is multiple ambiguity about every other feature—stem, conjugation, person, tense and the identity of its subject and predicate. This ambiguity is compounded by the addition of the relative clause ('…WHO I AM') in Exod. 3.14. It may be that this ambiguity is fundamental to the revelation of the Name: Yahweh has made himself known by his name; he can be known as he makes himself known and rational statements can be made about that knowledge; he can be invoked by name. Yet he can never be completely known as he is in himself or as he may be in his actions. This paradox of veiled mystery yet of knowledge revealed to his people is well expressed in Deut. 29.29[Heb. 28]. Some of the elements of the ambiguity will be explored below.

(i) Stem: Assuming the name to be a verbal form, there are four possible stems with which it could be associated: HWH 'fall' (of snow; Job 37.6); HWH 'desire' (cf. Mic. 7.3; Prov. 10.3, etc.); HWH 'become', rare synonym (Aramaic?) of the fourth possibility, the common Hebrew verb HYH 'be'.

While appropriate senses have been suggested for a name derived

from the first two roots—Yahweh as originally a weather God, cf.
Baal; Yahweh as passionate, 'jealous'—Exod. 3.14 interprets Yhwh in
accordance with the last. This may be a popular, rather than a scien-
tifically accurate, etymology, giving the Israelite stamp of understanding to an inherited term.

On the basis of biblical material itself the hypothesis has been put
forward that the name 'Yahweh' was of Kenite origin. Certainly it was
in the service of his father-in-law, Jethro, priest of Midian, that Moses
first encountered Yahweh at the mountain of God (Exod. 3). In
Exodus 18 Jethro takes the lead in sacrifice and in the communion
meal; he offers Moses counsel about the discharge of justice within the
community. Jethro is also called a Kenite (Judg. 1.16) and subsequent
Kenites in the Old Testament are notable for their Yahwistic zeal
(Judg. 4.11, 17ff.; 2 Kgs 10.15ff.; cf. 1 Chron. 2.55). B. Rothenberg has
discovered a Midianite tent-shrine complete with brazen serpent (cf.
Num. 21.8). The tradition of the knowledge of Yahweh since the
generation of Cain, the eponymous ancestor of the Kenites (Gen. 4.26),
in contrast to the traditions that the name was first revealed to Moses
(Exod. 3; 6), may then have historical foundation.

On the significance of a possible non-Israelite origin of the name
Yahweh, S.R. Driver has already said all that is necessary (*Exodus*,
p. li):

> The *source* from which either this or any other divine name was ulti-
> mately derived by the Hebrews, matters little or nothing: the question
> which is of importance is, What did the name *come to mean* to them?...
> We can await with perfect calmness whatever the future may have to
> disclose to us with regard to its ultimate origin, or its pre-Israelite use.

(ii) Conjugation: If the name is a 3rd s.m. imperfect verb with the
prefix ya-, the conjugation should be causative (hiphil; the intransitive
conjugation, qal, has the prefix yi-). In that case the name describes
the activity of a creator god, who brings into being. But, on the other
hand, Exod. 3.14, in providing the 1st s.c. imperfect prefix 'e-, interprets the name as derived from the intransitive stem of the verb (qal;
the causative conjugation, hiphil, would have the prefix 'a-).

The explanation in Exod. 3.14 thus understands the name in terms
of 'being', not of 'creating'.

(iii) Person: In form, Yahweh is 3rd person s.m., 'he...' However,
Exod. 3.14 interprets as 1st person s.c., 'I...' In thus emphasizing the
first person, it is comparable to the 'divine self-predication' formula 'I
am...', especially in the 'prologue' to the Decalogue (cf. the first part
of the 'covenant formula', 'I will be your God...', e.g., in Exod. 6.7). In

the explanation of Exod. 3.14, Yahweh is not an objective, indirectly referred to, 'he', but the personal, relational subject, 'I', who is not merely addressed as 'Thou' but who takes the initiative of addressing as 'I'.

(iv) Tense: Traditionally, the name is regarded as a verb in the present tense, 'he is'. Cf. the LXX of Exod. 3.14, 'I am the one who is'; Vulgate, 'I am who I am'; hence EVV, 'I am'. If so, the statement is primarily ontological, concerning the eternity of the being of God.

Nonetheless, the verb is more naturally taken in Hebrew in the future tense, 'he will be'. If so, the statement is primarily soteriological, a promise of continuing activity, even an eschatological affirmation.

(v) The openness of subject and predicate: The personal pronoun subject, 'I'/'he', and, thus, the deity who bears the name Yahweh, awaits identification. Hence, already in the Hebrew Bible, there are the possibilities of the equation of Yahweh with the patriarchal God of the father (Exod. 3.13ff.), and with El (Exod. 6.3), no doubt the supreme deity of the North-West Semitic pantheon (cf. Abraham's encounter with El-Shaddai at Hebron[?] in Gen. 17.1, and Jacob's at Bethel in Gen. 35.11).

Equally, the complement of the verb 'to be' needs to be supplied ('I am/he is…'). The name must be concretized through experience (e.g. deliverance from Egypt; gift of land) and is open to new experience in which former experience is renewed and revitalized.

(vi) The force of the relative clause in Exod. 3.14, '…who I am/will be': Some argue, on the basis of the syntax of the Hebrew relative clause (cf. GKC §138.d), that the translation should be 'I am the one who is'.

Exod. 3.14 is often elucidated on the basis of Exod. 33.19, where again relative clauses pose a similar syntactical problem: 'I will be gracious to whom I will be gracious; I will have compassion on whom I will have compassion'. Some take this as a paronomasia used to express totality and intensity, 'I am truly the one to have compassion and show pity'. Others object that such paronomasia expresses not totality but vagueness. Therefore, Exod. 3.14 ('I am/shall be who/ what I am') is to be regarded as a revelation which is also a conceal-ment, a statement of God's being or action which veils the fulness of that being or action, and safeguards the transcendence, otherness and freedom of God (cf. Gen. 32.29; Judg. 13.18). Herein lies the theo-logical basis for the ineffability of the divine name in Jewish tradition (cf. *b. Pes.* 50a on Exod. 3.15 which reads not 'this is my name for ever [*lᵉ'ōlām*]', but the same consonantal text with different vowels, 'this is my name to be concealed [*lᵉ'allēm*]').

Further Reading

Albrektson, B., 'On the Syntax of *'ehyeh '^asher 'ehyeh* in Exodus 3.14', in P.R. Ackroyd and B. Lindars (eds.), *Words and Meanings: Essays presented to David Winton Thomas* (Cambridge: Cambridge University Press, 1968), pp. 15ff.

Cross, F.M., 'Yahweh and the God of the Patriarchs', *HTR* 55 (1962), pp. 225ff.

Rose, M., *Jahwe: Zum Streit um den alttestamentlichen Gottesnamen* (Zurich: Theologischer Verlag, 1978).

Etymology marks only one stage, and particularly in this case not the most eloquent one, in the elucidation of meaning. The Hebrew Bible as a whole, not least the rest of the book of Exodus, is the exposition of the character of Yhwh, the deity who bears that name. In conformity with the redactio-historical argument pursued above, the nature of the deity who bears the name Yahweh may be expounded first in the terms of the D-version and then of the P-edition.

II. *The Theology of the D-Version*

The complementarity of the D-version and the P-edition noted at the end of Chapter 3.VI.5 in connection with the Decalogue, can be extended in a number of respects: the relative roles of Moses and Aaron, the religious institutions through which Israel focused their relationship with Yahweh (Firstlings, Passover and covenant in D; Passover, Unleavened Bread, Pentecost and sanctuary in P), Law, and the theological statement implied by these institutions ('justification' in D; 'sanctification' in P), with their associated eschatologies.

1. *Moses*

The heart of the D-version, in the parts of Exod. 19.3–20.21 attributable to it, concerns revelation, God's initiative of self-disclosure. Revelation occurs both in theophany, which inspires awe and the subjugation of the will, and in rational communication, expressed in instruction and personal guidance.

The whole people gathered at the foot of Mt Horeb share directly in overwhelming experiences of vision and audition. The narrative describes the essentially immediate nature of the relationship between Yahweh and people in terms of an original moment of preparation for covenant; at this moment of fundamental significance, Moses functions initially as marshal. The people see for themselves the terrifying appearing of God above them on the mountain-top. That terror is increased by the impenetrability of the storm-cloud by which the mystery of God is veiled: the appearance of God as he is in himself is beyond human capacity to conceive or endure. This vision is accompanied by a no less overwhelming experience of hearing, the crash of the thunder-roll and the trumpet alarms of cosmic battle transcending intelligible speech. The purpose of this vision and audition is to catch the people up directly into the unforgettable experience of an immediate encounter with God, to the utter limit that such an encounter is conceivable and endurable for ordinary humanity. This once-for-all experience of overwhelming direct personal encounter with their own very God, who has just rescued them from slavery and danger and brought them to freedom, is to be the basis and reference-point of their continuing life. The 'fear of Yahweh' is the basic posture expected of the people from now on (Exod. 20.20).

It is only in the service of this primary experience of the people's direct, unmediated, encounter with its God that Moses assumes his role. His role is that of supreme prophet: he is spokesman and agent for God, intermediary between God and people, mediator of covenant and intercessor for the people, even ready to offer himself vicariously on their behalf. The portrayal of Moses as prophet matches the definition of his status as prophet in Deuteronomy (see, especially, Deut. 5.23-26; 13.1-5; 18.15-22; 34.10-12). There are also close parallels to be drawn between Moses and other prophets in the Dtr corpus, especially Elijah, the first of the great reforming prophets of the northern monarchy (cf. the parallel experiences of theophany in Exod. 33 and 1 Kgs 19), and Jeremiah, the last of the reform prophets who lived through the terminal decline and final collapse of the southern monarchy (cf. the call narratives in Exod. 3f. and Jer. 1 – probably elaborated by the Dtr editors – with the motifs of the sign of the burning bush/almond tree and of the youth and inarticulateness of the two figures).

As Yahweh's agent, Moses receives his credentials ('how will they believe in me?') in the power to work signs (Exod. 4.1-9). His shepherd's staff becomes a wonder-working rod; by it he effects the plagues which are in principle the handiwork of Yahweh (e.g. Exod. 4.17; 9.23; 10.13). Their purpose is so to heighten the obduracy of Pharaoh that the manifestation of Yahweh's power and glory may be the greater (cf. Exod. 14.17). Moses' rod is instrumental again for the revelation of Yahweh's power through Moses at the Red Sea (Exod. 14.16, 21, 31 ['and they believed in Yahweh and his servant Moses']) and in the – now displaced – incidents of water from the rock (Exod. 17.5 referring back to the first plague, Exod. 7.17) and of deliverance from the Amalekites (Exod. 17.8ff.).

Moses' intimacy with Yahweh is indicated by his encounter at the mountain of God, Horeb (Exod. 3.1–4.17; 18.1-12), and by his lone converse (e.g. Exod. 19.3-9, 19; 24.12, 18; 31.18–32.20; 32.30–33.6; 34.1, 4-28) and unparalleled vision on the mountain-top (Exod. 33.12-23). Herein Moses receives his credentials as recipient of revelation (Exod. 19.9, 'that they may believe in you'). After Horeb, this intimacy continues at the tent of meeting (Exod. 33.7-11): revelation remains in the form of rationally accessible guidance through the mediator to the people.

Moses' role as mediator of the covenant is dramatically presented. He continually reports the speech of each side to the other (Exod. 19.3-9). It is he who has the task of transposing the people's ear-splitting experience of direct encounter with God into rational communication in terms of the 'ten words' (Deut. 5.5). He writes the terms of the covenant in the Book of the Covenant and organizes the covenant rite (Exod. 24.3-8). It is he who receives the tablets of the Decalogue engraved by the finger of Yahweh himself (Exod. 24.12, 18; 31.18). His mediatorial role rises to its greatest intensity in the aftermath of the golden calf incident in his intercession and offering of himself for vicarious punishment (Exod. 32.30-33) and reaches its conclusion in the remaking of the covenant on its original terms (Exod. 34.1, 4-28).

2. *The Deuteronomic Exposition of the Name of Yahweh in Terms of Exodus, Covenant and Renewal of the Covenant*
(i) Exodus: The D-version of the narrative of the exodus in Exod. 1.11–5.21 follows the sequence of Deut. 15.12–16.8, that is, the D legislation on the freeing of the Hebrew slave (Deut. 15.12-18), the dedication of the first-born (Deut. 15.19-23) and the observation of the passover (Deut. 16.1-8). It is the exposition in narrative form of this legislation. It opens with the resounding statement in Exod. 4.22f., which combines the themes of the three sets of legislation, 'Say to Pharaoh, "Thus says Yahweh, 'Israel is my first-born son... Let my son go that he may serve me. If you refuse to let him go, behold, I will slay your first-born son'."' This combination of the motifs 'firstborn', 'setting the slave free' and 'to serve', that is, 'be slaves' to Yahweh, sets the theme of the D-version of the exodus.

The institutional focus of the Deuteronomic Plague narrative is *not* the Passover as such but the offering of the first-born (cf. Chapter 3.IV.3[iv] [b]) (as, indeed, the connecting of these institutions in the narrative with the climactic tenth plague—the death of the Egyptian first-born—would lead us to expect). Israel is Yahweh's first-born, who at the cost of Egypt's first-born owes life, freedom and prosperity to Yahweh; in turn, they owe all their first-born to Yahweh as an expression of gratitude. Thus the slaying of the first-born of Egypt, both of human and of beast, leads directly to the legislation on Israel's offering of the first-born of their animals and the redemption of the first-born of their sons (Exod. 13.1-16). Because of the centralization of the cult in D, the offering of the first-born of animals no longer takes place locally on the eighth day (as in the earlier legislation of the Book of the Covenant, Exod. 22.29f. [Heb. 28f.]) but centrally and annually (Deut. 15.20) in connection with the festival of Unleavened Bread interpreted as Passover (Deut. 15.12–16.8). The commemoration of the exodus is thus two-fold: annually at the festival of Unleavened Bread/Passover, and also perennially in the visible preservation of the first-born male of every family. Hence in Exodus 13, while unleavened bread is indeed to be eaten annually in the month of Abib in commemoration of the exodus (vv. 3-10), it is subordinated to the perpetual recollection of Israel's redemption at the cost of the first-born by being enclosed within legislation for the offering of the first-born (vv. 1-2, 11-16).

It is perhaps within this context that the deeply enigmatic section Exod. 4.24-26, Yahweh's attempt on Moses' life, may be understood. It is fitting that Moses, the leader of Israel, redeemed at the cost of the Egyptian first-born and consecrated by the dedication of their own first-born, should himself be redeemed by the blood of the circumcision, the symbol of the dedication to Yahweh, of his own first-born son.

(ii) Covenant: In the D-version, the narrative passes directly from the crossing of the Red Sea to Horeb, that is, from deliverance to covenant. The 'prologue' to the Decalogue in Exod. 20.2, 'I am Yahweh, your God, who has brought you out of the land of Egypt, out of the house of slaves', succinctly states the essence of the matter. Everything depends on the nature and action of the God who reveals himself by the name 'Yahweh'. Israel find themselves in relationship with Yahweh not by choice on their part but thanks alone to his initiative. It is in this relationship that they are brought into being and into full status as a free people.

The formalization of this relationship in covenant now follows. It is the central contribution of the theologians of the D/Dtr school to have explored the concept 'covenant'. 'Covenant' is undoubtedly a term borrowed from everyday social and economic life for agreements which contain contractual obligations (cf. Chapter 2.V). But when this concept is turned from the 'horizontal' (inter-human) plane to the 'vertical' (the relation between Yahweh and Israel) the term has to undergo theological modification. How can Yahweh, inscrutable in his transcendence and sovereign in his autonomy, be bound as covenant partner? How can the people of Israel as human beings ever do anything for God, since all that they are and have they have received from him in the first place? If Israel cannot do anything for God in its obedience, how much less in its disobedience! However solemn the covenant and sincere the commitment to it at the moment of its original conclusion, however awesome the theophany of Yahweh, which accompanies it, however absolutely binding its terms, Israel falls away in the emblematic sin of the golden calf (Exod. 32).

The Dtr theologians write in the context of exile, where they reflect on the mystery of Israel's preservation in the midst of the exile, understood as punishment for sins committed ever since Horeb. Israel is Yahweh's first-born son, but in its long history it has proved itself rebellious. By law the refractory son should be put to death (cf. Deut. 21.18-21). How is it, then, that Israel has not utterly perished? The answer can only lie in the forgiving mercy and longsuffering grace of Yahweh himself. It is for this reason, therefore, that the Dtr theologians have reformulated the law-code of Exod. 20.22–23.19 as a covenant-code and called it the 'Book of the Covenant' (cf. Chapter 3.IV.3[ii]): the law-code with its penalties is now enfolded in the covenant-code; the penalty for breach of covenant-code now depends on the autonomous will of the divine covenant partner, 'who will be gracious to whom he will be gracious' (Exod. 33.19). The conventional term 'justification' (even without faith in the recipient!) can, with full appropriateness, be used of Deuteronomic theology.

(iii) Eschatology: But the terms of the covenant unilaterally abrogated by Israel remain valid. Therefore, the covenant is remade in Exodus 34 on the identical terms of Decalogue and B, as before (cf. Chapter 3.IV.3[iii] [c]). But the Dtr. theologians are aware that only if Yahweh himself in the end provides the conditions whereby Israel can be faithful to its terms can the covenant ever be maintained by them. Beyond the confines of Exodus, the D/Dtr school look forward to the day when God will inscribe the terms of the covenant, not on stone tablets but on the fleshy tablets of the heart of each member of the community, so that all God's people with immediate knowledge of his commandments will be enabled to keep the covenant (cf. Deut. 30.1-10; Jer. 31.31-34).

III. *The Theology of the P-Edition*

The P-edition of Exodus contributes especially the material on genealogies in chs. 1 and 6; itineraries in chs. 12–19; the emphasis on Aaron in chs. 6–11 and in subsequent chapters; the Passover in ch. 12 and sabbath in ch. 16, ritual purity and hierarchy in chs. 19, 24, 34 and the tabernacle in chs. 25–31.17; 35–40, along with a host of more detailed adjustments of the underlying D-version. Since this later edition of Exodus belongs to the final promulgation of the whole Pentateuch as Scripture in the postexilic period, it ought properly to be viewed as part of the overall statement of the final editors within the comprehensive chronological and genealogical schemata they provide for the Pentateuch, as well as within the rather narrower frameworks of the wilderness itineraries (cf. Num. 33) and of the large central block on 'the revelation of the Torah at Sinai' (Exod. 19.1–Num. 10.10). That can be done to only a marginal extent in this context. Put very generally and partially, the P-edition of the Pentateuch is concerned with the forms, projected into an idealized primal time for purposes of sanction, which continuing life under God should take in the period of 'realized eschatology' between the 'return from exile', which turned out to be limited in both scale and quality, and the definitive 'Return' which Israel awaits in the final jubilee.

For the P-edition, the revelation of the divine name 'Yahweh', deliverance from slavery and the covenantal relationship are as primary as for the D-version (though it is the prior covenant with the Patriarchs which P stresses, Exod. 6.2-9). The P-edition of Exodus, however, complements the D-version with a vast expansion of materials, particularly about the sanctuary in chs. 25–31, 35–40.

1. *The Status of Aaron*
The P-writer is naturally concerned with Aaron as the 'father' of the Aaronic priesthood of the Second Temple. He is as aware as the D-version that Aaron remains subordinate to Moses: the sacrificial cult, which can be observed in the name of any god (cf. the golden calf incident and Israel's Canaanite background), is ambiguous in itself and is only acceptable if given the normative interpretation of Yahwism, which stems from the revelation to Moses (cf. P's addition in Exod. 34.29-35 on the radiance of the face of Moses after he has communed with Yahweh). The Aaronic priesthood as officiants in the cult can then only operate within the more general 'Levitical' framework of the teaching of Moses, the Levite. This is put genealogically in

terms of the fact that the family of Aaron is only one branch within
the tribe of Levi (Exod. 6.16-25); it is expressed in narrative form in
the bloody ordination of the Levites as Yahweh zealots in Exod.
32.20b-29. The roles of the Levites are wider than cultic matters, concerning primarily instruction and the monitoring of Israel's obedience
to the precepts of the law (cf. Deut. 33.8-11).

Central to P's conception of the maintenance of the bond between
Yahweh and Israel are the sacrificial rites practised at the altar by the
Aaronic priests. By the rites of the Day of Atonement, sanctuary and
people are annually sanctified; thereafter, the stated round of sacrifice, whole burnt-offering, communion sacrifice, sin and guilt
offering—offered daily, weekly, monthly and at festivals—and the
numberless *ad hoc* sacrifices of vow and thanksgiving, by which the
restored bond between Yahweh and people is sacramentaly expressed
and maintained, can recommence (cf. e.g. Lev. 16; Num. 28; 29).
Equally significant for the maintenance of good order within the community is the priestly discrimination of 'the holy and the common, the
clean and the unclean' (Lev. 10.10). Thus in the P-edition of Exodus
the immediacy of Aaron's activity as Moses' agent in matters of
speech and miracle-working (e.g. Exod. 6.27–7.13) and his close proximity to Moses in the hierarchy on the mountain of God (e.g. Exod.
19.24) are stressed. The appropriate rites for the ordination of the
Aaronic priesthood and the specification of their vestments are duly
given in Exodus 28; 29; 30.30 (cf. 39; Lev. 8.1-36). The cosmic battles
which Aaron wages with Pharaoh's magicians are the prelude to the
renewal of the cosmos prepared by the construction of the Tabernacle.

2. *Realized Eschatology*

In the Pentateuch the D-version of the journey through the wilderness
is the dynamic, eschatological one of progression, from deliverance to
covenant to emblematic rebellion, and then from covenant remade
through repeated rebellions to covenant renewed on the plains of
Moab, so that Israel stands poised on the verge of entry into the land.
The P-edition's account is the static one of the prevailing situation of
human rebellion, despite the revelation of divine ordinances at the
heart of life. In the time of waiting between the return from exile and
the last Jubilee, Israel is in a constant condition of recalcitrant 'murmuring' against Yahweh, though he has done everything by the revelation of the Torah ordinances and institutions, that enables that
condition of holiness by which his people can proleptically anticipate
the end-time. Thus for the P-writer the Sinai pericope, Exod. 19.1–
Num. 10.10, stands centrally, with the incidents of the murmuring of

the people and the answering provision by Yahweh, repeatedly and unwearyingly granted, disposed somewhat symmetrically on either side (cf. Chapter 3.IV.3[iv] [a]).

It may thus be fairly claimed that whereas the D-version is about justification—the ever-renewed restoration of the rebellious people in the long-suffering grace of Yahweh till they stand poised on the verge of their inheritance—the P-edition is about sanctification, the possibilities of holy living now through observance of the Torah, even in the long in-between time of waiting for the final consummation.

3. *Institutional Focus*

As befits priestly preoccupation, the regulations for the domestic rites of Passover and the Temple rites of Unleavened Bread, combined in such unprecedented manner in Deut. 16.1-8 (cf. 2 Kgs 23.21-23 and Exod. 13.3-10), are carefully distinguished (Exod. 12.1-28, 43-50). The festival of Weeks/Pentecost, originally the occasion of bringing the offerings of first-fruits at the end of the grain harvest, is now reinterpreted in terms of Israel's history as the festival of the revelation of Torah (Exod. 19.1).

In accord with the theme of sanctification, the P-writer in the context of law-giving at Sinai in Exodus 19–24 stresses ritual purity for the encounter with Yahweh and strict hierarchy in those who dare venture towards his presence. Thus Moses, the recipient of direct revelation, stands at the apex of Mount Sinai; while Aaron and his sons and seventy elders share the covenant meal on the mountain, the young men and people share in the covenant rite on the plain below (Exod. 24.1-2, 5, 6, 8, 9-11).

Equally, the detailed specification of the tabernacle and its furnishings and equipment (Exod. 25.1–27.21; 30.1–31.11) and the meticulous execution of that specification in Exod. 35.1–38.31; 39.32–40.33 express the concept of the holy in spatial and material terms. But the mere external form, even when elaborated to this astonishing degree, is not the fundamental matter. The pervading purpose is that the external physical environment may be created wherein Yahweh, at his own behest, may fittingly bestow his presence. Exod. 40.34-38 thus forms the appropriate climax of the work: when all has been prepared by the action and revelation of Yahweh himself, his own presence is granted to his people for constant hallowing and guidance.

Further Reading

There are numerous *theologies* of the Old Testament available in English, e.g., L. Koehler (1957), E. Jacob (1958), T.C. Vriezen (1958), G.A.F. Knight (1959), W. Eichrodt (I, 1961; II, 1967), G. von Rad (I, 1962; II, 1965), J.L. McKenzie (1974) W. Zimmerli (1978), R.E. Clements (1978), C. Westermann (1982), W.H. Schmidt (1983), B.S. Childs (1985), J.D. Levenson (1985), H.D. Preuss (1995), W. Brueggemann (1997).

For the Deuteronomic movement in general, cf.

Weinfeld, M., *Deuteronomy and the Deuteronomic School* (Oxford: Clarendon Press, 1972).

For the theological impact of the Deuteronomic movement on the formation of Israel's literature during the exilic period, cf. e.g.

Vermeylen, J., *Le Dieu de la promesse et le Dieu de l'alliance* (Lectio Divina, 126; Paris: Editions du Cerf, 1986).

For the theology of P, see e.g.

Klein, R.W., 'The Message of P', in J. Jeremias and L. Perlitt (eds.), *Die Botschaft und die Boten: Festschrift für Hans Walter Wolff* (Neukirchen–Vluyn: Neukirchener Verlag, 1981), pp. 57ff.

Saebø, M., 'Priestertheologie und Priesterschrift', in J.A. Emerton (ed.), *Congress Volume, Vienna* (VTSup, 32; Leiden: E.J. Brill, 1981), pp. 357ff.

For a review of the history of the interpretation of the exodus, including its influence on Liberation Theology, see e.g.

Van Iersel, B., and A. Weiler (eds.), *The Exodus: A Lasting Paradigm* (Concilium, 198; Edinburgh: T. & T. Clark, 1987).

INDEX

INDEX OF REFERENCES

OLD TESTAMENT

INDEX OF MODERN AUTHORS

OLD TESTAMENT GUIDES

NEW TESTAMENT GUIDES

GUIDES NOW AVAILABLE IN NEW FORMAT:
BIBLICAL GUIDES